I1034065

APR 29 2005

by the same author

with Hans Keller
BENJAMIN BRITTEN:
A COMMENTARY ON HIS WORKS (1952)

with H. C. Robbins Landon
THE MOZART COMPANION (1956)

THE LANGUAGE OF MODERN MUSIC (1963)

ALMA MAHLER: MEMORIES AND LETTERS (1968)
Edited by Donald Mitchell
Translated by Basil Creighton
Third Edition further enlarged
with a new Appendix and Chronology by
Knud Martner and Donald Mitchell (1973)

GUSTAV MAHLER: THE WUNDERHORN YEARS (1975)

BENJAMIN BRITTEN 1913–1976:
PICTURES FROM A LIFE (1978)
with the assistance of John Evans

GUSTAV MAHLER
The Early Years

GUSTAV MAHLER

THE EARLY YEARS

DONALD MITCHELL

Revised and Edited by
Paul Banks and David Matthews

UNIVERSITY OF CALIFORNIA PRESS
Berkeley and Los Angeles

First published in 1958

Revised edition published in 1980 by
University of California Press
Berkeley and Los Angeles

Printed in Great Britain

© by Donald Mitchell, 1958, 1980
Appendix © by Paul Banks, David Matthews,
and Donald Mitchell, 1980

Library of Congress Cataloging in Publication Data

Mitchell, Donald, 1925–
Gustav Mahler: the early years

Bibliography: p.
Includes index.
1. Mahler, Gustav, 1860–1911. 2. Composers—Austria—
Biography. I. Banks, Paul. II. Matthews, David. III. Title.
ML410.M23M5 1980   780'.92'4 [B]   79-9694
ISBN 0–520–04141–0

For
KATHLEEN
Vienna, Easter
1954
and
in loving memory of
CHRISTA LANDON
(1921–1977)

"I think I have experienced your symphony. I felt the struggle for illusions; I felt the pain of one disillusioned; I saw the forces of evil and good contending; I saw a man in a torment of emotion exerting himself to gain inner harmony. I sensed a human being, a drama, *truth*, the most ruthless truth!"

> Arnold Schoenberg to Mahler, in a letter, after the performance in Vienna of Mahler's Symphony III in December 1904.

"He is among those who have enriched mankind with imperishable gifts; and although these do not transcend all other gifts, nor entitle him to those honours 'above all Greek, above all Roman fame', which by a natural reaction against the neglect and contempt of the world, many of his admirers were once disposed to accumulate upon him, yet to refuse an admiring recognition of what he was, on account of what he was not, is a much worse error, and one which, pardonable in the vulgar, is no longer permitted to any cultivated and instructed mind."

> John Stuart Mill on Bentham.

PREFACE TO 1958 EDITION

IT was not my intention to write a book about Mahler in two volumes. The division has happened as a result of writing more on the early years and the early works than I had at first thought possible. I hope this is not simply a matter of verbosity but, rather, a true reflection of the amount I found myself obliged to write about. Upon reaching 1880 it seemed to me that my biography had reached a cadence—not a full close, perhaps, but at least a point where one might rest; and with the music, too, I felt that a break which left us on the brink of Mahler's first period proper was not altogether inappropriate. Then there was the size of the book itself—already not negligible in bulk. A further consideration was the thought that waiting upon completion of the second part would mean delaying publication, for quite a number of years, of an account of Mahler's childhood and youth, of the environment, musical, personal and social, from which he sprang, which does, I trust, do something to fill in the very lightly sketched outlines proffered by earlier biographers.

We have known less of Mahler's early years than of most other composers' of equal eminence. For reasons which I think become clear in the development of the book I consider those years to be of the first importance for our understanding of the mature artist. It was these two related factors which really determined me to let this present book stand on its own legs, as conscious as I was of a certain disappointment that it scarcely touched upon the symphonies, song-cycles and songs which contain, when all is said and done, the heart of Mahler's genius. This book, none the less, though I think it unfolds a not unsatisfying shape, was written as a beginning rather than an end in itself; and was evolved, as it were, under the shadow of the impending masterpieces of Mahler's maturity. It is my hope that its chronological dives into the future mean that the impact of the later music is part, at least, of the reader's experience when assimilating Mahler's early years.

vii

I shall not labour the point here that Mahler's biography has presented—and still presents—many obscurities; so much is apparent from the text which follows. No less apparent, I think—hence the plethora of footnotes—is the fact that I have been obliged to rely extensively upon second-hand sources, but for a small region where I have been able to verify or discover facts and documents for myself. (A good many primary sources I fear have vanished for ever.) My main task has been to reduce into some kind of order a large but fragmentary, incoherent and often wildly contradictory Mahler literature; and out of that order, which entailed any amount of checking and cross-checking of data (dates, in particular), to try to build a reasonably continuous and detailed biography. I think that many of my dates are correct; since in many instances they run counter to those appearing in other biographies and standard works of reference, I have wherever possible shown the reasoning by which I have arrived at my new conclusion (which practice has proved another fertile multiplier of footnotes).

It may be my fate, of course, to have preserved between covers mistakes and misinformation which might well have been left to gather dust undisturbed. I hope this fear may prove to be exaggerated. But at the worst such an achievement would still represent an advance in Mahler studies; there, the first step must be to scrutinize what has been written about him, and this has been impossible in the absence of a work which comprehensively surveys the principal sources of biographical and musical information. I think this book has taken that first step and perhaps progressed a step or two beyond it in so far as its preliminary scrutiny has established not a few firm facts and dates, some of them new ones. (I shall gladly receive corrections of fact and substance and print them as an appendix to the second volume.)

When the continuation of this book will appear is largely a matter of simple economics. The writer without private means or other subsidy has to subsidize his own books with bread-and-butter occupations which, while earning him his freedom, consume his time. But I doubt if the urgent and undiminished fascination that Mahler has had for me since my schooldays will allow me to leave for long the job half done. It will certainly not be for want of admiration of his genius that completion of the second book may be delayed.

* * *

The Early Years owes much to the aid of friends—and friendly strangers—at home and oversea. I am specially indebted to:

H. C. Robbins and Christa Landon, whose hospitality in Vienna in 1954 made this book possible. They not only helped me to make the best use of my very brief stay in that city but have been unsparing since in the use of their own time on my behalf. They will realize that part of this book's dedication belongs, in a very real sense, to them.

Hans Keller, who has patiently and expertly translated extracts from many documents and answered innumerable queries arising from the text. He has been as generous with his skill, interest and encouragement as if my work had been his.

Alfred Rosé, Mahler's nephew, for his readiness to supply most valuable information about the autographs in his possession, at whatever cost in personal inconvenience. It is my hope that the generous spirit which has furnished me with much significant descriptive detail will one day permit the autographs themselves to become part of Mahler's creative legacy.

F. Charles Adler, the veteran conductor and champion of Mahler, for many acts of kindness.

Erwin Stein, for his friendly interest in the progress of the book and for many a perceptive comment and enlightening memory.

Laton E. Holmgren, who was generous enough to send me material from the United States which was not available in this country.

John and Alix Farrell, for preparing the index.

None of these good people can, of course, be held responsible for the uses to which I have put their warmly appreciated assistance. The same qualification applies to, but in no way diminishes, my thanks to the following, all of whom have aided me with information or the means of securing it:

Schulrat Rudolf Baldrian; Dr. Otto Blau, of Messrs. Josef Weinberger Ltd., London; Dr. Eric Blom, C.B.E.; Dr. Mosco Carner; Professor W. E. Collinson; Mr. Martin Cooper; Mr. Paul Hamburger; Dr. Hans Holländer; the late Dr. Ernest Jones, the biographer of Sigmund Freud; Frau Doktor Hedwig Krauss, librarian of the *Gesellschaft der Musikfreunde*, Vienna; Mrs. Alma Mahler Werfel, the composer's distinguished widow; Dr. Dika Newlin; Dr. Fritz Raček, of the *Stadtbibliothek*, Vienna; Professor Erwin Ratz, president of the International Gustav Mahler Society; Dr. H. F. Redlich; Mrs. Rudolph Reti; Mr. Eric Simon; Mr. Nicolas Slonimsky; Mr. H. C. Stevens; Mr. Frank Walker, upon whose immaculate biography of Hugo Wolf I have leaned so heavily; and Dr. Healey Willan.

I am grateful to the following music publishers for permission to quote from Mahler's works:

Dr. Alfred A. Kalmus and Universal Edition (London) Ltd., by arrangement with whom the quotations from *Das klagende Lied* and Symphony I are made;

Messrs. B. Schott's Söhne, Mainz, the publishers of the *Lieder und Gesänge aus der Jugendzeit*, from Book I of which my quotations in Chapter IV/(o) are taken.

It is by kind permission of the director of the *Wiener Stadtbibliothek*, Dr. Albert Mitringer, that I am able to reproduce part of Mahler's autograph score of an early version of *Das klagende Lied* (see Plates VIII, IX, and XI).

The sources of the illustrations are as follows:

Plates I, II(b) and (c), V(a): BGM; Plate II(a): RS[1]; Plate III, a print, is in my possession; Plate IV(b): FW; Plate IV(a): *Das*

Atlantis Buch der Musik, Zürich, 1946; Plate V(b): Baldrian, *op cit.* (see II/n. 3); Plate VI: Mr. Nicolas Slonimsky; Plate VII: by courtesy of Mrs. Alma Mahler Werfel; Plates VIII, IX and XI: *Wiener Stadtbibliothek*; Plate X: by courtesy of Messrs. Universal Edition (London) Ltd.

London–Vienna–London:
January 1954 – March 1958   D.M.

PREFACE TO REVISED EDITION

FIRST, I have to make an apology for the shamefully long interval between the first publication of this book and the appearance of the revised edition. I do not care to think of how many promises —how many date-lines—I have made and not kept. My sense of guilt makes all the stronger my gratitude to the editors of this revised and augmented text, Paul Banks and David Matthews. It is my good fortune, and also lucky for the book, that these two very able Mahler scholars of a younger generation should have been so generous with their time and skills. The critical appendix they have patiently compiled contains much information that is fresh and significant, and it takes comprehensive account of the vast amount of Mahler research in recent years that has thrown up so many new discoveries about the early period. All the same, it is a source of some satisfaction to me that the text as a whole seems to have held up remarkably well and has not, in my view at least, required major re-drafting. The book, I think, presented, and continues to present, a considered, coherent view of Mahler's early years and his early music; and by and large I have not felt the need to overhaul that view to any very radical degree. Indeed, I think the view was basically sustained in my second volume, *The Wunderhorn Years*, even if the method of approach changed somewhat; and I very much hope that the third volume, on which I am currently working, will show a similar consistency. It can all be only one man's view of Mahler, as I have always hastened to emphasize. But the enthusiasm with which the editors have tackled their often laborious task, and the many calls there have been over the years for *The Early Years* to be made available again, give me grounds for hoping that it is a view that can be usefully shared.

Barcombe Mills, Sussex
August 1978   DONALD MITCHELL

EDITORS' PREFACE

THIS new edition of *The Early Years* reprints the text of the first (1958) edition unchanged, except for some small corrections which it has been possible to make on the page without disturbing the original layout. All other corrections and all additional material will be found in the Appendix. An arrow in the margin of the main text refers to a note in the Appendix, which is identified by the page and line numbers of the passage on which it comments: thus note 1 *18* comments on line 18 of page 1.

The original list of works on pp. 116–20 has been retained; but we have supplemented it with a revised list (on pp. 322–4), based on the most up-to-date information available to us. The bibliography has also been updated.

Since *The Early Years* was published, a number of people have written to the author with corrections and suggestions: their help is gratefully acknowledged in the relevant places in the Appendix, but special thanks are due to Mr Knud Martner (Copenhagen), Professor Zoltan Roman (Calgary), and the late Deryck Cooke—whose death in 1976 was a sad event indeed for everyone concerned with Mahler's music. The *Musiksammlung* of the *Österreichische Nationalbibliothek* and the Library of the *Gesellschaft der Musikfreunde* in Vienna have both been very kind in placing material at our disposal. We should also like to thank Mr Bill Hopkins for translating various passages from the German.

PAUL BANKS
DAVID MATTHEWS

September 1978

CONTENTS

ILLUSTRATIONS

between pages 74 and 75

BIBLIOGRAPHY AND KEY

AG   Göllerich, August: *Anton Bruckner, ein Lebens - und Schaffensbild*, Regensburg, 1936.

AM⁰   Mahler, Alma: *Gustav Mahler* (hereafter referred to as GM): *Erinnerungen und Briefe*, Amsterdam, 1940.

AM   Mahler, Alma: *GM: Memories and Letters*, trans. Basil Creighton, London, 1946.

AM¹   Mahler, Alma: *GM: Memories and Letters*, trans. Basil Creighton, enlarged edition, revised and edited and with an Introduction, Preface, Appendix and Chronology by Donald Mitchell and Knud Martner, London, 1973, and Seattle, 1975.

AN   Neisser, Artur: *GM*, Leipzig, 1918.

BGM   Roller, Alfred: *Die Bildnisse von GM*, Vienna-Leipzig, 1922.

BW⁰   Walter, Bruno: *GM*, Vienna-Leipzig-Zürich, 1936.

BW¹   Walter, Bruno: *GM* trans. supervised by Lotte Walter Lindt, London, 1958 (new edition of BW²).

BW²   Walter, Bruno: *GM*, trans. James Galston, London, 1937.

BW³   Walter, Bruno: *Theme and Variations, An Autobiography*, trans. James Galston, London, 1947.

BWW   Wessling, Berndt W.: *GM, Ein Prophetisches Leben*, Hamburg, 1974. [Editors' note: This item would appear to contain substantial new information about Mahler's early years; but as the author produces no sources for his discoveries we have not thought it safe to quote from or refer to his text.]

CH   Hruby, Carl: *Meine Erinnerungen an Anton Bruckner*, Vienna, 1901.

DM¹   Mitchell, Donald: *GM: The Wunderhorn Years*, London, 1976.

DM²   Mitchell, Donald: Supplement to *GM: The Wunderhorn Years*, Ph.D thesis, University of Southampton, 1977.

DN   Newlin, Dika: *Bruckner-Mahler-Schoenberg*, New York, 1947. New edition, New York, 1978.

EJ   Jones, Ernest: *Sigmund Freud, Life and Works*, Vols. I & II, London, 1953 and 1955.

EK   Křenek, Ernst: 'GM', a 'Biographical Essay', in *GM*, by Bruno Walter, New York, 1941 (American edition of BW² above).

ER¹   Reilly, Edward R.: 'Mahler and Guido Adler', in *Musical Quarterly*, New York, Vol. LVIII, No. 3, July 1972, pp. 436–70.

ER²   Reilly, Edward R.: *GM und Guido Adler*, Int. GM Society and Universal Edition, Vienna, 1978.

FP   Pfohl, Ferdinand: GM: *Eindrücke und Erinnerungen aus den Hamburger Jahren*, ed. Knud Martner, Hamburg, 1973.

FW   Walker, Frank: *Hugo Wolf, A Biography*, London, 1951.

GA   Adler, Guido: *GM*, Vienna-Leipzig, 1916.

GAWW   Adler, Guido: *Wollen und Wirken*, Vienna, 1935.

GdM¹   *Bericht über das Conservatorium und die Schauspiele der Gesellschaft der Musikfreunde in Wien. Für das Schuljahr 1875–1876*. Vienna, 1876 (and successive years).

GdM²   *Rechenschaftsbericht der Direction der Gesellschaft der Musikfreunde in Wien . . . 1880–1881*. Vienna, 1882 (and successive years).

GdM³   MSS in possession of the *Gesellschaft der Musikfreunde*, Vienna.

GdM⁴   *Vollzugsvorschrift zum Statute der Grundverfassung des Conservatoriums*, etc., Vienna 1869 and 1876.

GdM⁵   *Lehrplan für das Schuljahr. . . .* (published annually, together with a *Stundenplan*, as a supplement to GdM¹), Vienna, 1875 (and successive years).

GE   Engel, Gabriel: *GM, Song-Symphonist*, New York, 1932.

GMB   *GM Briefe, 1879–1911*, ed. Alma Maria Mahler, Berlin-Vienna-Leipzig, 1924.

GMB¹   English translation of GMB by Eithne Wilkins, Ernst

Kaiser and Bill Hopkins, ed. Knud Martner, London, 1979.

HFR   Redlich, H. F.: *Bruckner and Mahler* ('The Master Musicians' series), London–New York, 1955; revised edition, 1963.

HG   de La Grange, Henry-Louis: *Mahler*, Vol. 1, New York, 1973.

HH   Holländer, Hans, private communications.

HH[1]   Holländer, Hans: 'Unbekannte Jugendbriefe GMs', *Die Musik*, Berlin, 1928, Vol. XX, No. 11.

HH[2]   Holländer, Hans: 'GM', in *Musical Quarterly*, New York, Vol. XVII, No. 4, 1931, pp. 449–63.

JD   Diether, Jack: 'Notes on Some Mahler Juvenilia', in *Chord and Discord*, Iowa, Vol. III, No. 1, 1969, pp. 3–100.

KB[1]   Blaukopf, Kurt: *GM*, trans. Inge Goodwin, London, 1973.

KB[2]   *Mahler, A Documentary Study*, compiled and edited by Kurt Blaukopf with contributions by Zoltan Roman, London, 1976.

KB[3]   Blaukopf, Kurt: 'Auf neuen Spuren zu GM', in *Hi Fi Stereophonie*, Kalsruhe, May 1971, pp. 356–64.

LK   Karpath, Ludwig: *Begegnung mit dem Genius*, Vienna–Leipzig, 1934.

LS   Schiedermair, Ludwig: *GM*, Leipzig, 1900.

MK   Kennedy, Michael: *Mahler* ('The Master Musicians' series), London, 1974.

NBL   Bauer-Lechner, Natalie: *Erinnerungen an GM*, Leipzig–Vienna–Zürich, 1923. English translation by Dika Newlin, ed. Peter Franklin, London, 1980.

PS[0]   Stefan, Paul: *GM, Eine Studie über Persönlichkeit und Werk*, revised edition, Munich, 1920.

PS   Stefan, Paul: *GM, A Study of His Personality and Work*, trans. T. E. Clark, New York, 1913.

PWB   Banks, Paul: *The Early Social and Musical Environment of GM*, D.Phil. thesis, University of Oxford, 1979.

RL	*Ritter's Geographisch-statistisches Lexikon*, ed. W. Hoffmann, C. Winderlich and C. Cramer, Leipzig, 1855.
RML	Riemann, Hugo: *Musik-Lexikon*, 10th edition, Berlin, 1922.
RS[1]	Specht, Richard: *GM*, Berlin-Leipzig, 1913.
RS[2]	Specht, Richard: *GMs VIII. Symphonie*, Vienna-Leipzig, n. d.
RS[3]	Specht, Richard: *GM*, Berlin, 1905.
SW	*GM in Vienna*, ed. Sigrid Weismann, London, 1977.
TR	Reik, Theodor: *The Haunting Melody, Psychoanalytic Experiences in Life and Music*, New York, 1953.

I

1860-1875

GUSTAV MAHLER was born in Kalischt (Kaliště), in the Royal Province of Bohemia, on 7 July 1860. The date has been the subject of dispute. Mahler celebrated the 7th as his birthday, his parents the 1st.[1] Mahler's birth certificate places the 7th beyond doubt.[2] The birth-village, in the district of Humpoletz (Humpolec), was near the Moravian border and close to the town of Iglau (Jihlava), a town not without a previous musical association. It was to the barracks there that Beethoven's nephew, Karl, was attached in 1827.

What was Kaliště like? Paul Stefan calls it "unpretentious".[3] Alma Mahler does not call it anything. Mahler himself said nothing about the place, but quite a lot about the house in which he was born (No. 9). Once, when out for a stroll at Steinbach am Attersee with his friend and confidante Natalie Bauer-Lechner (1858-1921), the sight of some peasant dwellings stirred his memory. He claimed then that in such a shack he was born, a house without glass to its windows and with a puddle at its front. All that was nearby was the village and a few dispersed hovels.[4] The prospect does not sound inviting.[5]

The memories Mahler had of Kaliště may have been early ones, but cannot have been immediate impressions. It was only a few months after Mahler's birth that the family moved to Jihlava, in December 1860.[6] But doubtless Mahler, when living at Jihlava, may have returned to Kaliště and reviewed, and thus remembered, the squalor of his old home.

There is no need to imagine that Mahler romanticized the poverty of his early days. All the evidence indicates that his home conditions, from every angle, were exceptionally depressing. I shall have a good deal to say of the conflicts which mark Mahler's music and his personality. Perhaps it was only appropriate, as it was most certainly formative, that conflicts of one sort or

I

another surrounded his childhood and youth. They may be usefully divided into three categories: territorial, social and familial. Within these three contracting circles of conflict, Mahler stood as a common centre. Territorially, the conflict was a matter of European politics. When Mahler was born, Bohemia was part of the great Austro-Hungarian empire. After the first World War and the collapse of the empire, it became part of the Czechoslovak republic. The region in which Mahler spent his youth had, through many changes of fortune, long been associated with the struggle for Czech independence, and there can be little doubt that the political restlessness of his environment—both in his youth and in his later years—added a further insecurity to the host of insecurities engendered by the conditions of his childhood. Mahler himself once put it thus:

> "I am thrice homeless, as a native of Bohemia in Austria, as an Austrian among Germans, and as a Jew throughout all the world. Everywhere an intruder, never welcomed."[7]

There Mahler shows acute awareness of what a sociologist would call his 'status problem'. Yet he himself neglects to mention what was, territorially speaking, the initial problem of status, that while he and his family may have been Bohemians in Austria, they were not Bohemians among Bohemians, but part of an alien minority whose rule was resented and finally, though after Mahler's death, thrown off. It is hard to determine how far political climates influence the development of personal characteristics. Mahler showed little interest in politics, and it is my belief that events much nearer home play a decisive rôle in the formation of character; too much in Mahler has too often been conjured up or explained away by seemingly convincing analogies drawn between his music and the collapsing Austrian empire. Nevertheless, I have no doubt that this outer ring of political ferment at the very least reinforced his inner tensions, the combination of which with musical, rather than social or political, history—developments in these fields do not invariably follow a parallel course—determined the nature of his idiom in substantial detail.

2

We approach a vital inner tension when we move in from the territorial to the social sphere. Mahler, as we have seen, could not be accepted as a Bohemian among Bohemians; further, he was not even accepted as a member of the minority of which he was part. He and his family were aliens among aliens. We have here the age-old problem of the Jews, ironically emphasized in this instance by their minority status within a minority. Ernst Křenek writes:

"The town of his birth was Kališt[ě], in Southern Bohemia, a purely Czech settlement. The nearby township of Iglau . . . , situated at the Western edge of Moravia, however, is largely inhabited by Germans, a 'linguistic island'. This condition was typical in many parts of Czechoslovakia and accounted for the interminable racial trouble ever freshly nourished by the increasing nationalistic tendencies of the 19th century. The Jewish minority, scattered all over the country, was at that time almost invariably counted into the German element. Most of the country Jews were merchants trading between the German centers in the towns and the solid mass of Czech farmers and peasants that surrounded those 'islands'. They spoke Czech with their rural customers but their social ambitions associated them with the German element because of its closer relations to Vienna, the center of the Empire."[8]

H. F. Redlich formulates it:

"Tolerated by their Slavonic neighbours, whose language Moravian[9] Jews usually mastered, but scorned by the officially favoured minority of resident Germans, they had to live in conditions of constant insecurity, expecting at any time to be submitted to excesses of racial prejudices from either side."[10]

Anti-Semitism dogged Mahler's footsteps from his early years onwards, and even today it is not a spent force: evaluation of his personality and achievements, judgments of his music, are still distorted by this antique feud. Gabriel Engel's suggestion that "although Gustav Mahler was of Jewish extraction, throughout his arduous, yet meteoric rise to the throne of music he never complained of religious discrimination"[11] is misleading in so far as it gives the impression that Mahler's Jewishness constituted no problem to himself—or others. There is ample evidence to the contrary; of hostile discrimination and anti-Jewish demonstration which plagued him both professionally and artistically:

"If Mahler's music would speak Yiddish, it would be perhaps unintelligible to me. But it is repulsive to me because it *acts* Jewish. This is to say that it speaks musical German, but with an accent, with an inflection, and above all, with the gestures of an eastern, all too eastern Jew. So, even to those whom it does not offend directly, it cannot possibly communicate anything."[12]

Anti-Semitism must be accounted a major tension in the constitution of Mahler's personality, though of course his birth as a Jew had, too, its positive side, both in the make-up of his character and his music. That practical awareness of the consequences of being a Jew must have been an early experience is stressed by the fact that the Mahlers were only able to migrate to Jihlava after the removal of restrictions on the movement of Jews from one place to another.[13] This climate of social sufferance plus an explosive political atmosphere can only have exerted a nagging pressure on Mahler during his most formative years. Though he may have slept, politically, through his adult life, he never rid himself of the most pressing of status problems—of the Jew, "everywhere an intruder, never welcomed".

We might think that here already, in these circumstances of double alienation, there was sufficient tension to test even a character of marked poise, one firmly based in an affectionate family life. The family, as an integrated unit, can do much to mollify the assaults of the outside world, sheltering the children when young and at the same time guaranteeing them a fund of emotional security which will last them a lifetime. But Mahler enjoyed no such good fortune. With the kind of iron fatality that we meet in Greek tragedy, his youth was flawed by conflicts at every level; and nowhere did conflicts rage more fiercely than in his home, the very centre of his fractured universe.

If Mahler himself proved to be a man of conflict, his father, Bernard Mahler, a Jew, born at Kaliště on 2 August 1827, was no less afflicted by a violently disturbed disposition. We can build up only a rough sketch of his background from the available evidence. Hans Holländer tells us that he was a freethinker, who "shut the door upon every religious usage of traditional Hebraism". Alma Mahler describes him as "a man of strong and exuberant vitality, completely uninhibited". His mother, Mahler's grandmother, "was a woman of masculine energy. She was a hawker and even at the age of eighty went from house to house with a large basket on her back".[14] Mahler's own account is more enlightening:

> "My father (whose mother previously supported the family as a pedlar of drapery) had the most diverse phases of making a livelihood behind him and, with his usual energy, had more and more worked himself up [the social scale]. At first he had been a waggoner, and, while he was driving his horse and cart, had studied and read all sorts of books—he had even learnt a bit of French, which earned him the nickname of a 'waggon scholar'. Later, he was employed in various factories, and subsequently he became a private coach [*Hauslehrer*]. On the strength of the little estate in Kalischt [Kaliště], he eventually married my mother—the daughter of a soap manufacturer from Leddetsch [Ledeč]—who did not love him, hardly knew him prior to the wedding, and would have preferred to marry another man of whom she was fond. But her parents and my father knew how to bend her will and to assert his. They were as ill-matched as fire and water. He was obstinacy itself, she all gentleness. And without this alliance, neither I nor my Third [Symphony] would exist—I always find it curious to think of this."[15]

Three important facts emerge from Mahler's fragment of autobiography—his father's very humble beginnings, his cultural ambitions, the misalliance that was his marriage. It is easy to see here the seeds of the conflict that soured Bernard's life and predetermined, and yet made a hell of, his marriage. Quite obviously, Bernard wanted to improve himself. Alma Mahler—who can only have had this biographical information from her husband—tells us that at Jihlava Bernard had "what might almost be called a library, and was goaded on by the ambition to better himself".[16] There is something rather pathetic about Bernard's attempts to become an intellectual, to climb out of his village rut, especially since racial prejudice probably both hampered his progress while intensifying his determination to overcome opposition, to prove himself to his antagonists. I think there can be little doubt that it was, in the widest sense, Bernard's obsessive desire to join the ranks of the cultivated that chose his wife for him. Marie, some years younger than himself—she was born on 3 March 1837[17]—was not only "all gentleness", as Mahler relates, but came "of a good Jewish family named Frank".[18] Her family, in fact, as Plate VI shows, was not named Frank but Hermann (Guido Adler has the right name in his book).[19] The birth particulars further reveal that she was the daughter of Abraham Hermann and Teresa "born Hermannová", an indication of inbreeding, doubtless a by no means uncommon practice in these small (and in any case minority) communities, but one that may well have contributed to the strain of instability, physical and mental, which was prominent in Marie's children.

Alma Mahler drops a significant clue to the unhappy marriage when she reveals that Marie, amid family circles, "was jokingly called the 'duchess'" because of "her superior refinement".[20] We know from Mahler's testament that his parents were as compatible as "fire and water"; we know that Marie did not love her husband—"she married . . . without love and with utter resignation"[21]—and can only presume from Bernard's treatment of his wife that he certainly did not love her. The secret of her attraction for Bernard reposed, I suggest, in "her superior refinement", in her superior social status; Mahler's father married, in his own social context, a "duchess"—many a joke conceals a deep truth—and it seems in accord with his cultural aspirations that he should have acquired culture in the shape of a refined wife of a good family. The prize would have flattered his vanity, soothed his feelings of inferiority, and swelled his self-esteem. But from his attitude to his wife, it is safe to assume that while the winning of her may have temporarily assuaged his consciousness of his own inadequacies, it was her very refinement that made the marriage an impossibility. Bernard, living with Marie's "gentleness", may have found himself continuously irritated and incensed by characteristics after which he yearned but did not possess. The pattern is a familiar one, and the will to marry Marie does not at all exclude his subsequently rough handling of her. If Bernard's choice of a superior wife was dictated by his own feelings of inferiority, it is logical enough to attribute his outbreaks of violence to the constant reminder of his inferiority implicit in his wife's refinement.

Those outbreaks must have haunted Mahler's childhood. His wife relates[22] that "the marriage was an unhappy one from the first day", that Marie had to suffer "unending tortures" as a consequence of "the brutality of [Bernard], who ran after every servant, domineered over his delicate wife and flogged the children". The father "gave way to his temper whenever the mood took him". Alma Mahler declares that the boy "saw nothing of the unending tortures his mother had to endure", and certainly it is noticeable that Mahler's own conversation with Bauer-Lechner makes no direct mention of the scenes that must have occurred between his father and mother. In the light of a later document, this omission figures as a significant suppression, the deliberate burial of unpleasant memories.

In the summer of 1910, Mahler sought an interview with Sigmund Freud, the psycho-analyst, who was then on holiday in Holland. Two sentences from Freud's report—made in a personal communication to Marie Bonaparte in 1925—give us a vivid glimpse of the relations between Mahler's father and mother:

"His father, apparently a brutal person, treated his wife very badly, and when Mahler was a young boy there was a specially painful scene between them. It became quite unbearable to the boy, who rushed away from the house."[23]

We shall see later that this event played a central rôle in the formation of Mahler's musical character. Biographically, his disclosure—and, of course, all the conditions of his conversation with Freud favoured disclosures of this kind—not only supports in detail the general accounts of Mahler's unhappy family background but shows, in fact, how violently he reacted to his parents'

7

"unbearable" incompatibility. It was the peculiar conclusion of this particular episode—the comment of the hurdy-gurdy[24]—which left its mark on Mahler's music; but the incident must have been repeated a hundredfold, and there can be little doubt that his personality was permanently scarred by witnessing such distressing scenes. Mahler, then, did not, as his wife claims, see "nothing of the unending tortures his mother had to endure from the brutality of his father"; on the contrary, he was an active, impressionable, agonized observer of a situation that inevitably intensified his Oedipal attitude towards his mother: hence, among many other things, his years of celibacy, his intense relation with his sister, Justine, and the severe crisis which profoundly disturbed his marriage in 1910—which, indeed, prompted his visit to Freud. His love for his mother, which his wife tells us "had the intensity of a fixation, then [i.e., in childhood] and always",[25] which Freud diagnosed as such, "You loved your mother, and you look for her in every woman" (though Mahler "refused to acknowledge his fixation on his mother"),[26] cast long shadows over the span of his life. The hostility between his parents completed the circle of conflicts which surrounded his early years; it hit him hardest, because deepest, and hurt him most. The wound never healed. Small wonder that his wife "never heard Mahler say an affectionate word of his father"; and as one might expect of a relation as intense as was Mahler's with his mother, his feelings there, too, were by no means void of hostile components. In a letter to his friend Friedrich Löhr, from Jihlava in July 1883, Mahler writes of his depression at returning home and finding those he loves "so wretched, so gloomy"—his parents, in fact, were seriously ill, already on the road of bad health that led to their deaths in 1889. He continues, "I myself, so hard and cruel to them—and yet I can't help it, and torment them to distraction", a comment indicative of the ambivalence of his emotions towards his parents and, at the same time, a measure of the guilt he felt at his "cruel" behaviour.[27]

I have offered a reason for Bernard's marriage of Marie. But why did Marie marry him? We know from Mahler himself that the marriage was no love match; it was not, it seems, even a one-sided love affair. Bernard's part was no more, surely, than an expression of his will to better himself? It was a strong will, as Mahler suggests, backed by pressure from her parents. Nevertheless, her acceptance of Bernard remains a little mysterious—especially so, since both Alma Mahler[28] and her husband[29] mention another man of whom she was fond—until we learn that Marie, despite her good family, had "no pretensions to a good match". She was "lame from birth".[30] The lameness did not deter Bernard, bent on acquiring superiority through marriage. But poor Marie, who was not only lame but of a delicate constitution, who suffered from a weak heart[31]—defects of physique inherited by her children—was simply obliged to accept Bernard *faute de mieux*. Thus did the Hermann family rid itself of its ugly—or, rather, crippled—duckling. The more one ponders on the facts of Mahler's early environment, the more one wonders at his survival. It would be hard to conceive a marriage more fraught with explosive tensions than his parents'.

One result of the nervous tensions that surrounded Mahler's childhood manifested itself very clearly as a tic in his right leg, which distinguished his gait: "peculiar, unrhythmical, urgent and stumbling" is his wife's description.[32] Alfred Roller, in a detailed account of this fidgety leg, wrote that Mahler never mentioned the matter to him, and assumed that this defect was a source of embarrassment to him.[33] Roller was probably correct. In this context, it is interesting, I think—even significant—that Mahler omitted any mention of his mother's lameness when reminiscing about his youth to Bauer-Lechner, only confiding the fact to his wife (it is a pity that Alma Mahler is not more explicit); in view of Mahler's *Mutterbindung*, it is hard not to conclude that there was some sympathetic relationship between his tic and his mother's limp.[34] Coincidences of this order are too bad not to be true.

It is a sign of the domineering, ruthless, even callous character of Bernard that Marie's frail constitution had to sustain the brunt of the housework—and the strain of bearing no less than twelve children. Five of the children died young, of diphtheria, writes Alma Mahler,[35] but perhaps as much of the family weakness of physique. Isidor, in any case, born in 1858, seems to have met,

9

when little, with an unspecified accident.[36] As for the rest, Arnold (b. 1869), Friedrich (b. 1871), Alfred (b. 1872), and Konrad (b. 1879), all died at an early age. These continuous deaths, which cut across Mahler's childhood and youth, must have been a depressing feature of family life in Jihlava. Mahler, who succeeded the luckless Isidor, was the eldest surviving child; his younger brother Ernst, born in 1861, died in 1874, "of hydrocardia after a long illness". Alma Mahler writes that this was

> "the first [?] harrowing experience of Gustav Mahler's childhood. He loved his brother . . . and suffered with him all through his illness up to the end. For months he scarcely left his bedside and never tired of telling him stories."[37]

The brothers and sisters who lived long enough to play a part in Mahler's adult life were Leopoldine, born in 1863, who married unhappily and died in 1889 of a tumour on the brain;[38] Justine, born in 1868, who, after the death of Mahler's parents, was to form part of his household, as was her sister, Emma, born in 1875; Louis (Alois), born in 1867, and Otto, born in 1873. Justine and Emma were to marry musicians who were, oddly enough, brothers. Justine married Arnold Rosé (1863–1946), who was long leader of the Vienna Philharmonic Orchestra and leader of a famous string quartet; he was Mahler's friend and close colleague. Emma married Eduard Rosé, Arnold's elder brother, a distinguished 'cellist.[39] These two sisters seemed able, eventually, to come to some sort of terms with life, though Justine's later relation to Mahler was an unduly fervent one, and in childhood her fantasies assumed a neurotic shape. Alma Mahler relates a story that, she claims, "is thoroughly characteristic of her":

> "While still a child, [Justine] stuck candles all round the edge of her cot. Then she lay down and lit the candles and firmly believed that she was dead."

Poor creature, she may well have wished that she were dead. She had, it seems, "an unusually vivid imagination", but "the practice of lying was systematically inculcated in her by her father's shortsighted harshness. It was long before she awoke from a nightmare of whippings."[40]

Mahler's two brothers, Otto and Alois, showed no capacity whatever to adjust themselves to the requirements of everyday existence. Alois, the elder—"rather a fool than a freak"—indulged in ridiculous but self-inflating impersonations, to the embarrassment of his family. A rather sad, because so remote, meeting in Vienna between the two brothers is recorded in a letter of Mahler's to his wife, written from Mannheim in January 1904:

> "At the *Westbahnhof* I encountered my fine gentleman of a brother, the writer and chief accountant. The poor wretch looked at me sideways, half-shy, half-curious. It did after all touch me more than I had expected. I was only afraid that he would end up in my carriage. Indeed, I already saw us in the same sleeper. Well, that was spared me."

Mrs. Mahler completes the story. Alois

> "called himself Hans, because it sounded less Jewish, ran into debt, forged notes and finally had to flee to America. When he wanted to look smart, he wore a top-hat, a flowered waistcoat and white spats."[41]

Otto's is a tale of squandered gifts. He showed exceptional talent for music, and Mahler, whose favourite he was, "employed a tutor and got him through his school-work by hook or by crook. In later years he found him jobs as répétiteur in small German towns, but all to no purpose".[42] We have a glimpse of Otto's musical perceptiveness from a letter of Richard Strauss, written to his parents from Weimar on 31 January 1892, in which he asks them whether they have read Hanslick's unfavourable citicism of his *Don Juan*, done in Vienna. He continues:

> "Mahler (Hamburg) sent me yesterday a letter of his nineteen-year-old brother in Vienna, who writes about the work with the greatest understanding, enthusiasm and thoroughness. The young are already going along my way!"[43]

"But all to no purpose"; despite Mahler's aid—and anxiety for his brother was a constant preoccupation, especially after the death of his parents in 1889—Otto's development was frustrated by a deep-seated inhibition which led him "again and again" to throw up "the livelihood provided for him". Self-destruction was a logical conclusion to what we may guess was a short life of acute self-distrust and anguished insecurity—expressed it seems, as lack of "seriousness and perseverance"—and, in February 1895, Otto shot himself.[44] "He left a note saying that life no longer pleased him, so he handed back his ticket."[45]

Bruno Walter tells us that in Otto's desk were found

> "two symphonies . . . , one of which had been performed but once, and only in part, the other having been received with total lack of understanding—nay, with derision. There were a number of songs with orchestra; three books of lieder, which nobody sang; a third symphony was nearly completed."[46]

Walter is the only writer on Mahler who refers to these MSS. of his brother which, comprising symphony and "songs with orchestra", offer an intriguing parallel to the development of Mahler's own music at this time. One wonders what became of Otto's musical remains.

If I have dwelled on Mahler's family at some length, and anticipated later events through tracing the little we know of the personal histories of his parents, his brothers and sisters, it is simply in order to provide as detailed a background as possible to his childhood, for though there are few references to the early years of the Mahler children apart from Mahler's, what Alois became and Otto's sad fate are suggestive enough of the childhood tensions that shaped their destinies. It only requires a little imagination brought to bear on some of the essential biographical facts—Mahler's status problems, the incompatibility of his parents, his mother's feeble health, the scenes of brutality, the death of Ernst, the swift yet spaced-out deaths of five other infant brothers, the morbid imagination of Justine, the neurotic indolence of Otto, the crazy ambitions of Alois—to gain a fairly clear picture of the almost grotesquely contorted background to Mahler's youth.

I feel that not even a Strindberg, Ibsen or Dostoievsky could have contrived a family charged with a greater variety of high-voltage psychic tensions.

Alma Mahler, rather curiously and misleadingly, makes much of Mahler's day-dreaming as a boy. "Indoors and out he lived in a dream; he dreamed his way through family life and childhood." It was this same dreaminess, she claims, that led him to see nothing of what his mother suffered at the hands of his father.[47] But we know from the structure of Mahler's own personality, from his confessions to Freud, how certain youthful impressions bit deep. We know from his limp, and above all, from his relation to his wife, that his identification with his *suffering* mother was, in fact, intense. Alma Mahler herself tells us that Mahler "wanted my face to be more 'stricken'—his very word", that he thought "it was a pity there had been so little sadness in my life"—all of which supports Freud's analysis when he told Mahler: "You loved your mother, and you look for her in every woman. She was careworn and ailing, and unconsciously you wish your wife to be the same."[48] When Mahler was a very small boy, he was asked what he wanted to be. Back came the reply: "A martyr!"[49] It is not fanciful, I suggest, to understand this strange remark as further expression of his overwhelming identification with his mother's lot—a "martyrdom" (Alma Mahler's word),[50] the impact of which he registered at both conscious and unconscious levels. We should be very misguided—and indeed flying in the face of what seems to me incontrovertible evidence—if we assumed that Mahler travelled through his childhood mysteriously untouched by its patent strife.

It is, of course, as a response to this strife that his established day-dreaming must be interpreted. It was undoubtedly a means of escape, of retiring into himself when the pressure of external events was otherwise intolerable; a method of sitting out an emotional storm, of conserving energies, of enduring unpleasant physical circumstances. Alma Mahler describes how, as a little boy, Mahler was left in a wood by his father. Bernard, who has forgotten to do some duty at home, returns to the house, becomes absorbed in other activities and forgets the child. Hours later he goes back to the wood and finds his son exactly where he was left, very much at peace with himself.[51] Stefan tells us that Mahler's "teachers and companions notice from time to time a certain indifference—not inattention, but simply a forgetfulness of his surroundings. . . . Once he whistles during school hours a long note to himself, and awakes thereby to the effect, not a little astonished".[52] We know, too, that in later life this capacity for complete self-absorption remained. Mahler could, at will, suddenly withdraw, during a rehearsal, when his attention was not required—with comical results[53]—or from a conversation that he no longer wished to sustain.[54] Mahler's dreaminess, variously manifesting itself as "obstinate endurance" (Alma Mahler), or "concentration" and "a quite staggering lack of consideration for others" (Bruno Walter), in one respect, at least, was inherited by his daughter who, in her childhood, "could sit and wait for hour after hour as though in a physical trance".[55] Though in Mahler's dreaminess we can see that genius, in the most adverse circumstances, will find means of self-protection, of subterranean development and nourishment—as an artist, we may say that he owed something positive and valuable to being thrown back, however roughly, on his own resources—it is also of interest that his dreamy forgetfulness, a marked absent-mindedness, could shape itself as disguised aggressiveness. The incident of the untidy drawer is a significant example:

> "Every day his father exploded over the untidiness of Gustav's drawer—the one and only place where tidiness was demanded of him; and yet every day Gustav forgot all about it until the next explosion burst about his ears. It was quite beyond him to bear this one trifling command in mind."[56]

This category of day-dreaming, I suspect, was motivated less by that characteristic self-absorption than by hostility to his father. It was forgetfulness—however unconscious—with a purpose. There is all the weight of psychological truth behind this resistance to an unloved father's authority, behind this seeming neglect of a simple duty which resulted in untidiness in "the one and only place where tidiness was demanded of him". There was, after all, every reason to remember his father's injunction—to avoid the daily row; and yet the reason not to remember was by far the more powerful. Multiply such an episode a hundred times, and it becomes easy to fill in the outline of the tense, disputatious relation that existed between father and son.

All these incidents from Mahler's childhood would have taken place at Jihlava which, undoubtedly, was a great improvement on Kaliště. There was a grammar school, a music library, a military barracks, a town theatre, newspapers, and a not insignificant local musical tradition (both ancient and modern), and some sort of local society, a petty bourgeoisie compounded, one imagines, of the professions and officials of the municipality. The Mahlers moved to Jihlava in 1860; a guide-book of 1896—published, that is, seven years after the death of the parents—describes Jihlava as "an old town on the *Iglawa*, with weaving and plush factories and important markets. . . . The municipal and mining code of laws of *Iglau* is the oldest in Moravia."[57] A later Baedeker, published in the year of Mahler's death, informs us that the town possessed "25,915 inhabitants, mostly Germans", and two railway stations.[58] According to Engel, Jihlava, when the Mahlers took up residence there, was "still untouched by the modernizing railroad",[59] and it seems probable that the town, smaller than it was in 1911, developed extensively during the lives of Mahler's parents, as indeed it has done since; after 1889, which brought the deaths of Bernard and Marie, Mahler's association with Jihlava ceased. That Jihlava was a thriving, expanding community is not merely of academic interest. Bernard Mahler, when he moved from Kaliště to Jihlava, "set up in his business again",[60] and doubtless the move itself was partly determined by the better commercial potentialities of the town. Stefan says that Mahler's parents were "shopkeepers".[61] But Alma Mahler endows Bernard with a "distillery",[62] jokingly referred to in family circles as the "factory";[63] and it was presumably the distillation and sale of spirits that Mahler's father pursued in Jihlava. What, in fact, the "factory" amounted to, it is difficult to judge—the joke suggests, to nothing much. The Mahlers' Kaliště home scarcely supports visions of plenty. Stefan states that the parents were "only fairly well to do";[64] Alma Mahler, that Mahler "did not come of a poor home, merely from one of soul-destroying narrowness".[65] It may well be that Bernard's fortunes took a turn for the better after December 1860. Certainly the distinctively period photographs of Mahler, taken in Jihlava,[66] and those of his parents,[67] evoke an atmosphere of invincible respectability, from Bernard's silk hat down to the twelve-year-old Mahler's bowler. Yet it seems that the house in Jihlava was not a very elegant one, that the products of the distillery were sold on the premises in a kind of bar where rough behaviour rather than bourgeois manners would have been witnessed by the children.[68]

What, in short, best describes the Jihlava dwelling is the description Dr. Hans Holländer gives the place, who has seen it—"a small pub". He refers on another occasion to the family dwelling as a "liquor-shop", and adds that, some years later, in order to accommodate their growing numbers, the Mahlers moved into

"the neighboring house (Pirnitzergasse 6). The roomy courtyard, the garrets of the sprawling houses, the cellars and storerooms, held a world of romance for the boy Gustav, evoking in his spirit dim presages and fantastic pictures. Among the children who gathered here for play, the pale and weakly Gustav Mahler was a leader. He suggested new games, was the strict arbiter of discipline and order."

That "liquor-shop" adequately represents both the building itself and the profession of Mahler's father is confirmed by a letter Mahler addressed to Richard Specht in 1904.[69] Specht had written a small book about Mahler and had asked the composer to check biographical data, etc., in advance of publication. We find Mahler protesting at Specht's endowment of his parents with a "pub" [Schank]—which seems to him to be "a somewhat trivial specification" (he does not deny its truth)—and suggesting that the "business-man status" of his father would be a sufficient designation (he follows here the anonymous "business-man" classification of his father in the birth certificate). Specht, of course, readily obliged, and in the book itself[70] we find Mahler's parents appearing as "poorish business people". Thus the true character of Bernard's profession and the environment in which his son grew up was kept hidden by Mahler's understandable sensitivity to his origins. We may now, I think, see the "distillery" for what it was—indeed, the family "factory" joke becomes more pointed—and regard Bernard stripped of the disguises which his son had created in an access of self-protection.

Whatever the degree of the Mahler family's poverty, whether moderate or intense—and Specht says that the parents "never had to let their children go hungry"—we do know for certain, from an early letter[71] in the archives of the *Gesellschaft der Musikfreunde*, that Mahler, *c.* 1876, applied for exemption from the Conservatoire's fees. The sixteen-year-old boy pointed out that his father was in no position to support him, not only unable to pay the Conservatoire's bill. Mahler himself could not pay; indeed he was finding existence in Vienna difficult enough, with too few [piano] pupils to help him make ends meet. With many regrets, he informs the Conservatoire that he will have to cease his studies there if his application is not granted. Should his circumstances later permit it, he would pay his fees.

The outcome of this matter does not concern us here.[72] What the letter seems to reveal is an impoverished state of affairs at Jihlava—sixteen years after the Mahler family had moved there— which tends to weigh against Alma Mahler's statement that the home was not a poor one. There is no reason to think that Mahler exaggerated his circumstances, since there is no reason to think that Bernard would not have paid his son's fees if he could have done; so far as we know, Mahler enjoyed parental encouragement of his career as a musician instead of the customary opposition. Perhaps, after all, the "factory" did not flourish as Bernard may have hoped. Alma Mahler tells us that at Jihlava his "pride and reserve cut him off from other people and he was left to himself".[73] Perhaps the burdens of a large family were too great; even after Mahler had left home, his parents still had a sizeable family to support. Perhaps Bernard, with his marked bourgeois aspiration, lived outside his means. For whatever reason, it seems probable that the Mahler family, at best, never achieved more than a pinched, lower middle-class status.

Mahler's parents appear to have encouraged his musical talents. There, in fact, we have a valuable example of the positive side to Bernard's cultural ambitions; the self-pride he would have taken in his son's achievements actively helped Mahler to realize himself, or as Alma Mahler puts it, Bernard "was goaded on by the ambition to better himself, but he was uncertain how this craving was to be satisfied. So he decided that his children should achieve what was denied to himself." An anecdote found in Reik's book illustrates Bernard's parental ambition:

> "The father of Julius Tandler, who became a famous professor of anatomy at Vienna University, and Bernhard Mahler, the father of the composer, once took a walk together in Vienna. They passed the Anatomical Institute, and Mr. Tandler remarked, 'My son is now a medical student, but he will some day be professor in this building.' Ten minutes later the two men went by the Opera on the Ringstrasse, and Mr. Mahler pointed to that impressive house, saying, 'My son is at present conductor at the provincial theater in Laibach, but he will one day be director of the Imperial Opera.' "[74]

As we shall see later, Bernard took very practical steps to develop his son's gifts.

What was the musical occasion that was decisive for the boy's parents? Alma Mahler writes:

> "Once on a visit to the parents of his mother . . . Gustav could not be found. After a long search he was at last discovered in the attic, strumming on an old piano. From that day on his father was convinced that he was destined to be a musician."[75]

The tale is confirmed by Stefan, who adds, however, that nothing could persuade the boy to leave the piano, "not even the call to meals".[76] "From that day on" is thus determined by Alma Mahler: "[Gustav] was then four years old."[77] The point is of no great moment—Mahler was certainly an infant when the event occurred—but the difficulty of establishing it chronologically amusingly illustrates the problems facing the most modest biographer. Alma Mahler relates the same incident in another place where Mahler is aged not five, but four.[78] Stefan, on the other hand, says that Mahler was six, as does Specht.[79]

It may be awkward accurately to place this early performance as a pianist, but that Mahler's talents manifested themselves early is in no doubt. He himself claimed that from the age of four onwards he was both making music and composing, even before he could play scales.[80] From Stefan we have an account of other musical impressions and activities (it was music, he tells us, which brought a liveliness to a little boy who was otherwise "quiet, shy, reserved", whose parents "would gladly have seen him livelier"):

"Moravian servants, both Germans and Slavs, sing willingly and well. Melancholy songs accompany getting up [sic] and going to bed. The bugles ring out from the barracks [at Litoměřice].[81] The regimental band marches past. And the tiny youngster sings each and every tune after them. At the age of four, someone buys him a concertina,[82] and now he plays them himself, especially the military marches. These latter have so much attraction for him that one morning, hastily dressed, he hurries away after the soldiers, and gives the market-women who come to fetch him[83] a regular concert on his instrument."[84]

Alma Mahler confirms that the small boy secreted himself about the barracks in order to eavesdrop on the military signals.[85] Specht records that between the ages of four and six[86] Mahler could sing already over two hundred [?] folk-songs, learnt from servants.[87] Dika Newlin warns us that "those trumpet-calls" which appear in Mahler's early songs (but not only there, of course) have been attributed to "the influence of the military barracks near which Mahler spent his childhood" by "over-imaginative biographers",[88] and thus raises the whole problem of the relationship between Mahler's music and the musical impressions derived from the environment in which he spent his youth. It seems clear to me that the part popular, part folk, part military musical atmosphere in which Mahler grew up did, in fact, exert a considerable influence on the formation of his style, that his imagination was stimulated and even permanently coloured by local musical events in a manner which owes nothing to the feats of reconstruction by "over-imaginative biographers", that the geographical context of his birth—his Bohemianism, let us call it—was more of an active force in his music (or in certain important works) than has hitherto been realized. It is, of course, the quite peculiar use to which Mahler put his popular materials which is of significance, which distinguishes his music at its most folk-like both from the nationalists and the cosmopolitans or Europeans (Brahms, for example, or Franz Schmidt) with gypsy leanings; the latter tendency was always a feature of the Austro-German tradition from the eighteenth century onwards. We must naturally beware of reading too much into a seemingly simple equation of style and environment—Mahler converted the musical experiences of his boyhood into highly complex symbols—but there is nothing gained in denying a vital source of inspiration.

We know, as it happens, from Mahler's interview with Freud how a certain region of popular music making became charged— lastingly so—with a particular emotional tension. To escape that "specially painful scene" between his father and mother Mahler rushed away from the house:

> "At that moment, however, a hurdy-gurdy in the street was grinding out the popular Viennese air 'Ach, du lieber Augustin'. In Mahler's opinion the conjunction of high tragedy and light amusement was from then on inextricably fixed in his mind, and the one mood inevitably brought the other with it."[89]

The mundane, as we know, is often a prime component of Mahler's symphonies. If we care to establish the "hurdy-gurdy" as a symbol of the mundane, the striking incident outlined above enables us to place the origin, and account for the presence, of that whole area of musical experience, which formed so substantial a part of the background to his youth, in the music of his maturity. A casual yet fateful sequence of events meant that the "hurdy-gurdy" was for ever associated with Mahler's intensest inner life. Small wonder, then, that his early musical impressions, endowed with so exceptional an emotional significance, proved to play a weighty rôle in the formation of his musical personality. Mahler's extensive recollections of his childhood impressions—though the central, searing experience was subjected over the years to endless permutations—were motivated by the most powerful of psychic tensions. Thus we do not need to exercise our biographical imaginations in an attempt to force a relation between Mahler's music and the environment of his youth, but merely to appreciate the musical consequences of a violent collision between two realms of experience, the impact of which continued to vibrate throughout Mahler's compositions. This direct link between childhood musical memories and a basic emotional situation seems to me to offer the best of all reasons for the prevalence of the mundane in Mahler's music, while, of course, it does not exclude the probabilities of other influences, both immediate—e.g., folk-song elements—and later—e.g., "the universality and grandeur of Bruckner's horns and trumpets", which Miss Newlin views as an influence as contributive to Mahler's "trumpet-calls" as the barracks at Litoměřice.[90] However, I think the validity of the attributions of origin to the mundane in Mahler's music must finally be determined by the specific function the mundane assumes within a given musical context; and here, it is my opinion that the music supports my general proposition that the region of the hurdy-gurdy, and all its affiliations, was charged with tension by a singular complex of occurrences, and derives its special meaning from the association of a particular musical event with a profound experience of childhood. In these circumstances, Mahler's remark to his wife in a New York hotel, on hearing a barrel organ playing in the street below—"took me straight back to my childhood"—takes more stress than would many a sentimental memory similarly expressed. His description of it as "such a lovely barrel organ"[91] suggests that in later life, Mahler's memories of childhood, as is so often the case, were sometimes warmly coloured; one recalls the aura of the loved one, the mother, and suppresses the contingent conflicts.

Whatever Mahler's childish talents for composition amounted

to, it was, from the outset, his gifts as a pianist that were concentrated upon; and there is ample evidence to confirm the view that his parents, to the best of their ability, helped to develop them. He started lessons, it appears, at the age of five with, rather oddly, a double-bass player of the name of Sladky.[92] When he was six, music lessons were continued with Herr Viktorin, the *Kapellmeister* of Jihlava's theatre, and later (or conterminously?) with Brosch, a piano teacher proper.[93] He must have learnt fast, because Specht tells us that at the age of eight he had a pupil of his own, aged seven.[94] Mahler's fees were minimal, but probably his demands were high. The end of the affair was prophetic: ". . . owing to the inattention of the learner, the teacher loses his temper and the instruction has to be broken off".[95] Further influences included industrious use of Jihlava's music lending library[96] and visits to the house of the family Fischer, through whom he came into contact with local musical society—in particular, the church choir. "On holidays", Holländer writes

"the *regens chori* of the parish church, Heinrich Fischer (whose son [Theodor] was Mahler's favorite playfellow and schoolmate), took him into the choir, where he became familiar with Haydn's *Sieben Worte*, Mozart's *Requiem*, Rossini's *Stabat Mater*, and other sacred compositions."[97]

Nevertheless, it must have been that Mahler's parents, while satisfied with the rate of his progress, were not satisfied that their talented son was receiving due recognition; or perhaps they determined to show Jihlava the youthful genius living unnoticed in its midst. Whatever the motive—and the parents may well have been prompted by the boy's teachers (Viktorin, however, seems to have left the town)—a subscription concert was organized, and on 13 October 1870 the ten-year-old Gustav Mahler made what seems to have been his public *début*, as a pianist, on a platform in Jihlava. The programme is not known, but the event was recorded thus in *Der Vermittler*, a Jihlava weekly paper:

"On 13 October 1870 there was, by way of an exception, an *Abonnement suspendu*, the reason being that a nine [sic]-year-old boy,

22

the son of a local Jewish tradesman named Mahler, was to be heard for the first time playing the the piano before a large audience. The great success the future virtuoso achieved with his audience did him honour; one could only wish that for his excellent playing he had had an equally good instrument at his service. If the young artist's former teacher, Herr Kapellmeister Viktorin, hears of yesterday's success, he can certainly be pleased with his protégé."[98]

The newspaper reporter's comments on the piano are suggestive of the environment in which the "future virtuoso" was expected to flourish. None the less, the success of this concert brought its rewards. The young Mahler was now in demand. He played the piano, accompanied choirs, and partnered a violinist, Milla von Ott, in her violin recitals. Patriotic occasions also brought Mahler into the public ear, for instance, the marriage in 1873 of the Archduchess Gisela, and in 1879, the celebration of the silver wedding of the Emperor and Empress. His repertory would seem to have included a fantasia on themes from Bellini's *Norma*, and pieces by Schubert, Schumann, Mendelssohn, Chopin and Liszt.[99]

This local activity as pianist which marked Mahler's childhood and early youth was not the only shape assumed by his music-making in Jihlava. In later years, he offered his small home town the opportunity to taste the talents for which he became famous— as composer and conductor. (Mahler conducted a performance of Suppé's operetta, *Boccaccio,* in Jihlava on 12 September 1882. The Jihlava *Grenzbote* praised the "precise ensemble" of the performance and Mahler's "spirited conducting". The leading lady was one Fräulein Hassmann, whom Mahler described as "the shallowest creature among women to have come my way for a long time". Doubtless Mahler's parents would have been among the audience.)[100] But up to the time of his entry into the Vienna Conservatoire, it was his piano playing which was the best evidence of his musical gifts and there can be little doubt that the "minor sensation" he caused at Jihlava gave his parents confidence in his future as a musician and smoothed the path towards the realization of his ambitions. An account of the impression Mahler's abilities as a pianist made on his acquaintances must await the next chapter.[101]

23

Mahler may have been rapidly developing into a musician, but there was still his formal education to be considered. He attended first Jihlava's *Volksschule* (primary school) and then, in 1869, the grammar school (*Gymnasium*), two years earlier than was customary.[102] The education there was of "public high school" standard, "with emphasis on the classical languages".[103] That Mahler entered the grammar school under age suggests that he was a bright child, but most accounts agree that he did rather badly in his studies; perhaps he found the atmosphere utterly uncongenial. One commentator writes that he was "unreliable", "scatterbrained", and achieved only "uneven results".[104] We know already of Mahler's capacity for self-withdrawal, and have quoted an instance of it from Stefan; such episodes, it is suggested, occurred as a consequence of musical day-dreaming. It may have been that Mahler, by the time he had grappled with his developing musicality and his emotionally strenuous life at home, had little energy to spare for school work. In 1871, when Mahler was eleven, he changed schools, spending the winter term (five months?) in Prague. There he attended the *Gymnasium* and was boarded out as a piano pupil in the home of Alfred and Heinrich Grünfeld,[105] brothers who became noted musicians, whose father, presumably, owned "the celebrated music firm of Grünfeld" mentioned by Alma Mahler.[106] Possibly Mahler's parents thought that the Prague combination of school plus musical training in an environment which obviously had more to offer than Jihlava was a practical step in the right direction—at least their action seems to show once more their care for their son's musical advancement. In the event, the scheme turned out badly. Though it is scarcely credible, Alma Mahler tells us that the boy's "clothes and shoes were taken from him and worn by others and he had to go barefoot, and hungry also"—all of which Mahler said he "took . . . as a matter of course". What, according to his wife, awoke Mahler from his childhood dreams and brought him into touch "with the ugliness of life for the first time" was acting as

"involuntary witness . . . of a brutal love-scene between the servant and the son of the house [presumably Alfred, born 1852], and he never forgot the shock of disgust it caused him. . . . This episode left a deep mark. . . . Gustav never forgave the young pianist who had given him this shock."[107]

I have suggested earlier that Mahler's day-dreaming was a re-action to the particular realities of his domestic life, that he was not as out of touch with aspects of the "ugliness" of his own environment as Alma Mahler seems to assume. Nevertheless, it may well be true that the distasteful incident in the Grünfeld home was Mahler's first awakening to this kind of "ugliness". The affair evidently affected him profoundly, and it seems probable from traits that manifested themselves in his adult character that this rough sexual revelation, coupled with the effects of his relation to his mother and the experience of his father's aggressive behaviour to his wife, played no small rôle in the formation of his emotional life. Though the reverberations of this episode were less far-reaching, and the "love-scene" itself an isolated occurrence, it is not altogether irrelevant to recall the inhibiting influence in later years of the young Brahms's unhappy experiences in the *Lokale* of Hamburg. With both composers, the resultant inhibitions had their musical consequences.

Bernard, "by a side-wind", heard of his son's plight in Prague and brought the uncomplaining, passive boy back to Jihlava, at whose *Gymnasium* he remained until he departed for Vienna. Mahler made his own laconic comment on his education in a letter of 1896: "My youth consumed by the Gymnasium—nothing learnt. . . ."[108] His mania for reading, a passion which developed early[109] and never left him, seems to have owed nothing to his schooldays. Here, perhaps, he was stimulated by his father's "library" and literary leanings.

1875 proved to be a decisive year. It must have been that Mahler's age and the state of his musical talents forced a family decision. It seems that a musician from Prague, Gustav Janowitz, was among those from outside who counselled Mahler's parents to send their son to Vienna; he had been much impressed by the boy's performance of Beethoven's sonata op. 81A (*Les Adieux*), and his positive opinion aided the final unfolding of their resolution.[110] "The family", says Stefan, "seems to have had no doubt as to what the boy's profession would be in view of his obvious talent, although a sacrifice would have to be made to allow him the necessary time for study, and there were other children to be considered." In any event, Bernard took Mahler to Vienna and called upon Julius Epstein (1832-1926), a celebrated piano teacher at the Vienna Conservatoire. Epstein, "not very willingly, but still struck by a remarkable look in the boy's face . . . invited the young unknown to play something, either of his own or otherwise. And after only a few minutes he told the father: 'He is a born musician'; and answered all objections with, 'In this case I am certainly not mistaken'."[111]

Epstein certainly was not; and on 20 September 1875 student No. 326, "Mahler, Gustav, aus Iglau [from Jihlava] 15 J[ahre]: [15 years]", [112] commenced his first term at the *Conservatorium der Gesellschaft der Musikfreunde* in Vienna.

II

1875-1878

THERE can be no doubt that, on the fifteen-year-old citizen of Jihlava, Vienna must have made an enormous impact. Apart from the journey to the capital for interview by Epstein, we have no record of visits to Vienna made by Mahler during his youth. The short period he spent in Prague during the winter of 1871 seems to have been the only occasion when he left the area in which he was born. In every respect, then, Vienna must have been brand new to him; the parochial atmosphere of Jihlava was exchanged for city life, a city moreover in which Brahms and Bruckner were residents, while the primitive musical amenities of his home were replaced by the rich, professional resources of the Vienna Conservatoire. We know, or can reconstruct in some detail, the history of Mahler's musical development in Vienna—the creative interrelation between place and personality. The influence of Vienna apart from the sphere of musical culture is more difficult to determine, but Mahler's later career neatly fits into Křenek's thumb-nail sketches of the city's ambivalent attitude to its outstanding personalities, all of whom

"brought up in the peculiar intellectual atmosphere of Vienna lived ever after in a dialectical syncretism of love and hatred for that city which offered splendid potentialities for the highest accomplishments, as well as the most stubborn resistance to their realization."[1]

It is probable that during Mahler's first years in Vienna he was most taken up by the "splendid potentialities", though "stubborn resistance", too, came his way—it was not until 1897 that, in one activity at least, he succeeded in conquering Vienna, and even then "stubborn resistance" dislodged him after ten years' exercise of no less stubborn power. We cannot, however, despite what must have been Mahler's total immersion in the student life of the Conservatoire, discount the possibly formative influence on his early years of that "peculiar intellectual atmosphere" to which Křenek refers, and which, in part, was due to the political and cultural unrest contingent upon the decline of the Austrian empire after 1750. It was a strand in that outer circle of conflicts already discussed in the preceding chapter. As Křenek puts it, in the later nineteenth century

> "the inability of coping with the increasing political difficulties on the part of the representatives of the imperial idea became more and more evident. A most peculiar attitude of hedonistic pessimism, joyful skepticism touching on morbid sophistication, became the dominant trait in Vienna's intellectual climate."[2]

I have suggested earlier that one must be wary of drawing strict parallels between intellectual (social, political) climates and characteristic features of an artist's personality. "Morbid sophistication" is just the kind of tag which has been tied on Mahler time and time again. But intellectual climates are notoriously difficult to define, and, if established, their effect on an individual is equally difficult to assess. In any case, too many foreboding climates are discovered after the storm has broken, whose existence would never have been perceived but for the ensuing catastrophe. It remains true, none the less, that the strains and tensions which were finally to snap the *status quo* in 1914, shortly after Mahler's death, were present in Vienna in the 1870s and even more intensively so in the 1890s and first decade of the twentieth century. They doubtless exerted considerable pressure. If, however, we readily admit a formative social influence—and the scope and character of Mahler's reading, for example, shows how specific a product he was, in some aspects, of the prevailing intellectual atmosphere—we must admit that it will not, in relation to his music, bear the degree of analysis to which his family influences may be subjected, nor return such promising results by way of verification.

The bare facts of Mahler's career at the Conservatoire, which

28

are exposed on a later page, must be read against a biographical background, of which it is less easy to offer a decisive impression. Facts are rather few, documentation is scanty, and some of the facts, I suspect, have become muddled or exaggerated or obscured with the passage of time. Mahler told both Bauer-Lechner and his wife quite a substantial amount about his student days, and though I have no doubt that his memories, in essence, were accurate, much of their detail is vague or contradictory. In the absence of knowledge based on primary sources, many of which, I fear, can now never be tapped, I can do no more than attempt to reveal the flavour, the general trends of Mahler's life as a student. Its precise chronology is as difficult to establish as the order of composition of his early works, most of which he destroyed.[3]

That Mahler was poor when he was a student all accounts confirm, including Mahler's own letter to the Conservatoire, which has already been quoted. Alma Mahler tells us that Mahler and his friends were "very poor"; by way of relief it seems that his parents sent him parcels of food, pocket-money and old clothes.[4] His economic conditions had many personal and some musical consequences. Epstein, for instance, Mahler's piano professor, who had advised Bernard to send his son to Vienna, countersigned Mahler's application to be excused his fees and agreed to pay half the fees himself. The letter is undated, but since, according to the Conservatoire records,[5] Mahler was on half-fees from 1876-7 onwards (his second year), it is likely that the document belongs to 1876—and that Epstein's generous offer was accepted. Whether Epstein paid half fees and Mahler half, or whether Mahler was excused paying anything at all and only Epstein was charged, is not clear; but in any event Epstein took a warm-hearted interest in the boy, befriended him, and gave him indispensable financial aid. Mahler, for his part, seems to have appreciated his piano teacher's exceptional kindness and to have kept up with him in later years.[6] Epstein, we learn from Stefan, was proud to call himself "Mahler's teacher";[7] this sympathetic, perceptive man deserves a special tribute both for his insight and his readiness to dip into his own pocket. He played, I think, a fatherly rôle in Mahler's student years, the extent and benefits of which have not been fully recognized.

Despite Epstein's assistance and contributions from home, Mahler still had to make ends meet. Here Epstein again, and his own pianistic gifts, were of help. From Mahler's letter to the Conservatoire about his fees, we know that his piano teacher had promised him pupils; indeed, he asked him to take on his own son, Richard Epstein, as a pupil—"probably for humanitarian as well as professional reasons".[8] Though Mahler apparently found it difficult to find enough pupils, there is no doubt that his piano lessons were an important activity and source of income throughout his student career, and beyond it; for example, in June 1879—almost a year after he had left the Conservatoire—we find Mahler on a Hungarian estate, hired for the summer to teach a boy the piano and promote the family's appreciation of music.[9] Alma Mahler gives an amusing instance of the solutions Mahler and his student friends had to hand when economic pressure became too severe:

> "When their money ran out, one of them gave a pupil notice. The plan was to ring the bell, say he was suddenly obliged to go away and request payment for the lessons already given. The ready money provided meals for all three for a day or two. On the other hand, a pupil was lost for ever."[10]

This sort of struggle for sheer survival marked not only Mahler's strictly student period in Vienna, but the years that followed, before he became inextricably caught up in the routine of life as a conductor; and it was not really until 1883, with his appointment at Olmütz (Olomouc), that his career as conductor assumed the remorseless continuity that shaped the pattern of the remaining twenty-eight years. There were, in fact, five years after the completion of his course at the Conservatoire to which the term student period may still apply; though these years were broken by intermittent theatrical engagements—his earliest—by journeys home, or by acting as a resident piano tutor outside Vienna or Jihlava. Vienna, where jobs were to be discovered, was the anchor to which he clung, and the general conditions of his life there

were essentially those which obtained between 1875–8, when
he was on the roll of the Conservatoire itself. I can only make
this brief excursion into the future because, as I have said above,
it is difficult to establish a precise record for Mahler's student
years; a typical anecdote, unless we are fortunate enough to have
a date, may well belong to any year between 1875 and 1883.

We can assume, however, that from 1875–8, Mahler's years
at the Conservatoire, his hands were full with the new life in
Vienna, with teaching and with being taught, and with the
assimilation of all manner of fresh experiences, though Schiedermair is explicit that lack of funds prevented him from using
to the full the musical amenities offered by the city's opera house(s)
and concert halls. We learn from Stefan, too, that "he seems to
have visited the theatre only seldom, and it is right to say that he
became acquainted with most of the operas he conducted later
only as their conductor". On the other hand, Holländer suggests
that this ignorance of the musical theatre must be qualified in
view of the repertory of Jihlava's opera company. Works played
there between 1870 and 1880 included *Figaro, Don Giovanni,
Fidelio, Der Freischütz, Faust, Ernani,* and *Il Trovatore*, besides
a full complement of operettas. It does seem improbable that
Mahler would have missed these productions on his own door-
step. Perhaps his opera-going days were curtailed when he
moved to Vienna?[11] Only Alma Mahler mentions an opera,
Götterdämmerung, in connection with Mahler's student days, and
Götterdämmerung was not performed in Vienna until 1879;
there must, I feel, have been many events of a like nature, both
earlier and later, which have gone unrecorded. In any case, the
Conservatoire possessed what appears to have been a thriving
opera school, and there can be little doubt that Mahler would have
come to terms with many new works—new to him, that is—
through student performances or study groups. For example,
from 1875–7, the opera school attended to, in whole or part,
Lucia von [di] Lammermoor (and other operas by Donizetti),
Fidelio, Die Afrikanerin [L'Africaine] (Meyerbeer), *Der Waffen-
schmied* (Lortzing), *Aida, Der häusliche Krieg* (Schubert), *Faust*
(Gounod), etc.[12] There is no reason to suppose that Mahler

31

missed any opportunities to expand what must have been the very limited boundaries of his musical background; indeed, his earliest compositions, which belong to his student period, in particular *Das klagende Lied*, are suggestive of a wide range of stylistic models with which he was familiar.

In addition, moreover, to his work at the Conservatoire, Mahler continued to study privately for his school-leaving examination. He had, it seems, a tutor by the name of Melion, who supervised his preparation for his matriculation, which he passed at his second attempt in 1877, in Jihlava.[13] The Mahler family, obviously, were not prepared to run any risks in the education of their gifted son; his formal studies were not to be neglected, however promising was his musical bent. His matriculation, as it happened, enabled him to enrol as a student at Vienna University, in the same year that he sat for his examination.[14] He registered there for lectures in philosophy, history, and the history of music, a choice of subjects that not only reflects intellectual trends characteristic of Mahler's questing personality but also the influence of his education at the *Gymnasium*, with its classical emphasis. I think we may count Mahler's laconic summing-up of his schooldays, "nichts gelernt", as something of an exaggeration. The learning he acquired (with whatever difficulty) proved to be a useful instrument in the pursuit of his interests outside music. It certainly coloured his reading.

Where Mahler lived in Vienna it is now probably impossible ever fully to determine. We have a few addresses for the years after 1878 which have mostly come into our possession through his association with Hugo Wolf. We may assume, in the absence of precise statistics, that the pattern of Mahler's moves from house to house was very much that of Wolf's, who indulged in an

> "endless succession of removals from one lodging to another, in search of cheap, yet decent and quiet 'diggings', where he could work at his music in peace. Between Wolf's return to Vienna in September 1876 and May 1879 . . . there are recorded no fewer than twenty-one addresses where he occupied rooms."[15]

It was doubtless as a peripatetic lodger that Mahler existed in

Vienna during his Conservatoire years and after. Alma Mahler relates an entertaining story that gives the reason for at least one of Mahler's moves to a new domicile. With two of his friends, he had heard a performance of *Götterdämmerung*—this anecdote, then, belongs to 1879, or later—and, "in their passionate excitement", the three of them

> "bawled the Gunther-Brunnhilde-Hagen trio [act two] to such effect that their landlady came up in a fury and gave them notice on the spot. She would not leave the room until they had packed up their scanty belongings, and then she locked the door angrily behind them."[16]

When we come to examine Mahler's record as a student at the Conservatoire, we have, fortunately, the archives of the *Gesellschaft der Musikfreunde* as a documentary backcloth, and though there are a few patches of obscurity, for the most part the facts are clear—a welcome relief amid the chaotic information that surrounds his early biography.

The winter term of 1875 commenced on 20 September. It was, it will be recalled, Mahler's piano playing that had been the plainest manifestation of his musical talent at home, that had earned him his entry into the Conservatoire; and it was on his piano studies that the stress was laid during his first year in Vienna. Stefan reports that "the Annual Report of the Conservatoire for the year 1875-6 shows that he skipped the preparatory class to enter the first finishing class for piano of Professor Epstein".[17] In view of Mahler's gifts, it is more than probable that he did jump a preliminary pianistic stage reserved for beginners; of more importance, perhaps, is the fact that the piano was marked as his principal subject, harmony and composition only as secondary subjects. At the end of his first year, the Conservatoire records show that Mahler had successfully completed his course of studies with Epstein and was admitted into the piano-playing competition (*Clavier-Concurs*) of 23 June 1876, at which he was unanimously awarded first prize for his performance of the first movement of Schubert's A minor Sonata.[18] This was not the only prize Mahler carried off; at the composition competition held on 1 July 1876, he won first prize for the first movement of a Quintet [?], a work which raises peculiar bibliographical problems of its own, besides introducing the confused topic of Mahler's student compositions. A fuller account of Mahler's *juvenilia* is attempted on another page, but it may be best to deal with this Quintet immediately since evidence concerning it belongs chronologically to Mahler's activities after the close of his first year at the Conservatoire.

When he returned home to Jihlava for the holidays—in 1875-6 there were excursions to Morawan, Ronow, Maierhöfe bei Časlau[19]—Mahler must have been reasonably satisfied with his first year's progress in Vienna. He had, after all, won two first prizes, and passed out of his three courses—piano playing, harmony and composition—with top marks. Perhaps it was these successes which determined him—or his parents—to display his prowess to the citizens of his home town as both pianist and composer. In any event, we know that on 12 September 1876, a concert was organized in Jihlava in which Mahler and some of his friends from the Conservatoire took part. The programme comprised contributions from Mahler the pianist—among other works, Schubert's *Wanderer* Fantasia, which he began (rather oddly) in the wrong key, and continued the transposition to the end of the movement—and two compositions, a piano Quartet and a Sonata for violin and piano. This concert was probably the first public performance of any of Mahler's own music.[20] About the violin Sonata, there will be more to say. The piano Quartet— or rather its first movement, which I suspect (but for a fragment of another movement) is all that was written—is of more immediate interest, not just because it happens to be one of the very few autographs[21] to survive from Mahler's youth, nor because of its prophetic, A minor key; but because it seems likely that this movement was the prize-winner of July, that the Quintet was, in fact, a piano Quartet. Holländer suggests that "the Quartet has some connection with the ostensible [prize-winning] Quintet movement", and Redlich plumps for the Quartet as the more probable choice, though without giving his reasons.[22] Most other commentators specify a piano Quintet's first movement as the prize-winning work.[23]

This matter is not of such moment to warrant pages of investigation, but it does appear to me to be most probable that the Conservatoire records are in error, although one cannot exclude the possibility that they may be correct. It would seem most natural that Mahler would, in his September concert, have put on the work that had won him a prize in July; and played it with those friends who doubtless were his colleagues in the competition in Vienna and thus already familiar with the music. The Conservatoire records, moreover, while detailing a Quintet, make no mention of a piano, nor do they list the performers, omissions which would not be especially striking were it not for the fact that the second prize-winning work dating from Mahler's Conservatoire years—a Scherzo for piano Quintet (1878)— is specified as such, with a double check in the shape of the five (!) performers' names.[24] Thus the rather scanty nature of the information concerning the first work raises doubts as to its reliability. Since, however, no piano was included in the movement's description, we have to explain why most commentators chose to describe it as a piano Quintet. Perhaps the solution lies in their establishing an automatic relation between the decisively recorded Scherzo for piano Quintet of 1878 and the Quintet of 1876, an impression which may well have been reinforced by unclear memories of a movement for piano and strings, a work both performed and circulated in MS. It would be easy, in these circumstances, for a piano Quartet to be converted retrospectively into a piano Quintet. In any event, until further evidence proves the Conservatoire records accurate I think it justifiable to view the extant autograph first movement of a piano Quartet as the prize-winning work of July 1876, as the piece that was revealed to such inhabitants of Jihlava as were interested on 12 September.

Mahler's first year in Vienna saw him launched as a composer; in his second, in which he renounced his participation in the year's composing competition, he doubtless consolidated his creative gifts, although he still took part in the piano-playing

▷ concourse of 21 June 1877, when again he won first prize for a
performance of Schumann's *Humoreske*, op. 20; on this occasion,
however, it does not seem as if the prize was unanimously awarded.
In his list of subjects, Mahler was credited with second year piano
studies (with Epstein) and second year composition; first year
▷ counterpoint now replaced the previous year's harmony course.
The whole entry is marked in the Conservatoire records with a
sign indicating that Mahler was excused half his fees.

While Mahler's name may be found in the relevant class
registers for the piano and composition, it is missing in the case
of counterpoint. Stefan reports that the director of the Conservatoire, "because [Mahler's] compositions showed so much
knowledge and skill", " 'let him off' counterpoint", "that Mahler even regretted it later".[25] I have not traced any regrets on
▷ Mahler's part and, as Stefan himself remarks, "how he mastered
counterpoint is best shown in his symphonies". (Alas, that fatal
act of excusal has been transformed into an instrument of unfavourable criticism, e.g., "Weakness in contrapuntal studies
hampered Mahler throughout his career[26]".)

This whole topic would seem to be a perfectly straightforward
and comprehensible event in Mahler's biography, despite the
fact that Guido Adler, an early chronicler, gives him a counterpoint professor without first verifying Mahler's attendance at
the professor's classes.[27] But there is, none the less, another point
of view—one to which I give little credence—related in a book
by Ludwig Karpath, an acquaintance of Mahler's in the later
Vienna years and music critic of the *Neue Wiener Tagblatt*. Karpath discloses a letter, dated 15 March 1912, from Dr. Robert
Hirschfeld, which purports to reveal the true reason for Mahler's
abstention from counterpoint:

". . . The 'Mahler boys', however, have written that he skipped his
counterpoint. But I offer proof, according to the archives, that he
reached Grade III [i.e., achieved no more than pass marks] and
consequently for reasons of tact was not mentioned in the final exam.
Please don't talk about this to anyone, since it is a great secret. At the
time, Bruckner [the composer] taught counterpoint. So he [Mahler]

was after all a pupil of Bruckner, but unsuccessfully so! With Professor Krenn [Mahler's composition teacher, and also a professor of counterpoint at the Conservatoire] it was easier to get full marks, to wit, in composition without counterpoint."[28]

The tone of this odd document, which appears in any case in a somewhat gossipy volume of reminiscences, is hardly free of bias, and further doubts as to its validity and intentions are intensified by Karpath's own reminder that Dr. Hirschfeld, music critic of the *Wiener Zeitung*, was one of Mahler's persistent opponents. That he should have bothered—only a few months after Mahler's death—to dig around in search of damaging revelations probably has no other significance than the evidence it offers of the hostile climate that surrounded Mahler's personality and continued to promote aggressive tactics even when he was no longer alive. I cannot refute Dr. Hirschfeld's statements. My investigations of the Conservatoire's archives do not in any respect support his conclusions. We have Mahler's own words on his relation to Bruckner, which explicitly deny a pupil status on his part, his name appears amid neither Bruckner's nor Krenn's counterpoint pupils, and if, for "reasons of tact" his name was dropped from Bruckner's class, would not that same tact have devised some means of covering up an otherwise inexplicable and prominent gap in Mahler's musical education—inexplicable, that is, only if we assume that there was something to hide? But this matter is scarcely worth a further thought. Mahler's counterpoint would not be undermined by Hirschfeld's burrowings, even if his "great secret" proved to be the truth. I reproduce his letter because Mahler's biographers customarily, and, I think, correctly, deduce that his skilful student compositions were the reason why he was excused a counterpoint class (see, for example, the development section of the piano Quartet's first movement, a model product of Mahler's first year as a composition pupil); and I thought it obligatory, if unrewarding, to take note of Hirschfeld's contradiction.

As we have already seen, Mahler, in addition to his work at the Conservatoire, was also studying for his matriculation. The close of his second year at the Conservatoire brought him to the summer of 1877 (the end-of-term piano-playing competition took place on 21 June), when, at the age of seventeen, he was expected to sit for his examination. His failure meant that he had to wait a further two months before finally grappling with and successfully accomplishing his matriculation. His third and best term at the Conservatoire would have begun towards the end of September, and it is probable that the re-examination can be allotted to the early weeks of that month. How Mahler spent the holidays we do not know, but doubtless, for part of them, he prepared himself for his matriculation; in his letter to Epstein, he speaks of a holiday task, set by the latter, that he was hoping to complete;[29] he may well have had other tasks of a like kind, and, of course, there was always the possibility of piano pupils.

For his last term at the Vienna Conservatoire, 1877-8, Mahler was listed for third year composition and history of music (*Geschichte der Musik*). Though he was no longer officially studying the piano, it was as a pianist that he appeared in a concert held on 20 October 1877, the whole programme of which gives us the period flavour of the musical taste prevailing in the Conservatoire:

1. Hummel: Septet (1st. mvt.)
2. *a.* [Julius?] Schulhoff: *Le Zephir* [sic] ⎫ for harp
   b. Zamara: *Aux* [sic] *Printemps* ⎭
3. Mozart: Aria from *Figaro*
4. Chopin: Nocturne (D flat major) [op. 27]
    Étude No. 4 (C♯ minor) [op. 10]
5. Verdi: Aria from *Maskenball* [*Un ballo in maschera*]
6. Xav. Scharwenka: Concerto for piano (B flat minor [no. 1, op. 3], 1st mvt.) HERR MAHLER
7. Mendelssohn: *Ich hör' ein Vöglein, Venetianisches* [sic] *Lieder* [*Venetianisches Gondellied?*]
8. Chopin: Concerto (E minor [no. 1], 1st. mvt.)
9. *a.* Brahms: *Liebestreu*
    b. [Th.?] Kirchner: *Es wäre so*, Lieder
10. Bach-Gounod: *Meditation*, for violin, 'cello and organ

Scharwenka's first piano concerto was composed only in 1877 —his compositions, we are told, "possess energy, harmonic interest, strong rhythm, many beautiful melodies and much Polish national character", and he was also celebrated as a pianist[30] —and thus Mahler's only recorded appearance as soloist in a concerto was in a contemporary work. It is odd that while Mahler's virtuoso ability as a pianist, so pre-eminent in his student days, came to nothing, his genius as a conductor apparently never disclosed itself.

On 11 July 1878, Mahler again appeared as pianist, but on this occasion as composer-pianist in a performance of the work that had won him a first prize unanimously awarded on 2 July, in his composition class. The entry for the concert of 11 July, when the final exercises (*Schlussproduktionen*) of the Conservatoire's composition pupils were performed, reads:

"[Item 6] Gustav Mahler: Clavier-Quintett (Scherzo). Clavier: der Componist und die Herren: Fried. Skalitzky, Stefan Wahl, Joh. Kreuzinger und Ed. Rosenblum."

There can be no doubt whatever that this Scherzo, unlike the obscure first movement of 1876, was conceived for the medium of the piano quintet.

The end-of-term concert in July brought Mahler's three Conservatoire years to a successful conclusion. Having fulfilled all the necessary conditions laid down by the institute's statutes— continuous attendance at a main course of study for not less than two years, submission to all prescribed examinations and the attainment of at least pass marks therein—Mahler was granted his matriculation; but more than that, he left with a Diploma, for which the regulations were even more stringent—i.e., success in the same conditions that applied for matriculation, with the provisos that the candidate should achieve "excellent" results in his principal subject and win a prize at the last concourse. It was doubtless Mahler's prowess as a composer that earned him this final distinction.

The bare facts of Mahler's career at the Conservatoire offer us only momentary glimpses of the development of his personality, his talents and his general musical education. We have to read very much between the lines, if we are to guess with any reasonable chance of accuracy at the variety of knowledge, experience and influences he assimilated during these early Vienna years. As Stefan puts it, "there is no information of how the Conservatoire influenced Mahler". What the Conservatoire's history of music course amounted to, I do not know; and if Stefan's information is correct, Mahler's name does not appear on the roll of those who heard the lectures.[31] Perhaps this particular gap was filled in by a parallel set of lectures which Mahler may have attended at Vienna University. It seems that he inscribed himself there from 1877-9 as an "auditor" of three groups of lectures: philosophy, history, and musical history.[32] Stefan tells us that "he heard . . . only a few of them, and his astounding knowledge was gained later according to his own plan".[33] It is not clear what Mahler had in mind by enrolling at the University, but it extended his education by a year—to 1879—and may well have stimulated his sympathies in spheres other than the strictly musical; besides, the university lectures must have brought him into contact with many new people. We know almost for certain that Mahler's close relation with Bruckner centres about his two university years. Altogether, in fact, the friends and acquaintances Mahler made as a student probably represented a vital and fertile breeding ground of new influences and new ideas, one not only in contrast to his own small-town upbringing but in opposition to the orthodoxy for which the Conservatoire stood. We must, then, take account of Mahler's circle, approaching it, however, by way of a few notes on his official teachers.

The director of the Vienna Conservatoire was Joseph Hellmesberger (1828-93). He took up his appointment in 1851. Frank Walker describes him as "additionally celebrated both as a witty man about town and as leader of an admirable string quartet".[34] The memoirs of the violinist Carl Flesch, who was also a pupil at the Conservatoire during the long reign of Hellmesberger, fill out the picture of the institute's director:

". . . the 'old' Hellmesberger . . . appeared to me to be a man of the world who, well on in years, tried at all costs to make a youthful impression, what with his wig and the jet-black dye of his whiskers *à la* Franz Josef. His tripping and stilted gait created the impression of a forced and coquettish grace which, according to Hanslick and [Arnold] Rosé, had characterized his playing too. . . . [He] is said to have produced a tone of captivating mellifluence. He conducted the students' orchestra and directed a chamber music class."[35]

Flesch continues, "three types of people were anathema" to Hellmesberger, Jews being one of them—a condition hardly conducive to happy relations with Mahler—while his musical character (he "was the naturally musical Viennese *par excellence*: he could do everything—even compose, although he had no creative talent. His *magnum opus* was a waltz-like salon piece entitled *Ballet Scene* and eminently suitable for the charity concerts of the Princess Pauline Metternich"[36]) represented much that was doubtless anathema to Mahler, as young as he was. We can see that such friction as there was between the Conservatoire's director and its fiery pupil resulted more from a radical opposition of musical ideals than the inevitable conflict between generations.

But Hellmesberger, of course, had many valuable positive qualities. As Flesch remarks,

"His real significance lies in the fact that he was the first who . . . introduced the Viennese public to the wonderland of quartet literature. The construction of his programmes at that time (i.e. round the middle of the century) was exemplary. As early as 1849 he performed Schubert's D minor Quartet, which had been virtually unknown; in later years, he played Schumann's and Brahms' chamber music and, above all, the Beethoven quartets, of which only the op. 18 set was generally known."[37]

There seems no doubt, however, that Mahler fully appreciated, indeed, revelled in, this side of Hellmesberger's musicianship. Adler recounts how much the Hellmesberger Quartet, and in particular their interpretations of late Beethoven, meant to the Conservatoire's students—"more than all the teaching".[38]

Less accomplished, it seems, was the director's conducting, which, according to Flesch,

> "did not seem to amount to much, at any rate from the point of view of our own contemporary standards. In my recollection, he appears as a pretty mediocre and impersonal time-beater of the roughest variety, and as a chamber music teacher, too, he showed a downright disarming negligence."[39]

Mahler and his 'Conservatoire' Symphony[40] suffered at the hands of Hellmesberger the conductor. It is curious that we have no news of students conducting the student orchestra. Adler's own memoirs give him an occasional place in the school orchestra (at the drums, with Mottl) but not a turn on the podium.[41] Can it be ironically true that Mahler passed through the Conservatoire without ever wielding a baton?

Hellmesberger's chamber-music activities earn him a niche in history. He was, moreover, among the examiners who, in November 1861, granted Bruckner his matriculation (though it was not until 1868 that he was appointed to the staff of the Conservatoire), and it was Hellmesberger who commissioned a work from Bruckner that finally emerged as the string Quintet of 1878-9. Hellmesberger's son, Joseph (1855-1907), was to cross Mahler's path in later years.

That Hellmesberger, the "witty man about town", "a legendary figure in Vienna" who was "an excellent artist of the traditional type, but also one of those 'good Viennese musicians' of the old stamp",[42] seemed to show some appreciation of the highly unpolished and idiosyncratic Bruckner's gifts, speaks in his favour. But he must have found the volcanic young Mahler a tough customer; while Mahler, for his part, and like Hugo Wolf, doubtless viewed Hellmesberger with suspicion. As Stefan has it, the director would hardly have been regarded as a pioneer by the "young and impetuous", the "rising talents", by whom he was surrounded.[43] In Wolf's case, his impetuosity strained "Old Hellmesberger's" patience and he was expelled from the Conservatoire "for offences against discipline" in 1877, during Mahler's second year. Wolf left to the announcement that he was quitting the establishment "where he was forgetting more than he was learning".[44] From Mahler, too, there was a loud rumble of insubordination, which is authenticated by an unpublished [?] letter in the archives of the *Gesellschaft der Musikfreunde*. In it, Mahler apologizes to Hellmesberger, in unusually humble tones, for a rash step and asks to be once again received into the Conservatoire. He assures the director that he will try to earn his approval by means of industrious study, and to make him as contented as his [Mahler's] teachers. The letter closes with further expressions of penitence. If, as seems probable from this document, Mahler felt for some reason or other obliged to leave the Conservatoire—the circumstances of the incident are not known, of course, but a collision between Mahler and authority must have been at the root of them[45]—then this fiery action of the sixteen-year-old student (the letter belongs to 1876[?])[46] counts as the first of the many resignations which were so marked a feature of Mahler's future career, a career that progressed by means of a series of explosive resignations, the last of which always propelled him to the next phase of his achievement. The furious rows that enveloped Mahler's musical life at every level were not only part of his temperament but part of the very machinery that enabled him to realize his artistic ambitions.

Mahler's early clash with the Conservatoire is probably symptomatic of the unruly tensions that governed his student days there, and those of his intimates; it also affords a fleeting glimpse of his own wilful, impulsive personality (fewer signs of the indrawn day-dreamer at this period!) and its response to the Conservatoire's environment.

The incident with Hellmesberger suggests that Mahler's characteristic aggressiveness was beginning to reveal itself in his behaviour, a conclusion supported by reminiscences of Julius Epstein, his piano professor, who also proved himself a good friend. It was Epstein who had advised Bernard Mahler to send his son to the Conservatoire and who later encouraged Mahler to accept his first engagement as a conductor. With Epstein, who was a notable piano teacher and one of the editors of the Schubert *Gesamtausgabe*,[47] Mahler always seemed to enjoy the most cordial relations which are reflected in the student's warmhearted letter of 1877[48] and in a later letter from Cassel, dated 26 March 1885, in which Mahler, the ambitious young conductor, writes "in old veneration" as Epstein's "grateful pupil".[49] Stefan records that "Epstein proudly calls himself Mahler's teacher, and tells how he from the first had a preference for this somewhat unruly and inspirational rather than hard-working pupil. We may also trust his kindness to have overlooked much that others do not usually pardon in enthusiastic youth."[50] "Unruly and inspirational" was probably putting the case mildly. Significantly enough, Mahler, in the Cassel letter to Epstein, in which he wishes to be remembered to "H[err]. Hofkap[ellmeister]. Hellmesberger and Professor Krenn", says: "True, is it not, that I am still as 'arrogant' as I was?" Though he places the revealing word between quotation marks and makes half a joke of it, we can sense that the adjective still has some force behind it, even in 1885, as a pointer to Mahler's youthful personality. Arrogant was a charge that was often to recur, and not all of those with whom Mahler was later associated were as kindly disposed towards him as Epstein was.

His harmony teacher, during his first year at the Conservatoire, was Robert Fuchs (1847-1927), a prolific minor composer now chiefly remembered for his serenades for string orchestra (hence he was known as the "Serenade Fox").[51] I doubt that Fuchs wrote the kind of music Mahler would have welcomed, but there is no evidence of friction between professor and pupil. Mahler's instructor in composition was Professor [Franz] Krenn. Krenn, so far as biographers of Mahler are concerned, has been misnamed ever since the early days of Mahler studies. It is as Theodore Krenn that he appears in Stefan's book of 1913[52] and as Theodor Krenn in Adler's monograph of 1916,[53] and it is with the wrong name that he has rolled down the years, from 1913, or earlier, to 1954, in the fifth edition of *Grove*. Thus, until challenged, are errors in musical history perpetuated. *Franz* Krenn (1816-97), who taught at the Conservatoire from 1869-93—not only composition, but also harmony and counterpoint—numbered both Mahler and Hugo Wolf among his pupils. He was a theorist and also a minor composer, mainly of church music, with no less than twenty-nine masses to his credit.[54] His creative ideals, we may presume, were hardly of a character to fascinate either of the two adventurous geniuses who came under his supervision, while his personal disposition seems to have been forbidding. Frank Walker describes him as a "dry-as-dust, monosyllabic pedant". " 'Old Krenn', everyone called him, for he gave the impression of never having been young at all."[55] Stefan, quoting Ernst Decsey, marks him down as "hardworking, taciturn and dry".[56] The "pedantry of Professor Krenn" eventually became "irksome" to Wolf, and doubtless contributed to his impatience with the Conservatoire and his voluntary or enforced retirement in 1877.[57] There is no knowing whether Mahler's act of insubordination was, like Wolf's, involved with his attitude to Krenn, or Krenn's to him, but in any event it did not lead to a fatal breach. Mahler survived the rigours of his most disciplinarian teacher with every evidence of outward success—two first prizes for composition—whatever the inward strain may have been.

If fewer of Mahler's student compositions had been destroyed or lost, and if those that remain were more freely available, then it might be possible to give a clearer picture of the relation between the development of his own musical personality within and without the Conservatoire. We should be able to measure, with some degree of accuracy, the influence exerted by his teachers, to contrast the probably conservative trends of his student efforts, sanctioned and initiated by authority, with the probably more radical traits exhibited in his first private creative labours. But while we have the cantata, *Das klagende Lied*, as an example of the latter, we have only the first movement of the much earlier piano Quartet, on the official, Conservatoire side, with which to compare it. Though we have a fairly full and documented account of Mahler's student career, most of the musical documents that formed part of it seem to have vanished. Thus it is difficult to assess, in musical terms, how much Mahler as a youthful composer owed to his institutional training and how much he was stimulated by events outside his curriculum and very probably in opposition to it. Certainly the first movement of the piano

45

Quartet, if it is representative of the compositions of Mahler's studenthood which pleased his teachers, is indicative of the conservative character of the Conservatoire's instruction—instruction not conservative enough for Brahms, however, who wrote in 1879:

> "Our conservatoire is in a terrible state as regards the teaching of composition. You only need to see the teachers [Krenn, of course, would have been active at this time] and not—as I often do—the pupils and their work. . . ."

(Mahler himself once described Brahms in a letter as "wedded to conservatism".)[58]

We may guess from *Das klagende Lied*—especially since the work was rejected when offered to the committee of the coveted Beethoven Prize—that Mahler's ideals as a composer were not shared by his teachers, that while the Conservatoire may have endowed him with adequate basic techniques, a sympathetic audience and artistic experiences of a calibre likely to have provoked his curiosity and aroused his inspiration were found outside the sphere of the Conservatoire's influence. In short, Mahler's growth as an artist almost certainly owed most to himself and his wider environment and comparatively little to his academy, though the strictly utilitarian function of the latter is not to be underrated. Adler, however, it must be recorded, had no high opinion of certain aspects of the Conservatoire's teaching. His comments on the institute stand in amusing contrast to Brahms's or Hirschfeld's. Brahms probably thought the instruction defective because it produced pupils whose music he deplored. Hirschfeld thought Mahler was not up to the standard of the Conservatoire's instruction. Adler, on the other hand, declares that the Conservatoire, ultimately, was not good enough for Mahler. He writes:

> "When at the age of fifteen he came to the Conservatoire in Vienna, he brought with him more talent than accomplishment. Good as were the piano and harmony teachers there, the instruction in the higher theoretical subjects (in counterpoint and composition) could

46

not have been less searching and to the purpose. Talent had to overcome this incomplete education, and only many years later was Mahler able to erase these deficiencies through iron industry and resolute personal study."[59]

It is interesting to have another point of view. None the less, in the face of the actual achievement of the early music, of the early songs, of *Das klagende Lied*—even the modest but very musicianly competence of the piano Quartet's first movement—one wonders not at any "deficiencies" but at the young composer's astonishing expertness and facility.

But we may assume, I think, that the musical atmosphere in which Mahler breathed outside the Conservatoire was more fertile and stimulating than that within. Unfortunately, however, that wider environment, reflected as it is in *Das klagende Lied*, is very thinly documented. In fact, we have a case almost the exact opposite of the Conservatoire years. There we have a fair amplitude of records, but no music. When we move outside the Conservatoire, we have some music—though only a little of what Mahler must have composed—but few sources of detailed information. We have to build up an account of the wider environment from biographical fragments and from parallel and better-documented studies of his intimate friends, of Hugo Wolf, in particular.

The artistic climate, outside the Conservatoire, inhaled both by Mahler and his acquaintances, was topical rather than period, and breezy rather than stuffy. As Stefan puts it, the "rallying-point" of these young people

"was the Wagner Society, and there the Master's cause was upheld in word and deed. It is not known how far Mahler took part in the struggles of that wonderful period; he was often enough looked upon as a fanatic, because, no doubt owing to Wagner's writings about Regeneration, he was at that time both an abstainer and a vegetarian."[60]

Hugo Wolf, no less than Mahler and even more explicitly,

47

became involved with the Wagner party, to which was opposed a substantial body of conservative opinion led by two famous and influential critics, Eduard Hanslick, of the *Neue Freie Presse*, and Ludwig Speidel, of the *Fremdenblatt*. 1875, the year in which both Mahler and Wolf started their first term as students at the Conservatoire, was, writes Frank Walker, "one of importance in the long conflict which raged in [Vienna] around Wagner, his theories, and his works". He continues:

"In the eyes of the young men of that day Wagner represented modernity, freedom, and progress; to conservative parents and pedants he was the great iconoclast and seducer of youth. Not only the man's music, but every shade of opinion that could be associated with his name, from anti-Semitism to pan-Germanism and, later on, even vegetarianism, was embraced wholeheartedly by the young Wagnerian party. The Vienna Wagner Verein [Society] had been founded in November 1872 and was wholly the product of this youthful enthusiasm. Felix Mottl [the well-known conductor, 1856–1911], the leading spirit in its foundation, who had sought and obtained the master's blessing upon the enterprise, was himself barely sixteen years of age at the time, and almost all the members, in the early years of the society's existence, were drawn from the ranks of the Conservatoire and university students. They were wholly under the spell of that mighty magician and demonstrated their allegiance with all the emphasis of which youth is capable. Max Burckhard [later director of Vienna's *Burgtheater*, a Privy Councillor and High Court judge, and a friend of Mahler and his wife][61] once waited for three days at a railway station, having heard that Wagner was expected to arrive there, simply for the honour of setting eyes upon the great man himself. To be young at that time was to be a Wagnerian, with all the earnestness and intolerance, the follies and the exaltations that the term implied."[62]

Mahler, as Stefan suggests, and like Wolf, succumbed to certain Wagnerian follies. In October 1880, for example, Wagner had published an essay in the *Bayreuther Blätter*, 'Religion und Kunst', "in which he had expounded for the first time his astonishing and newly acquired beliefs that in meat-eating lay the cause of the decline of the Christian religion and its influence, and in vegetarianism the only hope for the regeneration of man-kind". As Mr. Walker remarks, "the effect of this article on the faithful had been widespread and immediate".[63] Wolf was not long in establishing himself as a vegetarian, but Mahler must have been one of the first in the field, with views as convinced and claims as wide as Wagner's; we find him writing to a friend as early as 1 November 1880:

> "I have become, since a month ago, a complete vegetarian. The moral effect of this way of life, in consequence of the voluntary subjugation of the body . . . is immense. You can imagine how convinced I am by it when I expect thereby a *regeneration of mankind*."[64]

There is no record of Mahler interesting himself in any other of the extra-musical aspects of the extensive Wagnerian credo; one article of faith of the ultra-Wagnerian party, moreover, was its anti-Semitism,[65] but despite the fact that Mahler was a Jew, he does not seem to have been embarrassed by a conflict of loyalties, nor does the fanaticism of his support seem to have embarrassed Wagner's supporters. But it may well have been that as a Jew he felt a distaste for concerning himself with political and cultural ideals in which he, and his race, would have no part. Conforming to vegetarianism raised no problems of status.

The thought that the salvation of the world might be accomplished, so to speak, by nibbling at a carrot, formed part of the lunatic fringe of Wagnerianism. Mahler, as we have seen, did not fail to manifest the minor extremes of devotion, but it would be absurd to imagine that even at this early stage he did not respond creatively to what mattered most about Wagner—not his faith in the regenerative effect of the vegetable, but his music.

The case of Wagner was dominant in Vienna during Mahler's student years. It was a topic

> "to which no one could remain indifferent, and it seemed that, in considering it, scarcely any one was even able to preserve an open mind and a sense of humour and proportion. It resolved itself into a warfare of the generations, in which even family loyalties were frequently sacrificed to musical party politics."[66]

The much-discussed case was, in Mahler's formative Vienna years, mightily reinforced both by the presence of Wagner in the city and the performance of his works. It was in 1875, the year that Wolf and Mahler entered the Conservatoire, that Wagner returned to Vienna after an absence of three years to conduct two concerts of his own music in March; he "was received in state by the local Wagner Verein".[67] The programme comprised the *Kaisermarsch* and extracts from the *Ring*, which included "the first performance anywhere"[68] of the closing scene of *Götterdämmerung*. The first concert "ended with a demonstration of enthusiasm by the great audience that surpassed everything of the kind in Wagner's previous experience of Vienna".[69]

Later in the year, in May, he gave a further concert, while in November, Wagner came again to Vienna to supervise at the Opera performances of *Tannhäuser* (the Paris version, revised) and *Lohengrin*. Excitement in the city was intense, and we have a measure of the response of the enthusiastic student in Hugo Wolf, who wrote in a letter:

> ". . . on Monday, 22nd November, I was initiated into [Wagner's] wonderful music. It was *Tannhäuser*, performed in the presence of the great Richard Wagner himself. . . . The overture was wonderful, and then the opera!—I can find no words to describe it. I can only tell you that I am a madman. After each act Wagner was tempestuously called for and I applauded until my hands were sore. . . . More about Wagner in my next letter. I am quite beside myself about the music of this great Master and have become a Wagnerian."[70]

Wagner, in the autumn of 1875, "spent six weary weeks in Vienna". "Hanslick and Speidel once more showed themselves at their most contemptible in their treatment of him . . . but the majority of the critics were with him." Though in the midst of collaborating in these performances of his works at the Opera, Wagner found time to take note of other musical events in the city, and occasionally his path crossed the Conservatoire's; indirectly, when he went to one of "Hellmesberger's chamber concerts at which Brahms played the piano part in his own new C minor quartet", directly, if abortively, when "Hellmesberger tried to persuade him to pay a diplomatic visit of quasi-inspection to the Marchesi singing classes[71] at the Conservatoire", which Wagner "bluntly refused to do. It would take more than that, he told Hey, to rid 'these out-and-out Italians' of their prejudice against his music: Madame Marchesi in particular had distinguished herself by declaring his operas 'unsingable', the ruin of the human voice and so on."[72] The influential Madame Marchesi's attitude to Wagner's music, promoted within the classrooms of the Conservatoire, is suggestive of that institution's conservative character. Wagner, assuredly, was very much part of the radical, outside environment which absorbed our students' imaginations; it was their exercises, perhaps, not the products of their imaginations, that the Conservatoire's teachers initiated and received.

This is not the place for a detailed account of Wagner's turbulent relations with Vienna. His visits in 1875 were not his first nor his last, though his next, in March 1876, proved to be his final Viennese appearance—"it was a weary, disillusioned Wagner" who then departed, "firmly resolved never to set foot again in the town 'where every scurvy cur can fall with impunity on a man like myself and void his foulness on me . . .' ".[73] But if Wagner did not emerge again in Vienna in person, his music most certainly did, and it advocated his cause no less eloquently and perhaps more persuasively. Vienna, during Mahler's student period, was not only enlivened by performances of the early Wagner operas—we know, for instance, from a diary, that in 1875-6 Wolf heard *Der fliegende Holländer*, besides *Lohengrin* and *Tannhäuser*—but also by the first Viennese performances of the *Ring*, though the latter cycle was not first heard in its correct sequence. *Das Rheingold* and *Siegfried* were performed in 1878 (at opposite ends of the year!), *Die Walküre* in 1877, and *Götterdämmerung* in 1879; and while *Die Meistersinger* had been performed in Vienna as early as 1870, *Tristan* was not done there until 1883 (a year later, in fact, than the first London performance)[74] after no less than seventy-seven rehearsals.[75] We have learned already from Stefan that Mahler, in Vienna, appears to have visited the theatre "only seldom", unlike Wolf who, from the outset, was an inveterate opera-goer. None the less, we know that Mahler heard *Götterdämmerung* in 1879, probably in Wolf's company, and it is impossible to believe that he did not attend other performances of Wagner operas between 1875 and 1883. Mahler, after all, was renowned as a "fanatic", and his fanaticism he must have owed to his acquaintance with Wagner's music, however scantily documented are his visits to the opera house. There was, moreover, not only the possibility of encountering stage productions of the operas, but opportunities for hearing fragments from the works in concert performances, in both orchestral programmes and chamber recitals;[76] and, of course, the music itself was in circulation, presumably in the shape of vocal scores.[77] There can be no doubt—otherwise *Das klagende Lied* and a good deal of Mahler's development are inexplicable— that Wagner's music, by whatever means it was communicated, made a profound and fresh impact on the young composer. It is not simply for reasons of background history that I have stressed at some length and in some detail the record of Wagner in Vienna during the years of Mahler's apprenticeship, though as background the account is indeed of both biographical and musical importance, especially in so far as the Wagner case and its concomitants—the notorious Brahms-Bruckner feud, for example— expose a typically Viennese cultural situation of co-existent convention and revolt.[78] The relation between, say, the Wagner Verein on the one hand, and the conserving Conservatoire on the other, must be seen in this light. What is of specific significance *vis-à-vis* Mahler is the influence on him of Wagner's *early* operas, without an understanding of which (both the influence and the operas) it is difficult to comprehend the character of Mahler's own early music, not only *Das klagende Lied*, but the world of *Des Knaben Wunderhorn* and even, in part, the first three symphonies. We correctly assume Mahler to be a Wagnerian but forget that Wagner's range was wide. Today, the label Wagnerian summons up thoughts of the later Wagner, of the composer of *Tristan* and *Parsifal* in particular; it is only natural that we tend to identify 'Wagnerian' with that part of Wagner's achievement that has had most relevance to the growth of twentieth-century music. But for the youthful Mahler, early Wagner was new and affecting—he was developing as an artist while Wagner's music was still winning acceptance and, not least, performances—and it is *Lohengrin* and *Tannhäuser* and *Der fliegende Holländer* that we must bear in mind as vital stepping-stones on the way to Mahler's creative emancipation and fulfilment. All the musical evidence points to his comparatively late assimilation—in the song cycles and symphonies of his maturity—of late Wagner. It is true, of course, that Wagner, though the prime influence in Mahler's early music, was one among many, nor must we discount the prompt emergence of the authentically Mahlerian voice. None the less, the eclecticism of Mahler's first pieces is in itself a reflection of the eclecticism of Wagner's early style. Mahler took not only what Wagner had to offer, but also what Wagner had taken from others—hence some seemingly surprising stylistic trends in Mahler's first phase were his, so to speak, at second hand. We hear this process in reverse, in Wagnerian idiosyncrasies he received through his admiration of Bruckner and his music, when the Wagnerian Bruckner rather than Wagner himself may have been the more potent source of inspiration.[79]

So much for the general musical atmosphere that prevailed outside the Conservatoire. No less important than this environment, in fact part of it, were Mahler's friends and colleagues, who ranged from Bruckner, in his fifties, to Wolf, who was just a few months Mahler's senior. We have been able to extract from Wolf's account of his student days and the devoted labours of his English biographer something of the authentic taste of these Vienna years. Trifling incidents recorded on Wolf's behalf or by Wolf himself, that "as early as November 1875 he had found his first pupil in an engineer, who took lessons from him for three hours weekly, at a gulden an hour" (we can assume that Mahler, in his search for piano pupils, was no less prompt),[80] that "Professor Fuchs . . . gave me [Wolf] a ticket for a reserved seat in the circle [for a Philharmonic concert of 9 January 1876]",[81] must equally have been Mahler's experience; and though Mahler, it is said, was no

53

great concert- or opera-goer, the list of events Wolf attended during his Conservatoire period (Wagner's concerts and operas apart) throws further light on the musical atmosphere in Vienna in the 1870s and is suggestive of the composers that the students might have debated among themselves. We know from Wolf's diary that he heard at the opera in 1875 *Figaro, Oberon, Robert le Diable* (Meyerbeer), *Die Zauberflöte, Don Giovanni,* and *Fidelio*; concerts included Liszt's *Gran Mass* and Mozart's Mass in C (which Mass—there are several in C—is not identified). In 1876-7, Wolf heard *Der Freischütz, Lucia* (Donizetti) and *Les Huguenots*; Liszt's oratorio, *St. Elizabeth,* was performed at the *Musikverein,* and at a Philharmonic Concert the programme comprised Mendelssohn's overture, *Meeresstille und glückliche Fahrt,* a violin concerto by Viotti, Berlioz's orchestration of Weber's *Aufforderung zum Tanz,* and Beethoven's Symphony VI.[82] All this, doubtless, was but a fraction of the music Wolf assimilated out of and in the Conservatoire—we learn, too, of his enthusiasm for Conradin Kreutzer's *Das Nachtlager von Granada* and Suppé's overture to *Dichter und Bauer*;[83] but it suffices to give us some idea of what music was, so to speak, in the air when Mahler was a student.[84] With no diary at our disposal, we can do no more, no better, than sketch in the musical background against which he moved. Wolf, of course, is not only of use to the biographer of Mahler as a model who has fortunately been documented with some method. He was also, for a time at least, Mahler's fairly intimate friend, and in altogether later years he was to figure again in Mahler's life, though in the most unhappy circumstances. Both Mahler and Wolf during their first year were harmony pupils of Professor Fuchs. Their careers at the Conservatoire, however, did not run on parallel lines, though in 1876, in their second year, they were both in Krenn's composition class—Mahler for his second year and Wolf for his first. But it was during this second year—in the first quarter of 1877—that Wolf fell out with the Conservatoire authorities and was dismissed or retired of his own accord. There can be little doubt that these two young composers, sharing many common ambitions and ideals, and thrown together in the same classes, must have been on reasonably good

terms. It was, none the less, towards the end of the 1870s that
Mahler and Wolf renewed this preliminary stage of their friendship with increased familiarity.

1879 "seems to have been the period of [Wolf's] closest association with the young Mahler".[85] By then, Wolf had returned
to Vienna after the interlude at Windischgraz which followed his
departure from the Conservatoire; while Mahler, for his part,
had successfully completed his studies, though he was possibly
still attending lectures at the university. To whatever interests
they shared before was now added the certain aim that both of
them, free agents in Vienna, were bent on making their marks
there as composers—and both were hindered in the realization of
their ambitions by economic difficulties and the indifference or
hostility of the establishment; in Mahler's case, the economic
crisis was solved only by his undertaking his first appointment
as a conductor.

We have already noted an anecdote of Mrs. Mahler's which
implies that Wolf and Mahler lived in the same lodgings about
1879. The ex-students must have met again before then (Wolf
returned to Vienna while Mahler was still at the Conservatoire),
and it may well have been an identity of situation—both, as it
were, at a loose end in Vienna, seeking their musical fortunes—
that brought them together, rather than any fresh discovery of
mutual artistic or temperamental sympathies. Frank Walker writes
that Mahler "shared with Wolf the miseries of unquiet Viennese
lodging-houses"—Mahler remained ever acutely sensitive to the
disturbance of extraneous noises—and adds that "Heinrich Werner
records a story that Mahler lived with Wolf, and even shared a
bed with him, on the fourth floor of Opernring 23".[86] It is once
more through Wolf's biography that we catch a further glimpse
of Mahler's movements in 1879, information that again suggests
a close acquaintance between the two composers at this time.
Wolf writes home on 17 December:

"I move to-morrow to Cottage, near Vienna, in order to live more
cheaply. . . . Write therefore to Währing Cottage-Verein, Karl-

Ludwigstrasse 24. . . .[87] I have a dwelling—living-room, closet, lobby, kitchen, loft, and cellar—at the cheap price of 45 florins quarterly, that is 15 florins monthly, furnished of course. I have also a fine piano, for which I shall not need to pay any rent yet, because my friend Mahler, who leaves my future dwelling to-morrow, has paid up to the 1st. The instrument is excellent."

Mr. Walker continues:

"A letter of Mahler's, written on 22nd September of this year,[88] gives his address as Rennweg 3—the very house in which Wolf had been living before his return to Windischgraz for the summer, and to which he seems to have returned from October until he followed Mahler out to the Cottage-Verein at Währing, a settlement of detached villas in the English style, at that time still outside the city boundaries and probably used chiefly as a summer resort. In the winter months some of these villas, owing to their isolation, would be let at very low rentals."[89]

We have then at least three addresses for Mahler in 1879, with all of which there is some connection with Wolf. That it was "the first half of 1879, when, according to tradition, Mahler lived in the same room as Wolf on the Opernring", that "the first performance of *Götterdämmerung* in Vienna[90] took place on . . . the very day on which Wolf first moved into the lodgings on the Opernring", enables us to assign to this period, with some confidence, Mrs. Mahler's reproductions of her husband's reminiscences of his friendship with Wolf. The *dramatis personae* who figured in the *Götterdämmerung* fracas appear in another tale of Mrs. Mahler's, which almost certainly belongs to 1879. She writes that Mahler, Wolf and Rudolf Krzyzanowski

"shared a room for a few months. They were very poor and, as all three were musicians, extremely sensitive to noise; so when any of the three had any work on hand, the other two had to tramp the streets. Once Mahler composed a movement of a quartet for a competition while the other two spent the night on a bench in the Ringstrasse."[91]

The character of this incident is authentic, but its details are hard to verify. Mrs. Mahler does not specify the nature of the quartet or the prize. There is no reason whatsoever to think, as Dr. Redlich does, that this quartet movement is related to the prize-winning exercises (for piano quartet and piano quintet) of 1876 and 1878.[92] We know that Wolf was working at his string Quartet in D minor (1878-84) at this time. "Was it, perhaps," asks Mr. Walker, "originally intended for the same competition as Mahler's?"[93] We, in our turn, may wonder whether Mahler, in this context, was not working at a *string* quartet, as was his friend. But there the matter must rest. We have no documentary evidence that Mahler ever wrote or intended to write a string quartet, apart from this obscure reference by his wife. No such work forms part of the list of his lost or destroyed *juvenilia*.[94]

Another story of Mrs. Mahler's raises wider implications:

> "One day . . . Wolf got the idea of writing a fairy-tale opera. This was long before Humperdinck and undoubtedly an original inspiration. They considered many themes and finally hit on Rübezahl. Mahler was young and impulsive and he began on the libretto that very night and finished it next day. In all innocence he took it to Wolf for him to see. But Wolf also had made a start and was so put out by Mahler's having stolen a march on him that he threw up the whole idea and never forgave him. Outwardly they remained on friendly terms for some time longer, but they avoided each other's society. Many years later they met on the way to the Festspielhaus at Bayreuth and passed by with a curt: 'Hallo.' "[95]

This was not the end of *Rübezahl* by any means—there is more to be heard of the libretto and the music, in so far as Mahler proceeded with the latter—but it does seem that the opera marks, if it was not the cause of, the beginning of the end of Mahler's amicable relation with Wolf. If Mahler, as his wife remarks, "took" the libretto to Wolf, then the two composers were probably no longer living together, though still closely acquainted (as the exchange of addresses above supports). Even after 1879, Vienna's closed society still resulted in occasional meetings, and that the fairy-tale opera idea lived on is proved by Mahler's attempts at composing the music around 1881-2(?)—in Vienna—

and by Wolf's efforts, in the spring of the same year at Maierling, to settle down to an opera based on the legend of the fairy princess Ilse, a subject that had been suggested to him by reading Heine's *Harzreise*.[96] Neither project came to fulfilment, though Mahler took his work further than did Wolf, but that both composers, at roughly the same period, displayed various degrees of liveliness in the matter, seems indirectly to confirm the authenticity of Mrs. Mahler's reminiscence (while qualifying her comment that Wolf "threw up the whole idea"). Mahler and Wolf shared a common social circle in 1882 and the fairy-tale opera might well have been still a topic of discussion.

Thereafter, Mahler was swallowed up by his career as a conductor, and his removal from Vienna made final his break with his former companion. Mrs. Mahler tells us that Wolf, unlike the twenty-year-old Mahler, who undertook his first conducting appointment in 1880, "would not accept any job and said arrogantly that he was going to wait until he was made 'God of the Southern Hemisphere' ".[97] After 1882, apart from the Bayreuth encounter written of by Mrs. Mahler, there is no record of the two men meeting again until the tragic events of 1897 when Mahler, rather than Wolf, was the 'God'—he had just begun work at the Vienna Opera—and like all 'Gods' behaved, perhaps, with rather less than the requisite amount of human tact.[98]

Though Mahler's relation with Wolf was at length to explode, the conflagration lies fifteen years ahead; this account must rest at the point where their mutual regard, for whatever reason, died or frittered away. The episode remains as a curious, only temporary, commingling, at the most formative period in their lives, of two men of vital creative genius, each of whom was to make a substantial mark in very different spheres—Mahler's preoccupation with the symphony was almost as exclusive as Wolf's with the *Lied* (we have here an example of the specialization typical of the nineteenth century). I have suggested elsewhere, though now I would press the case far more diffidently, that there are certain aspects of Wolf's and Mahler's musical characters —so opposed in so many fundamentals—that will bear the weight of comparison.[99] It is, of course, their common Wagnerian allegiance that offers the most obvious source of stylistic identity, but that said, we are left with no more than a basic language employed by two masters whose methods are widely divergent. An inspection of Mahler's earliest songs (the first volume of the *Lieder und Gesänge aus der Jugendzeit*), and those songs of Wolf, some of which were published posthumously in 1936,[100] surviving from his student period and its aftermath, will, however, reveal an early stage of development when both composers shared more, creatively, than was ever to be the case in the future —their common musical traits,[101] like their common apprenticeship and habitat, belong to the years of their youthful friendship. As composers, they became, later, more and more remote, and one is obliged to ponder on their singularities, not their similarities, a fact which should engage the attention of those who believe that the social context is of such prime importance in the formation of an artist's personality and its mode of expression. Mahler and Wolf were both born in the same year, underwent, in part, the same training, were subjected to many of the same social pressures, and acquired, at the most impressionable time of their lives and in an almost strictly identical social environment, much the same range of experience. Despite their similar social contexts, Wolf turned out to be Wolf, and Mahler to be Mahler, and it is significant that we have heard little analysis of Wolf's music in terms of that disintegrating society supposedly mirrored in Mahler's, though we might have expected both composers to exhibit like social symptoms. It is hard to avoid the conclusion that, while society may exert its influences, it is another category of pressures that moulds the uniqueness of the composer's character.

None the less, if we extend our concept of character outside the strict sphere of musical idiom we shall find a characteristic common to the mature Wolf and Mahler (though the latter developed it the more fully), one the more notable since affinities are few and the characteristic itself—a capacity for irony[102]—met with but infrequently in music. For the rest, we are likely in attempting comparisons, to uncover opposites—Wolf's fastidious taste, for instance, and Mahler's lack of it. Wolf's good taste was as much an intrinsic feature of his musical character as the lack of it was an imperative condition for the effective functioning of Mahler's idiosyncratic talent. But it may well have been taste that prevented either composer from appreciating the other's gifts. They were not only free of mutual influence, but of mutual affection for each other's works. "There is no evidence", writes Mr. Walker, "that Wolf ever seriously considered Mahler as a creative artist, though he recognized his wonderful powers as an operatic conductor."[103] I suspect that Wolf may have thought Mahler's music inflated and vulgar. Mahler was not more enlightened about Wolf's songs; he remarked to Oskar Fried, the conductor, in 1910, "Of Wolf's one thousand songs, I know only three hundred and forty-four. Those three hundred and forty-four I do not like."[104] Did Mahler find Wolf's music text-ridden and anaemic? His comment, in any event, was a silly one; no sillier, it is true, than many of Wolf's opinions delivered in the *Wiener Salonblatt*, but as silly, simply, as many a composer's judgment of his colleagues, dead or alive, with whom he is out of sympathy. Few composers may be trusted as critics, least of all when apportioning blame; and even their praise is not above suspicion.

Wolf, as we have seen, was a whole-hearted Wagnerian, and in this enthusiasm Mahler was no less an equal partner. In 1904, in the midst of a bout of revaluations, Mahler wrote to his wife, "There are only [Beethoven] and Richard [Wagner]—and after them, nobody. Mark that!" He had previously been examining Brahms, with not very fruitful results:

> "All I can say of him is that he's a puny little dwarf with a rather narrow chest. Good Lord, if a breath from the lungs of *Richard Wagner* whistled about his ears he would scarcely be able to keep his feet. But I don't mean to hurt his feelings. You will be astonished when I tell you where I get more completely bogged than anywhere else—in his so-called 'developments'. It is very seldom he can make anything whatever of his themes, beautiful as they often are. Only Beethoven and Wagner, after all, could do that."[105]

Mahler's comment represents a typical composer's judgment,

revealing more of the commentator's character than insight into the character of the artist who is criticized. I doubt whether, in fact, this hasty appraisal of Mahler's may safely be read as his considered view of Brahms. It would doubtless, however, have pleased Wolf, whose battling for Wagner—and perhaps a rather unfortunate personal encounter with Brahms[106]—resulted in his undying hostility to the latter's music. But Mahler was more independent, less swayed by the great feud, in his approach to Brahms's work than was Wolf, and his personal relations were calmer, indeed, cordial, in later years. (Brahms's eventual admiration of Mahler the conductor is, of course, well known. It surprised Mahler at the time.)[107] Bruno Walter tells us that Mahler "was a passionate admirer of Brahms's *Variations on a Theme of Haydn* and loved to explain how high a standard Brahms in this composition had given the whole concept of variations". Alma Mahler writes of an impromptu performance of Brahms's horn Trio (op. 40), with Mahler at the piano, that took place in the Mahlers' New York apartment in 1910: she recalls its perfection as a rare experience.[108] It was Brahms's chamber music that Mahler found most appealing. He liked the G minor piano Quartet (op. 25)—"the only work of [Brahms] I can wholly accept"—and part of the C minor (op. 60), whose first two movements were "wonderful. . . . A pity that the last two movements fall off so sadly."[109] At an earlier stage in this survey of Brahms's chamber works—they were turned to at Maiernigg because bad weather kept Mahler indoors ("so for a change I played the piano")—it was the "charming sextet in B flat major" (op. 18) that unexpectedly modified his opinion that this region of Brahms's composing was "utterly barren music-making"; but for the Sextet, "I should have given [Brahms] up in despair, as I do myself at present".[110] Mahler's changeable, volatile judgment is again evident in a note of Bauer-Lechner's, from 1899, in which she records performances by Mahler and Arnold Rosé of Brahms's clarinet Quintet (op. 115) and clarinet sonatas (op. 120)—all three works in arrangements for violin and piano.[111] Mahler, previously, had not had much taste for these pieces: now he found them "splendid"—

and, in view of his own altered opinion, professed himself less surprised at the stupidity of artistic evaluations offered by the public.

In another of Bauer-Lechner's reminiscences, from the same year, we read that it was indeed in the chamber music that Mahler found Brahms revealing himself as a Master. On this occasion, Mahler expressed no qualifications, in contrast to his comments on Brahms's Symphony III which he had conducted in a Philharmonic concert in Vienna on 3 December (the work was "wonderfully played", Bauer-Lechner tells us). Mahler was enraptured by the symphony but dissatisfied with its instrumentation (and thus, presumably, with its sound). It was Mahler's feeling that Brahms's instrumental abstinence, his deliberate refusal to avail himself of the advantages and resources of 'progressive' orchestration, was all part of his hostility to Wagner. This, albeit intelligent, misunderstanding of the characteristic sound of Brahms's music emerges, it is plain to see, from Mahler's own instrumental approach, the character of which was bound to close his ears to the validity of Brahms's. Other thoughts of Mahler on Brahms, from the same source—in general, that he found Brahms's music wanting in unworldly, rhapsodic spontaneity—only consolidate the impression that Mahler was more sensitive to Brahms's inhibitions than his inspirations, a predictable consequence if the two composers' personalities are juxtaposed.[112]

Mahler's recorded views of Brahms show in some detail that he was far less committed to an extreme antagonism than was his friend Hugo Wolf; he maintained, in fact, a mid-stream position that would doubtless have excited Wolf's wrath. Wolf, of course, as I have mentioned, had not only artistic but personal motives for his vitriolic opposition to Brahms. But Wolf was an exceptional figure, and Mahler, I feel, with his often ambivalent attitude towards Brahms *and* Bruckner, is more truly representative of a climate of opinion more blurred at the edges than the history books would have us believe: that is, I doubt if the Wagner case, with its dependent feud between the disciples of Brahms and Bruckner, was as sharply defined in partisanship as appears at this distance in time. Epstein, for example, Mahler's piano teacher, was an intimate member of the Brahms circle, and yet, as we have seen, he was generous in his encouragement of his rebellious—and Wagnerian—young pupil. Hellmesberger, the director of the Conservatoire, to take another instance, was no less closely involved in the circle, and yet, though he exclaimed "This is Beethoven's heir" upon playing in Brahms's piano quartets (opp. 25 and 26),[113] he was not prevented from commissioning Bruckner's string Quintet nor aiding in the grant of Bruckner's matriculation.

The purpose of this brief digression is no more than to suggest that the background to Mahler's wavering judgments was itself far from being etched in black and white, that while his loyalty to Wagner was unshakeable, he retained a good deal of flexibility in his response to the 'Hie Brahms—hie Bruckner!' affair: such conditioning as existed in his case, was artistic rather than dogmatic, and, as I have hinted, dogma was the portion of the principals in the dispute—their disciples, perhaps uneasily and not always overtly, though perhaps more sensibly, kept more open minds.

The flexibility that Mahler displayed in a conversation about Brahms and Bruckner with his brother Otto, noted down by Bauer-Lechner in 1893, would most certainly have appalled Wolf had he heard of it, especially so in view of the conclusion Mahler reaches in his second sentence. We have already, I think, sufficient evidence of the momentary significance of Mahler's judgments—it does not diminish their interest—and there is no reason to take this longish utterance as a final evaluation; indeed by 1904, having worked through Brahms, Mahler had "fallen back on Bruckner again"; he decided then that they were "An odd pair of second-raters. The one was 'in the casting ladle' [*Peer Gynt*] too long, the other has not been there at all."[114] Mahler's conversation of 1893—Bruckner was still alive, and Mahler closes his remarks with an assertion that he would do what was in his power to gain the senior composer a hearing, who, in his lifetime, had not enjoyed his proper reward—neatly carries us on to a consideration of the two composers' singular friendship. "In order to judge a composer's *œuvre*", said Mahler,

> "you have to view it in its entirety. If you do so [in the case of Brahms and Bruckner], there is no doubt that Brahms emerges as the greater of the two, with his extremely well-rounded compositions which, incidentally, are in no way obvious, but disclose their depth and wealth in proportion as you delve into them—not to speak of his enormous fertility which, after all, you have to take into account when considering an artist's work as a whole. True, you are carried away by the greatness and wealth of Bruckner's invention, but every now and again you are disturbed and carried back, as it were, by its piecemeal character."[115]

Mahler's relation to Anton Bruckner (1824–96), with whom he is so often thoughtlessly coupled as a composer of similar character, is a complex one. Apart from his views on Bruckner's music, we have to consider Mahler's approach to his eminent predecessor as composer and conductor, and define his personal friendship with Bruckner, which was at its strongest during Mahler's student years. Bruckner's musical influence on Mahler can remain to be discussed as and when it arises in the course of examining Mahler's own works. His efforts on Bruckner's behalf as a conductor and his youthful friendship with the fifty-four-year-old master, who had already completed his Symphony V, may be treated here.

It is necessary, first, to trace a few of the steps that led Bruckner to Vienna. It was from Linz, at whose cathedral he was first organist, that Bruckner travelled to Vienna in 1861 to take the Conservatoire's final examination that would make him "eligible . . . for appointments as a teacher of harmony and counterpoint at conservatories throughout the monarchy".[116] As we have already noted, Hellmesberger, director of the Conservatoire during Mahler's studentship, was one of the examiners of Bruckner's powers of improvisation at the organ, an ultimate test that occurred in November and after the triumphant completion of which Bruckner received his long-sought-for diploma. Stimulated by his success, he made various attempts to secure a position of wider influence and greater responsibility, but it was not until 1868, after many failures and hesitations, that he finally gained an appointment in Vienna, as successor to his old teacher, Simon Sechter (1788–1867), at the Conservatoire. As professor of harmony, counterpoint and organ, Bruckner assumed his new duties on 1 October 1868.[117]

Mahler was not to arrive at the Conservatoire for another seven years, and Bruckner, meanwhile, was again agitating—he had commenced in 1867—for an appointment at Vienna University. Since his candidature was opposed by Hanslick, some years passed before Bruckner won his objective. He was appointed (unpaid!) lecturer in harmony and counterpoint in the University and "seems to have begun his lectures on 24th April 1876, although there is no absolute certainty about the date".[118] Bruckner continued activities in both institutions for many years, retiring from the Conservatoire only in 1891 and delivering his last lecture at the University in November 1894.

We are fortunate in possessing a letter of Mahler's—perhaps prompted by the currency of the myth that he was Bruckner's pupil[119]—in which he states very plainly how he himself regarded his friendship with Bruckner. It could scarcely be clearer in its refutation:

> "I was never a pupil of Bruckner. The world thinks I studied with him because in my student days in Vienna I was so often in his company and was reckoned among his first disciples. In fact, I believe that at one time my friend [Rudolf] Krzyzanowski and I were his sole followers. In spite of the great difference in age between us, Bruckner's happy disposition and his childlike, trusting nature rendered our relationship one of open friendship. Naturally the realization and understanding of his ideals which I then arrived at cannot have been without influence upon my course as artist and man. Hence I believe I am perhaps more justified than most others in calling myself his pupil and I shall always do so with deep gratitude."[120]

Mahler, in this document, while mentioning a most singular feature of his relation to Bruckner, "the great difference in age" between them—when Mahler was seventeen, Bruckner was fifty-three—makes no specific reference to attendance at the latter's lectures at the University or elsewhere. We must, I think, discount the probability of Mahler coming into contact with Bruckner at the Conservatoire, though he must certainly have been aware of Bruckner's presence and perhaps been intrigued by what he heard from friends who were in the great man's classes— from Hans Rott, for instance, who was enrolled as an organ pupil of Bruckner's for the year 1876–7. But the first impressions of the great composer may have been like those of Carl Flesch and his colleagues: "Among the teachers I used to meet in the corridors of the Institute, Anton Bruckner must be mentioned first; with his incredibly wide pants, he then seemed to us students a ridiculous figure."[121]

Though there may be no "absolute certainty" of the date when Bruckner commenced his lectures at the University, there can be no doubt that he was firmly installed there by 1877, the year in which Mahler enrolled as an auditor of various courses. We have no decisive information of Mahler's attendance at, or reaction to, any university classes but for Bruckner's, and even here commentators are cautious: Stefan, for example, writes that "there is little doubt that Mahler attended Bruckner's lectures"[122]—at the other end of the biographical scale Stefan's cautious assessment has become "attended religiously"[123]—while Alma Mahler, who offers some Bruckner anecdotes presumably related by her husband, mentions nothing of the older composer's University activities and confines herself, indeed, to the somewhat ambiguous statement that Bruckner "was not, strictly speaking, Mahler's teacher".[124] Guido Adler fills out the scant amount of documentation relevant to this topic by asserting that Mahler's visits to Bruckner's harmony (not counterpoint!) classes were "sporadic" and belong to 1878, the year in which Mahler's "more intimate association" with Bruckner developed.[125] It may well have been in 1878, then, that Bruckner always entered his lecture-room in Mahler's company and likewise quitted it[126]—or so Stefan recounts, although he does not reconcile his "always" with his former hesitant speculation. But while it may have been that 1878 was the period of Mahler's intensest friendship with Bruckner, there was already an event in 1877 that brought them close together, out of which, almost certainly, flowed the warm association of subsequent months.

On 16 December 1877 Bruckner himself conducted the Vienna Philharmonic Orchestra in the first performance of his Symphony III (in a revised version—the original had been found "unplayable").[127] The *première* proved to be a complete disaster. The audience thinned away during the performance, and at the end there were hardly more than ten people left in the *Parterre*. Worse still, open laughter marred the proceedings, in which Hellmesberger, true to his markedly ambivalent attitude to Bruckner's music, set an unfortunate example.

In the standing places, however, was a group of ten to twenty young Bruckner enthusiasts, most of them his pupils, who, at the symphony's end attempted to console the depressed composer.[128] Among them was Mahler, for whom the whole affair must have been a lesson in Viennese musical politics. Though Bruckner's inexpert conducting may have been a drawback, the real reasons for the catastrophe were quite extraneous to the quality of the music or the character of its execution. The fiasco was primarily the result of the feud between the Wagner party and their opponents; a secondary factor was the hostility of the orchestra. With the latter, Mahler, in later years, was himself to come into conflict; his own path to success, however, though it did not run smoothly, never encountered a humiliation so crushing as this *première*. His music at least kept his audiences in their seats, whatever their resistances.

Bruckner, at first, gave way to despair. "Leave me alone," he said. "People don't want to have anything to do with me." But among those present at the *débâcle*, and impressed by the work nevertheless, was the music publisher, Theodor Rättig—of the Viennese firm, Bussjäger & Rättig—who offered to take the work into his catalogue. Not only a score and parts appeared, but also a piano-duet version, the preparation of which was entrusted to Mahler: he was aided in his task by his friend Rudolf Krzyzanowski—who was also present at the ill-starred *première*—and

67

his piano professor, Epstein, who supervised the reduction.[129] This four-handed edition of the symphony, "one of the first piano-duet arrangements of Bruckner's symphonies", was published in 1878; it was Mahler's first publication. Already, it seems, Mahler's unbending idealism guided his approach to his work. "[His] piano score", writes Stefan, "follows the orchestral one exactly, and attempts to keep the various parts in the characteristic pitch of the instruments, even at the expense of not being easily playable."[130]

We may assume, I think, that out of the dismal *première* of Bruckner's Symphony III, an occasion for the demonstration of sympathies no less than antipathies, blossomed the composer's sincere regard for his younger colleague. That Mahler was invited to undertake the piano-duet arrangement is proof of it; and to 1878 the various stories recorded may be assigned. Alma Mahler relates that when Mahler took Bruckner his reduction of the symphony's first movement, "Bruckner was childishly pleased and said with a roguish smile: 'Now I shan't need the Schalks any more!' "[131]—the brothers Schalk, Franz (1863–1931) and Joseph (1857–1901), were Bruckner pupils and ardent disciples whose agreed, enforced, or arbitrary revisions of the composer's scores (like Ferdinand Löwe's) have perpetrated an almost insoluble textual confusion. Mrs. Mahler's perhaps exaggerated claim that the Schalk brothers at this time "made all the piano scores of his symphonies" lends point to Bruckner's comment. Since Joseph was Mahler's senior by three years, and Bruckner apparently welcomed the younger man's assistance, there is no reason to register surprise at the youthfulness of Bruckner's circle—though it is hard, indeed, to imagine the need fulfilled by the then fifteen-year-old Franz.[132]

Mahler, we are told, "used often to foregather with Bruckner at midday. Bruckner stood the beer and Mahler had to pay for his own rolls; but as he generally had no money, he had to make his midday meal on beer alone. Bruckner was always surrounded by large numbers of young musicians, to whom he talked with childlike unrestraint. But if there were Jews present, he always—if he had occasion to say anything about Jews—gave them the

courtesy title of the Honourable Israelites [*die Herren Israeliten*]."[133]
This suggests a convivial artistic and personal relationship,
heightened, no doubt, by mutual interest in work in progress on
the duet arrangement; so friendly an atmosphere provides a
background against which the amiable entry into and exit from
the lecture-room, *à deux*, seems natural rather than legendary, and
even promotes belief in Stefan's tale that "when Mahler had
visited him at his house, the far elder Bruckner insisted upon conducting the young man down the four flights of stairs, hat in
hand".[134] Bruckner's exaggerated courtesies are, of course,
notorious. Into that very category falls the gift which Bruckner
presented to Mahler in appreciation of his efforts—as an arranger—
nothing less than the autograph of Symphony III's second
version.[135] Bruckner's gesture, a characteristically unrealistic
reward for services rendered, neatly rounds off the piano-duet
episode and pays its own tribute to the warmth of these
two oddly-assorted men's association. It is probable, indeed,
that Bruckner was "very fond" of Mahler, as Alma Mahler
states.[136]

We have seen something of Mahler's later views of Bruckner's
music. While it appears that Bruckner played "various compositions of his, old and new" to his young colleague,[137] there
is no record of Mahler seeking Bruckner's judgment on his
youthful pieces or works he had composed up to 1896, the year of
Bruckner's death. Though Mahler was in touch with Bruckner
in the 1890s, it is not likely that the latter was familiar with
Mahler's developments as a composer. Thus we have no pro-
nouncements from Bruckner upon Mahler's music—which would
certainly have been of considerable interest: only the general
colour of his attitude at this early period, that he regarded Mahler
"as a young man of promise",[138] that he "always spoke of Mahler
with the greatest respect".[139]

Mahler's later relation to Bruckner's music was twofold: he was
involved with it as both conductor and composer. The extent and
nature of Bruckner's musical influence—some general stylistic
and formal parallels are obvious and have been wildly over-
stressed, while subtler relations have been overlooked—will be

dealt with as and when they arise in regard to specific works of Mahler's wherein Bruckner's influence is a factor to be taken into account. As a conductor, and eventual patron, of Bruckner's works, Mahler's record is a reasonably generous one that may be dispatched forthwith.

Křenek has written that Mahler "manifested his esteem for Bruckner actively as soon as he could, by including Bruckner's compositions in the programs of his concerts".[140] What may have been the earliest instance of his promotion of Bruckner's music was a performance, in Prague, in April 1886—when Mahler was conducting at the *Landestheater*—of the Scherzo from Symphony III, in a programme that included some of Mahler's own songs and works by Mozart and Wagner. It was about this time that Mahler wrote to Bruckner:

> "I know you are angry at me, but I have not altogether deserved it, for tossed about on the tide of life I still regard you with the deep affection and reverence of old. It is one of the aims of my life to help your glorious art to the triumph it deserves."[141]

Mahler's tossing about "on the tide of life" obviously refers to the conducting engagements he had undertaken since 1880, engagements that successively and with a growing intensity must have disrupted the continuity of his connection with musical life in Vienna and his Viennese friends. Mahler's admission—"I know you are angry at me"—suggests a lack of contact between him and his old friend, even that Bruckner was disappointed, perhaps even resentful that the younger man was not doing more on his behalf. When Mahler moved to Hamburg in 1891, to conduct at the opera house there, he was able to fulfil his "aim" to assist Bruckner's "glorious art to the triumph it deserves" through performances of the *Te Deum* (twice), the D minor Mass, and Symphony III.[142] Mahler, it appears, while in Hamburg, was still in affectionate touch with Bruckner, to whom he addressed a letter on the day after the *Te Deum*'s performance. The first sentence of the letter—which begins "Honoured Master and Friend!"—seems to confirm the fact that Mahler had something of a sensitive conscience about his Bruckner performances, that the elder composer had been restive:

"At last I am so fortunate as to be able to write you that I have performed a work of yours. Yesterday (Good Friday) I conducted your splendid and powerful *Te Deum*. Not only the whole public, but also the performers were most deeply moved by the mighty architecture and the truly noble ideas. . . ."

" 'Bruckner'," Mahler continues, after describing the public's profound response, "has now made his triumphal entrance into Hamburg." A Bruckner disciple, Wilhelm Zinne, living in Hamburg, wrote to his master about the performance in the Municipal Theatre "under Kapellmeister Mahler's inspired leadership":

"As I found out from personal association with Mahler, he is a true admirer of your works. . . . While Mozart's *Requiem* (doubtless because it was presented with nervous haste) did not make any very great impression, your work was positively enkindling, particularly because of its final chorus, moving with irresistible force."[143]

From Hamburg, Mahler moved to Vienna, in 1897; the year before, Bruckner had died there, thus this link was finally snapped. None the less, Mahler's appointment, during his first years in Vienna, as conductor of the Opera orchestra's Philharmonic concerts meant that he had an orchestra (the Vienna Philharmonic Orchestra, as it is today) at his disposal, and he was not backward in attempting to gain a hearing for Bruckner's symphonies—no easy task, since Bruckner was not a popular composer and Mahler himself, as a conductor, was not particularly popular with the orchestra. With the Vienna orchestra, Mahler performed Symphony VI on 26 February 1899; though it was the work's first complete performance (the middle movements had been played in 1883 under Wilhelm Jahn), Mahler did not spare the symphony substantial cuts, surgery which Brucknerians still feel disinclined to forgive. In more favourable circumstances, perhaps, Mahler might have respected Bruckner's *Urtext*; but his attitude towards the inviolability of original versions was, in any case, strangely inconsistent: for example, he insisted on Wagner without cuts in Vienna but was willing to restore the excisions in America.[144] His fidgety approach to other composer's instrumentation (and his own) is, of course, notorious; indeed, it is hard not to believe that his Bruckner performances did not include some of his famous touchings-up. The cuts in Symphony VI—and they seem to have been extensive—must be deplored; on the other hand judgment of any of Mahler's exploits as a conductor is always complicated by the fact that he was also a composer, and inclined to re-create, to re-compose, as it were, according to his own image, a process sometimes beneficial, sometimes dubious in effect. At the very least, it appears that Mahler's performances of Bruckner were coloured by the revisionary and 'improving' ideas of the master's editors and pupils current at this time. Mahler, in some respects, was unexpectedly entangled with the artistic assumptions of his period.

In 1900 and 1901 Mahler was responsible for further Bruckner performances; he conducted Symphonies IV and V in Vienna,[145] and the Scherzo from the fourth in the Trocadero, Paris, on 21 June 1900, when the orchestra visited the French capital as part of the World Exhibition; this brave gesture must have been one of the first occasions, if not *the* first, when Bruckner's music travelled outside Austria or Germany. Thereafter, Mahler's connection with the Vienna orchestra ceased (as conductor of the Philharmonic concerts, that is), and though he continued to lead a busy life as a conductor in the concert hall, the loss of an orchestra of which he was artistic director inevitably brought with it a certain loss of freedom. The possibility of pioneering was restricted by the taste in programmes of the agency extending the invitations, and resistances to Bruckner's music during the early years of the twentieth century were still influential in many quarters. There was, of course, similarly active opposition to Mahler's music, but in relation to his own works Mahler, as a conductor, stood in a naturally favourable position. It was not until some years later, when Mahler was working in America and—significantly enough—once again in possession of his own orchestra, that he was able to resume his championing of Bruckner's "glorious art": in 1908,[146] in New York, he "gave performances of all [Bruckner's] symphonies one after the other . . . , although they had a very bad press".[147]

Mahler's work on Bruckner's behalf did not cease there. In 1910, Universal Edition, the Viennese publishers, had taken into their catalogue Mahler's first four symphonies. Mahler, though about to receive the not insubstantial royalties due to him for these works, agreed to forgo his profits in order to help Universal Edition publish and publicize the symphonies of Bruckner. "He thought it only right", comments Mrs. Mahler, "that he should sacrifice his profits for another fifteen years out of love of Bruckner, without of course receiving, or expecting, a penny from the sale of Bruckner's works. This was a great sacrifice to make to Bruckner's memory and shows how deeply he revered him."[148] Mahler's financial generosity was a marked aspect of his character; it is illustrated at its best in his relation with Arnold Schoenberg, in an incident that belongs to this same year.[149]

"Mahler's love of Bruckner was lifelong", writes Mrs. Mahler; and despite Mahler's revaluation of 1904, which I have already quoted, I see no serious grounds on which Mahler's attachment to Bruckner may be challenged. What he wrote on the title-page of his copy of the *Te Deum*—he deleted the customary vocal and instrumental specification and substituted: "For the tongues of angels, heaven-blest, chastened hearts, and souls purified in the fire!"[150]—must be given as much weight as his more critical utterance. There is doubtless a paradox here, as in many of Mahler's judgments. But then there is something altogether paradoxical about Mahler's friendship with Anton Bruckner, a friendship whose common centre of interest was, as Křenek suggests, a common enthusiasm for Wagner, while "the mutual attraction between Jewish intellectuality and endemic *naïveté* is also a peculiarly Austrian phenomenon". One may well wonder, along with Křenek, "with what feelings the elder musician . . . looked upon the nervous, talkative Jewish boy from Bohemia";[151] but the brief history of their personal association contains, in fact, the basic constituents of their musical relation: some common ground, and certainly a major degree of genius in either case—and, for the rest, profound *contrasts* that are none the less strangely complementary. It was the complemental nature of the relation that enabled two composers in many respects so opposed to work with equal success within the same medium, to sustain, despite intense differences in character and procedure, a great symphonic tradition for a further forty-four years, from the date of Bruckner's Symphony I to the date of Mahler's Symphony X, an extension that maintained the status of the Viennese symphony until the first decade of the twentieth century.[152] An anecdote of Stefan's rounds off the account:

"... When the Viennese made an appeal for contributions for a Bruckner Memorial [Viktor Tilgner's monument], and the Director of the Opera was asked to sign the petition, he refused and said to the orchestra: 'Let us play his music instead. Amongst people who would hear nothing of Bruckner whilst he was alive, and stood in his way, is no place for me.' "[153]

I. Gustav Mahler, 1878

II. (a) Mahler's parents; (b) Mahler in 1865;
(c) With a friend, 1872 (Mahler is standing)

III. The *Ringstrasse*, Vienna, at the time of Mahler's youth

IV. (b) Hugo Wolf, 1877

IV. (a) Anton Bruckner

V. (a) The house in Kaliště in which Mahler was born

V. (b) The Summer Theatre at Hall

ČESKOSLOVENSKÁ REPUBLIKA

Obvodní .... NÁRODNÍ VÝBOR V Praze 1

OKRES ...... P r a h a

Ex offo "RODNÝ LIST

Rady židovských náboženských obcí

V RODNÉ MATRICE ~~XXXXXXXXXXXXXXXX~~

v P r a z e

Dolní Kralovice
VE SVAZKU III ROC. 1860 NA STRANĚ 42 POD ČIS. RADOVYM 16
JEST ZAPSÁNO

Den, měsíc a rok narození	7.7.1860 Sedmého července jeden tisíc osm set šedesát
Místo narození	K a l i š t ě čp 9, o.Humpolec
Jméno a příjmení dítěte	G U S T A V M A H L E R
Pohlaví	mužské
Státní občanství	. - .
Jméno a příjmení, den, měsíc, rok, místo narození, povolání a bydliště otce, jména a příjmení jeho rodičů	Bernard M a h l e r,obchodník v Kališti čp 9
Jméno a příjmení, den, měsíc, rok, místo narození, povolání a bydliště matky, jména a příjmení jejich rodičů	Marie M a h l e r o v á,roz.Hermannová, dcera Abrahama Hermanna a Terezie roz.Hermannová
Poznámky	. - .

Předseda:
v z.

V Praze dne 26.11.1953.
zást. matrikáře.

VI. The particulars of Mahler's birth: an extract from the "Birth Register of
the Council of Jewish Religious Congregations in Prague"

VII. A page from the first movement of Mahler's piano Quartet

VIII. A page from an early sketch for *Das klagende Lied*

IX. The comparable page from an early score of *Das klagende Lied*

X. The comparable page from the published score of *Das klagende Lied*

XI. The last page of the early sketch of *Der Spielmann*

XII. The courtyard of the Mahler house and 'distillery' in Jihlava (Iglau)

III

1878-1880

THE last section, especially in its accounts of some of the most important of Mahler's friends, took many leaps into the future. We must now pick up the threads of his life again, from the point where they were dropped.

Mahler, as we have seen, successfully completed his course at the Conservatoire in 1878. He had matriculated a year earlier, in 1877, and enrolled at the University, attending lectures there until 1879. Apart, then, from one year of university classes which, but for Bruckner's, he may well have treated lightly, Mahler, after the summer of 1878, was a free agent, a qualified young musician of recognized gifts, eking out an existence in Vienna while he sought an opening for his talents.

Such is the impoverished state of Mahler's biography, that it is difficult, for the next few years, to pin down his movements or describe his achievements in any substantial chronological detail. It is a particular loss, perhaps, that this formative, post-Conservatoire but still, in effect, student, period is so under-documented. Composing, at which Mahler had shone at the Conservatoire, undoubtedly absorbed more and more of his attention, though it failed to earn him, or even promise him, a living. His creative ambitions, indeed, must have very forcibly crystallized at this time—one text of *Das klagende Lied* was probably begun in or before 1878, in March of which year it was finished; shortly after the work's completion in 1880, Mahler undertook his first engagement as a conductor. The latter proved to be the first step on the long road that eventually brought him back to Vienna as director of the opera, while *Das klagende Lied* was the first work —or at any rate the first work to have been preserved—in which Mahler's potential genius as a composer was apparent (not so, however, to the establishment presiding in the Vienna of Mahler's youth). Thus between the end of his course at the Conservatoire and 1880, in a space of not more than two years, there developed those twin features of Mahler's career—composing and conducting —that became permanencies. From thenceforth, the basic pattern was unvaried. Mahler, in 1880 at least, can little have guessed that at this early stage the essential shape of his life was already set. The bare—very bare—facts known to us are simpler than the situations they inadequately represent ever can have been. We are acquainted with the conclusions, as it were, but not the complex texture of life and art from which they were drawn.

The biographer's problem is how to dispose the few facts and the mass of information which is apposite but unattached to precise dates or events. We were helped out in the immediately pre-ceding section by the records of the Conservatoire functioning as factual anchors in a flow of relevant though somewhat dis-embodied anecdote; and the lives of other musicians, impinging upon Mahler's chronology, were of aid in determining, if only approximately, valid inferences. The position eases again, as it must, as soon as Mahler is regularly employed—the institutions plot a defined course across the tangled biographical map.

To the years that bridge the gap between Mahler's last term at the Conservatoire and his first appointment as a conductor—their very incoherence is suggestive of the predominantly indecisive, uncertain atmosphere of this period—the best approach is perhaps the following: first, a general word on Mahler's manner of life in these years, together with such biographical and musical data as are available, the whole account carrying us forward to the summer of 1879; secondly, a note on Mahler's student circle, his friends and acquaintances, a topic which, as will be seen, arises naturally from its context; and thirdly, a return to chronology, which will take us to 1880 and Mahler's engagement at Bad Hall in Upper Austria. This last event will round off the biography, which will be followed by a retrospective survey of Mahler's early works—delayed to this point both because the works extend to it and because their origins are so muddled, their sequence so obscure, their dates so vague, that a discussion of them is only possible *en masse*; it would be impossible to attach many of the

works to a definite chronological scheme without hopelessly con-
fusing the few facts concerning Mahler's *juvenilia*.

Stefan has written that the "holiday months of the summer
[Mahler] spent in this [i.e., *c.* 1878] and the following years at
home with his parents". Stefan thinks the area rather unattractive;
none the less, "the widespread ranges of hills, the restful forests,
the numerous streams and lakelets round about Iglau" must have
made good holiday country, especially for so keen a country
walker as Mahler. Peasant customs were a lively part of the land-
scape. Holländer writes that "the traditional roundelays of the
German peasantry, called 'Hatschon' ", were "performed in
summer in specially prepared circular clearings in the forest.
In these round dances something of the spirit of the ancient
German *Springtänze* still survives." Löhr, who mentions the
partly Slav architecture of the peasants' villages and houses, further
fills out the picture of rural festivities which, he claims, were a
vital formative experience in Mahler's early youth—the Sunday
afternoon excursions into the vicinity of Jihlava, for instance,
where, in the open air, genuine Bohemian musicians played for
boys and girls dancing in the circular clearings described by
Holländer. Bauer-Lechner recounts that once, when out on a walk
with Mahler, it happened that a great jumble of sounds was heard
from a distance—military music, men's chorus, Punch and Judy
shows, shooting booths, merry-go-rounds, swings, all mixed up
together. Mahler cried: "Do you hear it? That is polyphony, and
that's where I got it from!—Already as a small child in the woods
of Iglau it impressed itself upon me and moved me so strangely."[1]
We need not take this Charles Ives-ish conception of polyphony
too seriously, but something of Mahler's childhood impression
of mingled sounds does make itself felt in the counterpoint of his
Symphony III.
    It is certain that Mahler returned to Jihlava for the summer
of 1878, after the triumphant completion of his studies at the
Conservatoire. So much we know from an appendix to Mahler's
correspondence, supplied by Dr. Emil Freund, a lawyer and boyhood friend of Mahler's, with whom the latter kept in touch to

the end of his life. The home of Freund's parents was at Seelau, three hours' journey by wagon from Jihlava. There, from 1878 until 1883, Mahler spent part of his holidays in Freund's company. The visit to Seelau in 1878 accounts for the only domestic incident that has been recorded from this summer. The incident itself—a young girl's (a relative of Freund's) marked enthusiasm for the eighteen-year-old composer—is scarcely significant; but that Mahler's puritanical earnestness evidently prevented him from embarking on a mild flirtation stands as precedent for the severe inhibition that seemed to characterize his attitude to women in later years.[2]

In this same appendix, Freund specifies piano-playing as one of Mahler's holiday pursuits, and there is no doubt that at this time the piano occupied much of his attention: teaching the piano, for instance, facilitated, if perhaps rather insecurely, the possibility of his spending time at composition. Tutoring, indeed, brought him in his basic wage, though there may have been other sources of income; in 1878, for example, his finances might have been increased by payment for his work on the published piano-duet version of Bruckner's Symphony III (the commission was, in any event, a trophy that probably gave satisfaction at home). It is likely that Mahler, even when home on holiday, attempted to supplement his pocket money, or wholly support himself, by means of piano lessons (this was certainly true of later years, though by then Mahler had moved outside Jihlava for his pupils). We must remember that the Mahler household, excluding Gustav, already accommodated five children, that there must have been considerable pressure brought to bear upon the eldest son to maintain himself, especially so in view of his academic success: cleverness exacts its own penalties. What the atmosphere of Mahler's home was like at this later stage of his youthful life, it is impossible to determine in detail; the passage already quoted from a letter of 1883[3] suggests that the adolescent would have had to deal with the same tensions and conflicts that had marred his childhood. Economically, on the other hand, there was doubtless every good reason, as of old, for Mahler making himself finan-cially independent; and if Jihlava, as was probable, divulged too few piano pupils, then that was another good reason for Mahler's return to Vienna at the end of the summer, where a further session of lectures awaited him at the University, where piano tuition was more sought after, where his friends were, and where music might be heard and discussed; and where he might succeed or fail unobserved by his family and unencumbered by their expectations.

We have some knowledge already of the kind of life that Mahler would have led in Vienna after his vacations in Jihlava and Seelau in the summer of 1878—Wolf's biographer has furnished us with an authentic background. In the previous chapter, I have given a fullish account of Mahler's friendship with the young Wolf. As we saw there, *c.* 1879 was the period when the friendship was most close. Wolf, we know, returned to Vienna on 21 September 1878. The date of Mahler's return to the city from his summer holidays is not recorded, but he was probably back there in time for the start of the University session (in October).

For what remains of 1878 we can do no more than sketch a life of probabilities—probable attendance at the University, composing, concert-going, participation in the activities of a large student community, and, of course, teaching the piano: the pursuit of pupils and their instruction must have consumed a fair slice of Mahler's time. We have learnt from Wolf's biography how seriously he was obliged, by economic circumstances, to apply himself to this industry. Mahler, no less; and it was a close friend of Mahler's, Rudolf Krzyzanowski, who asked Wolf (in 1879) to teach his piano pupils during his absence from Vienna; this particular scheme fell through,[4] but who can doubt that these three young musicians formed at times a kind of tutoring syndicate, procuring and exchanging pupils as the situation demanded?

Vienna, in the 1870s, was a comparatively small capital city, large though the surrounding empire was. The society on the fringes of which Mahler and Wolf lurked as potential tutors was correspondingly small and thus facilitated the interrelation of pupils, clients and instructors. And in other ways, too, this almost village society crossed and intercrossed its personnel who,

79

with their mutual if varied interests in music, must have been known to one another, if no more than by name, reputation or the conversation of shared friends. Piano teaching was not the only bond. In 1880 we find that Wolf's string Quartet was played—murdered, according to its composer—"in private at the house of Natalie Bauer-Lechner, who played second violin in the Soldat-Röger Quartet";[5] and Natalie Bauer-Lechner was, of course, to become an intimate friend of Mahler's and keeper of a diary of enthusiastic reminiscences. In these early years—she was two years older than both Mahler and Wolf—she must have been very much part of the musical circles in which our composers moved.

A more piquant, though more remote, relation rests in Wolf's tutoring of the Breuer children from 1878 to 1883. Dr. Josef Breuer was a well-known Viennese physician and man of science with whom Freud collaborated in a now-famous book, *Studien über Hysterie*, published in Vienna in 1895, "from which it is customary to date the beginnings of psycho-analysis". Freud and Breuer met in the late 1870s—when Wolf had just begun his instruction of Breuer's children—and they "soon became friends".[6] It is an odd coincidence that Wolf, when he was probably most friendly with Mahler, should have taught the piano to the family of a man whose own just budding friendship with Freud was to result in those first stirrings of psycho-analysis from which Mahler himself was to benefit, at Freud's own hands, after the turn of the century. Thus two important composers, one indirectly, the other directly, were involved in turn with a significant figure in the history of psycho-analysis and the movement's founder. I am not, of course, suggesting that there are any conclusions to be drawn from what were no more than accidentally related incidents widely separated in time; but the intertwining of events and personalities does give some idea of the close-knit texture of Viennese society, that might, at any moment, jumble together a number of creative figures-to-be, creative in very different spheres, throw them apart, and then later bring them into a more meaningful pattern. At the very least, the Breuer-Freud:Wolf-Mahler complex is indicative of the turbulent new thoughts adrift in Vienna at the end of the nineteenth century.

We have seen earlier from a letter of Wolf's that one piece of furniture he inherited on moving into an apartment recently occupied by Mahler (in December 1879) was "a fine piano". If Mahler expended much energy on teaching the piano, he also played it, for his own edification and that of his friends. Since his piano playing was a marked feature of his student period in Vienna, perhaps there is some justification for examining here his accomplishments as a pianist.

There is nothing more difficult than writing about performances that have not been personally experienced (the same problem faces us with Mahler's conducting). The development of recorded sound came just too late to help us out in Mahler's case: to the best of my knowledge, the only 'sound' document that exists is a pianola-roll transcription of the finale from Symphony IV, which rather amusingly rolls into one Mahler's talents as composer, conductor and pianist: it must have been manufactured just after the turn of the century.[7] What we know of Mahler's conducting comes from the memories of those who heard him in the opera house or on the concert platform; however fresh those memories may be—it is remarkable how the impression of a Mahler performance does not seem to fade with the years—it is scarcely reasonable to expect more from them than an account of the general atmosphere of a Mahler interpretation: if we are fortunate in having a pair of trained musical ears as witness, then a few concrete interpretative details may be recalled, but the reconstruction, even in rough outline, of a characteristic Mahler performance is an impossibility. It is hard enough to describe music musically; we should need to devise a new system of notation if an interpretation were to be successfully documented, if only a meaningful approximation to it. Distance in time, moreover, is not the controlling factor. Immediate press reactions to Mahler performances are, in fact, no more enlightening in detail than the cherished memory released perhaps after forty years or more.

But at least in the case of Mahler's conducting we have two possible sources of evidence that are of concrete musical signifi-

⇨ cance—certain of his carefully annotated scores, whose wealth of written-in dynamics and expression marks conveys something of the character of his interpretations, and the example of those conductors (e.g., Otto Klemperer, Bruno Walter (in Mahler's

⇨ own music), and F. Charles Adler), whose personal familiarity with, and admiration for, Mahler's interpretative genius was to a degree reflected in their own interpretations: we could, I think, still hear the Mahler tradition in some aspects of, say, Klemperer's performances of Beethoven or Walter's of Mahler.

There is nothing of this sort, however, to help us out when considering Mahler the pianist. We shall see that the piano had an influential rôle to play in his student compositions, and I have already touched on the odd fact that it was his achievements as a pianist that marked Mahler's Conservatoire years, not his talent as a conductor, a talent which remained latent and unsuspected until it was more or less accidentally released. All evidence of his pianistic prowess comes to us very much at second hand, from the enthusiastic but undiscriminating testimonies of his friends. Certain achievements, of course, speak for themselves. There was the successful recital he gave in Jihlava in 1870 when he was ten years old. It was his pianistic ability that won him his entrance into the Conservatoire and two of that institute's first prizes for piano playing. He was billed there as soloist in the first movement of Scharwenka's new piano concerto. Indeed, the more the pieces of the picture are fitted together, the clearer it becomes that composition apart—which, in any case, must have meant more to Mahler than to his professors or his family—it was as a pianist that he shone most outwardly and convincingly as a musician of promise. No doubt the sudden and amazing burst of adolescent creative exuberance that resulted in the composition of *Das klagende Lied* left him wholly decided as to his future, that composing was to be his artistic destiny, whatever other activities economic circumstances might dictate. The stage, in a subsidiary sense, was set for a career as a pianist, but chance, as it were from the wings, intervened, and Mahler became a conductor. (I distrust that last verb. Great conductors are born, not made. They 'become' what they are.) It remains strange, none the less, that Mahler's piano playing, so notable a feature of his youth and student days, died so complete a death in later years but for spasmodic, domestic returns to the keyboard; and in his maturity as a composer, the instrument (Symphony VIII and the piano arrangements of the songs excepted) had no rôle at all.

In these student years, however, it was not so. Stefan writes:

"The young artist gave the best of himself at the piano. All who heard it speak of his playing with veneration. At the Conservatoire they said that a pianist of exceptional gifts was latent in him, one of those who might enter the lists with Rubinstein and Liszt. But it was on account of the spirit, not of mere technique. The enormous will-power, the genius which exhausts every possibility of the music, broke out in the pianist's spirit, as later the conductor's power. The whole dread of the mystical abyss enveloped his Beethoven, and Mahler's friends have never again heard the last sonatas played in such fashion. He fled to Beethoven out of the sordid atmosphere of the theatre—to Beethoven and to Bach. And however much he was plagued with performances and rehearsals, he was always ready for chamber music—the more the better."[8]

This rather intoxicated style is typical of the unhelpful (from the musical point of view) verbal imagery sponsored by Mahler's piano playing. We are left in no doubt of its majesty—one can, perhaps, imagine a little of his grasp of a late Beethoven sonata— but there is nothing to aid us in forming a clear idea of his inter-pretations. A mystical mist, alas, envelops the testimony of a friend, Dr. Friedrich Löhr, whose experience of Mahler as a pianist was intimate and intensive; but a few comments, prompted by a piano session of 1884, allow us a glimpse of Mahler's per-formances:

"I have never experienced a like dematerialization of a human-technical process. Mahler knew nothing of the work of his hands and could never have accounted for the way in which he arrived at his interpretation. Every thought of technical difficulties was absolutely excluded; he was spell-bound, disembodied, passionately given over to what he assimilated from the notes without conscious material contact. . . . Thus in Beethoven's sonata, op. III, the

tempest of the opening maestoso burst frighteningly and precipi-
tously increased with a wild impetuosity that I have never heard
again, while the conclusion ebbed away, intensely transfigured in
exquisite beauty, softly and ever more softly, from all earthliness
to eternity."[9]

"But what", asks Dr. Löhr, "can words say about the effect of his
playing?" What, indeed! None the less, Dr. Löhr gives us some
indication of the extent and character of Mahler's repertory. He
heard him play all Beethoven's sonatas, Bach's 'Forty-Eight',
"and many another work by the beloved Master", and, on one
"unforgettable" afternoon, Beethoven's Mass in D. Mahler, he
adds, soon after (i.e., *c.* 1884: at about this time the *Lieder eines
fahrenden Gesellen* were composed) abandoned the piano and
piano music, having mastered the orchestra—which may be true,
though it is not certain that it was in the aforementioned cycle that
this mastery was first achieved.[10] Dr. Löhr's conclusion—that to
those acquainted with Mahler's piano playing, the spirit of his
conducting was familiar—rings true.

Natalie Bauer-Lechner was another close friend who remembered, as Dr. Löhr remembered the performance of the Mass in
D, an occasion on which Mahler, then a student, played through
the prelude to *Die Meistersinger* in so commanding a fashion that
"a whole orchestra" seemed to lie under his hands.[11] Doubtless
this sort of piano playing was a common event in Mahler's youth,
and it was one that he—or rather his occupation—maintained in
later years: his work at the opera house must often have entailed
recourse to the piano, for study or rehearsal purposes. When composing he certainly had a piano at hand—for instance, in his work-
shop (his *Schnitzelputzhäusel*) on the Attersee, in the 1890s, a
Bösendorfer baby grand piano, supplied by the Viennese manufacturers, was part of the furniture[12]—but it must not be supposed
that he composed at the piano, a practice of his student period that
he deprecated in a conversation with Bauer-Lechner.[13] On the
other hand, as one might expect, Mahler was known to play
through his compositions at the piano: to Bruno Walter, for
example, at Steinbach in the summer of 1896, he played the just
completed Symphony III. "The force and novelty of the musical

language fairly stunned me, and I was overwhelmed to feel in his playing the same creative fervour and exultation which had given birth to the work itself."[14] These piano *premières* must have been exciting experiences.

Dr. Löhr makes an intelligent discrimination in implying that what Mahler pointedly renounced in the 1880s was piano music. On the whole, in later years, Mahler's piano playing seems to to have been confined to his work (creative or theatrical), to study, or to pure recreation in the company of congenial musicians. The solo element completely disappears. If some piano music still claimed his attention, it was, it seems, for its recreative possibilities. Walter recounts as a "particularly precious" recollection his piano-duet playing, with Mahler as partner. Schubert was their "favourite". "We had great fun; Mahler sitting on the right, would play my top notes with his left hand, and leave his own lower line to my right; each of us thus had all the time to read both *primo* and *secondo*, which introduced amusing complications. He used to invent words to go with various marches, singing as he played."[15]

We have seen earlier on, when discussing Mahler's attitude to Brahms, that his private revaluations of composers involved him in playing the piano; but it was, perhaps, taking part in chamber-music, as accompanist to Arnold Rosé, or as pianist in Brahms's horn Trio or Beethoven's op. 70, no. 1, that gave him the keenest satisfaction. Stefan tells us that the Czech composer J. B. Foerster (1859–1951), who lived in Hamburg during the period Mahler conducted at the opera house, still remembered, years after the event, "the impression he had from Mahler's piano-playing in the 'Geister' trio. He had never before been so conscious of the supernatural element in the music." It was at this time, we learn, that Mahler "loved to delight [his friends] with chamber music at his house"; later, he may have had less leisure thus to indulge them, but his friends' tributes speak eloquently of the memorable quality of the performances that spasmodically studded a busy life.[16]

The shifting pattern of Mahler's life in 1878 must have been continued in 1879. The first half of the year did not unfold a permanent engagement, and piano teaching was again Mahler's principal means of support in his summer vacation. It is not, however, in Jihlava that we find him, but c/o "Herrn Moritz Baumgarten in Tétény, Ungarn"—probably for two or three months Mahler lived on this Hungarian estate teaching the piano to Herr Baumgarten's son and satisfying the family's musical enthusiasms.[17]

Mahler, it need hardly be said, was not particularly happy there, but it is difficult to separate his discontent with his employment from a general feeling of romantic despair promoted by his personal situation. The source of our knowledge of Mahler's agitated state of mind at this time lies in letters he wrote from Hungary to an intimate friend, Josef Steiner. Mahler, on the whole, kept his friends, but Steiner, after a close association with Mahler in the 1870s, seems to have faded out of Mahler's life. (Mahler certainly knew him as early as 1876.)[18] He wrote the text for Mahler's opera, *Ernst von Schwaben*,[19] and these letters from June 1879 show that he was then still very much a recipient of Mahler's confidences. But after 1879 the correspondence ceases (the possibility that other and later letters exist cannot, of course, be discounted) and we have no further mention of Steiner's name. Even to what circle Steiner belonged is obscure; he was not a student at the Conservatoire, and it is unlikely that he was one of the group of Mahler's University acquaintances. The portrait we have of him is most incomplete.

The letters Mahler wrote to Steiner are most valuable characterdocuments. They are fairly well known in translation (the most significant parts, at least), and I do not intend to duplicate the work of previous biographers: a few crucial extracts will suffice. First and foremost there is, throughout these turbulent, highlystrung letters, ample evidence of Mahler's extraordinarily intense conception of the Earth (all Nature, that is to say) as "Universal Mother", to whose bosom lonely, forsaken man clings for consolation. Mahler's love of Nature was profound and, so far as his music is concerned, mainly non-pictorial: there is nothing in his symphonies as pastorally evocative as, say, Beethoven's

Symphony VI, which is not, in any case, an especially pictorial 'Pastoral' symphony. There was, in Mahler's relation to Nature, something distinctly elemental, something downright religious, and little or nothing of the graphic—nor of the head or sentimental heart. He experienced the Earth and its seasons, D. H. Lawrence-like, in his bowels; and it is, indeed, in the bowels of the earth that some of his music—the elemental march for orchestra alone in the *Abschied* from *Das Lied von der Erde* for instance, or the introduction (*Adagio*) to the first movement of Symphony VII—seems to have its roots. Such pastoral elements as there are in his works—a few songs or relaxed symphonic movements excepted, perhaps—belong to a very different set of feelings than that normally found in rustic music, even in the music of such rural masters as Dvořák or Smetana.

But if Mahler loved (ambiguous word!) Nature, Nature, no less, distressed him: not only her tooth and claw aspects[20] but also her beauty, which can sear as much as it soothes. Mahler was wont to contrast the human predicament with smiling or sublime Nature: sometimes he was consoled, but as often her sublimity and in particular the perpetual renewal of her beauty only sharpened in his eyes the human lot of frailty, magnified its terrors and tragedies, intensified its transience. It was, of course, in *Das Lied von der Erde*, Mahler's song of the Earth—a revealing creation in itself—that he gave most poignant expression to his feelings about Nature and his "beloved Earth" (one of his greatest compositions and certainly, in this context, one of his most personal). It is interesting that in *Das Lied* there is only a minimum of pictorialism, while the landscapes, as it were, are always inhabited, literally so, by the wandering, seasonal singer, e.g., *Der Trunkene im Frühling* ('The Drunkard in Spring') or *Der Einsame im Herbst* ('The Lonely One in Autumn'). Mahler never fails to juxtapose Nature and Man, and from that duality spring the peculiar tensions of his 'Lied von der Erde', both in the great symphonic song-cycle and elsewhere.

It is not mere accident that Mahler's youthful letters to Steiner entail a few words about *Das Lied*, a composition belonging to his last years. On the contrary, the letters are deeply imbued with the spirit that was to motivate the creation of the song-cycle. Other biographers have already called attention to the parallel that exists between Mahler's passionate oration to Steiner of 18 June 1879 and the text of *Der Einsame im Herbst* from *Das Lied* (but not only *Der Einsame*—also the very content and atmosphere of *Das Lied*'s *Abschied*). The Steiner document runs:

"Oh my beloved earth, when, oh when, wilt thou take the abandoned one unto thy breast? Behold! Mankind has banished him from itself, and he flees from its cold and heartless bosom to thee, to thee! Oh, care for the lonely one, for the restless one, Universal Mother!"[21]

The prophetic tone of this passage enables it to bear a weight that one might otherwise consider disproportionate; were it not for the letter's fulfilment in *Das Lied*, one might be disposed to dismiss the letter as so much adolescent attitudinizing and rhetoric. But, as **Dr.** Newlin correctly observes, the letter tells us that Mahler "at eighteen had already entered into the spiritual realm where he was to dwell all the rest of his days. We cannot but admire this consistency of character; it shows us that no matter how mercurial and temperamental he may have appeared to outsiders, he was always true to himself. . . ."[22]

The text given above is not the only occasion on which Mahler seemed to anticipate in detail the world of *Das Lied*. In a letter to Anton Krisper, dated 3 March 1880,[23] he wrote of the coming of spring in terms that inevitably call to mind a particularly charged moment in *Der Trunkene im Frühling*:

1880	1908–9
"Der Frühling ist über Nacht gekommen und mit ihm die alte Sehnsucht und Wehmut." ("The Spring has come overnight, and with it the old yearning and melancholy.")	"Der Lenz ist da, sei kommen über Nacht!" ("The Spring is here, has come overnight!")

88

The parallel is striking; and in *Das Lied* it is, of course, the *music* that contains the "yearning and melancholy": the missing part of the letter has been musicalized—words have become superfluous. Then again, the extract from the Krisper letter illustrates aptly what I have written above, that while on the one hand Nature could bring Mahler comfort—

". . . with the strength of distress I cling to sorrow, my only consolation. Then the sun smiles upon me—and the ice has melted from my heart, I see the blue heavens once more and the quivering flower, and my scornful laughter dissolves in the tears of love. And I *must* love it, this world with its deception and light-mindedness and eternal laughter"[24]—

on the other, she could, at her most beautiful, at the onset of spring, arouse Mahler's melancholy.

If nothing else, these letters to his friend and librettist show how early Mahler's nervous, easily-wounded, precariously-balanced sensibility exposed itself; it was to remain essentially unchanged throughout his life, as was the predicament he expressed thus in 1879:

"The highest ecstasy of the most joyous strength of life and the most burning desire for death: these two reign alternately within my heart; yes, oftentimes they alternate within the hour. . . ."[25]

The terms in which the predicament was stated may have altered, but the conflict at the heart of it was constant, from the 1870s to 1911.

For the rest, these effusive, lyrical documents discharge a high-pitched rhetoric, amidst which we recognize familiar traits of personality and characteristic Mahlerian symbols. We read of his 'Liebling', a solitary lime-tree on Herr Baumgarten's estate, from the top of which Mahler could survey the Danube, and are reminded of the 'Lindenbaum' in the *Lieder eines fahrenden Gesellen*/4 and its instrumental evocation in Symphony I/3:

"Auf der Strasse stand ein Lindenbaum,
da hab' ich zum ersten Mal im Schlaf geruht!"

We read of a curious vision, cast in processional form—it is interesting that Mahler's musical visions often took shape as processions, e.g., Symphony I/3, Symphony II/5—in which "shadowy memories of my life pass before me like long-forgotten ghosts of departed happiness".[26] There is, in this dream-like sequence, a mention of Mahler's much-loved younger brother, Ernst (d. 1874), coupled, significantly, to a memory of *Ernst von Schwaben*—a joint project of Mahler's and Steiner's it will be remembered; and no less significant, perhaps, is the image from which these painful memories grow: a hurdy-gurdy man, with outstretched hat and withered hand, whose tuneless music suggests "the Greeting[27] of Ernst von Schwaben".[28]

Stefan tells us that Mahler

"took the man of the soil seriously. Once he meets a shepherd and his flock—what may such a man's thoughts be? Somebody replies: About the next market-day. But Mahler becomes angry: the shepherd lives with nature, he dreams and broods; he surely has ideas of his own. . . ."[29]

Mahler's irritation is characteristic of the man. It is not enough for a shepherd to be a shepherd; he must have ideas about his status. The perpetual self-examination, the implied sense of predicament—whether one is cowman or composer one's relation to the universe must be defined—is typical of Mahler's nagging, inquisitorial personality. But he could also take the shepherd at his romantic-pastoral face value, as the Steiner letters demonstrate:

"I've just come from the meadow where I was sitting by the hut of Farkas the shepherd listening to the music of his shalm. Ah, how sadly it sounded, and so passionately ecstatic, the folksong he played! The wildflower that grew at his feet trembled beneath the dreamy fire of his dark eyes and his brown hair waved about his sun-tanned cheeks."[30]

This ambivalence in attitude to the shepherd as a pastoral symbol—the pastoral convention—is as characteristic of Mahler (it is much present in his art) as is the duality of his response to Nature, to which I have already referred, a duality that is strikingly represented in the Steiner correspondence, the first part of which (17 June) ends with a passionate denunciation of the falsity of the Earth-spirit "who knowest not how to still the sorrow of a single tortured soul", while the last lines (19 June) unfold a mood of reconciliation:

"Ah, Steiner! You are still asleep in your bed and I have already seen the dew on the grass. I am now so peacefully content and quiet happiness steals into my heart as the spring sun into wintry fields. Will it now be spring in my heart?"[31]

I have commented upon the fact that of Josef Steiner, the recipient of these remarkable character-documents, we know little. Who were the other members of Mahler's Vienna circle of student friends? We have had notes on Mahler's teachers, an extensive survey of his relations with Wolf and Bruckner; but what of his youthful companions whose names intermittently and obscurely crop up in accounts of Mahler's early life? Stefan gives us a clue to some of them. He lists:

"Guido Adler, now professor of the History of Music at the Vienna University [Stefan was writing in 1912]; Rudolf Krzyzanowsky, who died as Hofkapellmeister at Weimar only a few weeks later than Mahler; the writer Heinrich Krzyzanowsky, Rudolf's brother; the archeologist Fritz Löhr, and his since deceased brother; and a musician of genius, Hans Rott, who died unrecognized and in want on the very threshold of his career."[32]

Guido Adler was Mahler's senior by five years, but like him, was born in Moravia. He first studied and then taught (1881) in Vienna, at which time he made Mahler's acquaintance, joined the staff of Prague University in 1886, and succeeded Hanslick in Vienna in 1898. Adler, who died in 1941, was a famous musicologist, supervisor of the *Denkmäler der Tonkunst in Österreich* and author of many books, one of which (GA) was a short study of Mahler, published in 1916; he also contributed to Stefan's anthology, *Gustav Mahler: Ein Bild seiner Persönlichkeit in Widmungen*, published in 1910. The former work is sometimes musically perceptive and valuable for its chronological table, though for one who claimed to stand so close to Mahler and was writing of events, as it were, near at hand, his biographical data are curiously scanty and even unreliable. It is one of the dismaying features of Mahler biography that personal sources of information, such as Adler, J. B. Foerster or Franz Schmidt, all of whom survived Mahler by many years, were not asked to expand their reminiscences or verify recorded utterances—hence the growing difficulty of accurately defining dates and circumstances. The Mahler era has been allowed to fade away without methodical documentation of the memories of its principal *dramatis personae*.

Adler himself said that sheer physical distance often disturbed the continuity of his relation with Mahler; none the less, this enforced separation did not result, it seems, in an exchange of correspondence across the years; while some letters doubtless have been lost, GMB contains only one communication to Adler, written from New York in January 1910.[33] References, otherwise, are sparse and mostly belong to the recollections of Alma Mahler who, from 1907, reports a telephone conversation— amusing in historical retrospect—in which the musicologist professed himself distressed not only by Mahler's public defence of Schoenberg but by Schoenberg's music.[34] Certainly the link between Adler and Mahler was never broken; but one may take leave to doubt whether the association was altogether without friction, perhaps because the musical historian and the composer are destined, by reason of their occupations, to mutual suspicion. So much, at least, is suggested to me by a clear reference to Adler made by Mahler in 1904 when he was in the midst of the rehearsals for the *première* of Symphony V. The letter is full of occupational preferences:

> "Oh that I were a Russian police agent! Oh that I were town councillor of Cologne with my box at the Municipal Theatre and also at Gürzenich, and could look down upon all modern music!"

The list ends—and the irony is explicit—

> "Oh that I were a Professor of Music and could give lectures on Wagner and have them published."[35]

But irony, though it makes a tempting finale, must not be allowed the last word. It was due to Adler's support, in the shape of "a detailed report", that the *Gesellschaft zur Förderung deutscher Wissenschaft, Literatur und Kunst in Böhmen* ('Society for the promotion of German Science, Literature and Art in Bohemia') granted a subsidy which facilitated the publication of Mahler's Symphonies I and III.[36] Adler, moreover, was prominent among those who agitated for the appointment of Mahler to the Vienna Opera; and he was horrified at Mahler's eventual abandonment of Europe:[37] it had been his hope, indeed, that Mahler, who was given an honorary place on the Conservatoire's management committee when the institute came under Government control (in 1908?), would become director of the Conservatoire upon relinquishing his work at the theatre. But all Adler's plans came to nothing.[38] (An interesting aspect of the affair was Mahler's "positive" reaction to the idea that he might take up teaching, an idea, according to Adler, that he (Mahler) had already had himself.)

As we have already seen, the name Krzyzanowski has cropped up frequently throughout these pages. There were two brothers, Heinrich (who studied at the University)[39] and Rudolf: the former a writer, the latter a musician. Rudolf was a student at the Conservatoire, and a member of Professor Krenn's third year composition class. At the same concert in which Mahler's prize-winning Scherzo for piano quintet was played, an *Adagio* for string sextet by Krzyzanowski was also performed: it, too, was awarded a prize.[40]

The date of Krzyzanowski's birth is uncertain.[41] After leaving the Conservatoire, he seems to have held a number of conducting appointments, the most important of which were at Prague, where he succeeded Karl Muck as first conductor from 1892–5, and Weimar, where he was *Hofkapellmeister* from 1898–1907. He died in 1911, as Stefan has told us, "only a few weeks later than Mahler".

Mahler's early friendship with the Krzyzanowski brothers was warm and intimate. He had interests and ambitions in common with Rudolf, and his holiday plans on occasions included both brothers.[42] His correspondence for some years makes frequent reference to Rudolf's career and he was always ready to advise, or use his influence on his friend's behalf, where such was required. (He suggested to his agent, for instance, that Rudolf should fill his post at Cassell when he moved on to Leipzig.) Until the 1890s, at least, his letters show that he kept in touch with these companions of his youth. At one stage, Heinrich wrote to Mahler suggesting an operatic project, but it appears that nothing came of the idea.[43]

Dr. Friedrich Löhr, the archaeologist, was a lifelong friend of Mahler's: he annotated the volume of Mahler's letters gathered together by Alma Mahler.[44] Löhr did much to help Mahler in his troubled family affairs. For some while he concerned himself with supervising the studies of Mahler's brother, the unhappy Otto. Another long friendship of a like kind was Mahler's association with Dr. Emil Freund, a lawyer. Freund lived in a neighbouring village in the Jihlava days, and Mahler sustained a cordial relation with him across the years. There is a bunch of letters from 1909-10 in which Mahler discusses his publishing contracts with Freund.

Two young musicians remain to be mentioned, Anton Krisper and Hans Rott, the latter that "musician of genius" listed by Stefan; they were both Conservatoire pupils. Little is known about Krisper, who died, we know, in 1914.[45] He was born in Laibach (Ljubljana), and when Mahler conducted there (in the winter of 1881-2) it was with the family of Krisper—the "victim of an incurable disease"—that he lodged. Krisper's later career did not altogether fulfil its musical launching. He wrote, it appears, an opera that was unsuccessfully produced at Prague, but then studied philosophy at Leipzig; and after only a year of philosophy he abandoned his course to enter a mining institute.[46] The instability of his character seems to be reflected in the changing patterns of his life. Krisper's unbalanced mental constitution earns him his only reference in Mahler's collected correspondence, where, in November 1880, in a letter to Freund, Mahler writes of the onset of Rott's insanity and fears that Krisper is similarly threatened.[47] What really endows Krisper with some significance as a member of Mahler's youthful circle are the letters addressed to him by Mahler and published in Die Musik by Hans Holländer.

That extract which I have quoted earlier shows him to have been the recipient of documents as personal and intense as the Steiner letters, which allow us so profound a glimpse of Mahler's adolescent character; Krisper, moreover, had the distinction of receiving, as an enclosure, stanzas that formed part—the eventually abandoned part—of Mahler's cantata, *Das klagende Lied*.

Hans Rott (1858–84),[48] who died insane, must have had considerable musical gifts. In the Conservatoire records for 1877-8 we find him a member, like Mahler, of Krenn's third year class in composition. From 1876-7 he was Bruckner's organ pupil and, in Redlich's words, "a declared favourite . . . as may be gathered from an informative letter from Bruckner to Ignaz Traumihler, the chorus-master of St. Florian, in which Bruckner recommends [Rott] as a candidate for the post of organist there".[49] (Close association with Bruckner was characteristic of this Mahler circle: Rudolf Krzyzanowski, who had worked with Mahler in preparing the piano-duet version of Bruckner's Symphony III, was also one of the composer's organ pupils. Rott, doubtless, was among the sympathizers who witnessed that symphony's ill-starred *première*.)

Mahler esteemed Rott's talents highly. Natalie Bauer-Lechner reported that "Mahler talked about Hans Rott, whose symphony he had taken with him to look through it with a view to possible performance in the Philharmonic Concerts:

"What music has lost in him cannot be estimated. Such is the height to which his genius already soars in this first symphony, which he wrote as a twenty-year-old youth and which makes him—I am not exaggerating—the founder of the new symphony as I see it. To be sure, what he wanted is not yet quite achieved. It is as if somebody raised his arm for the farthest possible throw and, still clumsy, falls far short of the target. But I know *where* he aims. Indeed, he is so near to my inmost self that he and I seem to me like two fruits from the same tree which the same soil has produced and the same air nourished. He could have meant infinitely much to me and perhaps the two of us would have well-nigh exhausted the content of this new time which was breaking out for music."[50]

Mahler also spoke well of Rott's songs, which, unfortunately, were never written down; a sextet also existed, but that work Mahler had never heard.

A symphony by Rott is mentioned by Mrs. Mahler in her memoirs:

> "Mahler had a friend whom he looked up to and admired. His name was Hans Rott; it was he whose symphony, although the better of the two, failed to win the prize."[51]

The context of this passage is obscure. It seems to refer back to her previous note on Mahler's Conservatoire days when Mahler "won the first prize for composition", which statement is correct in outline. She continues:

> "His fellow-student and friend, Hans Rott, an extraordinarily talented musician, was unsuccessful. Mahler went home and told them proudly of the prize he had won. His mother wept tears of indignation and said: 'All the same, Rott's work was better than yours.'"[52]

The first prize that Mahler won at the Conservatoire was certainly not for a symphony: moreover, the symphony we know he was presumed to write while a student was conspicuously unsuccessful. Thus both the work and the prize at the centre of this competitive anecdote are in doubt—another possibility is Rott's entry for the Beethoven Prize, for which Mahler submitted *Das klagende Lied*. Mahler said that Rott was a candidate, but did not specify his friend's work.[53] As for the comment of Mahler's mother, it was, Mrs. Mahler claims, "just like" her. Was she, perhaps, on occasions, envious of the attainments of her brilliant son, a "marvel" and "another Schubert" as his fellow-students described him?[54]

Poor Rott died in an asylum, where he kept up his composing but "used the sheets of music-paper he had written on for a very different purpose and said with a grin of delight: 'That's all the works of man are worth.'"[55]

Many biographers have remarked upon the macabre fact that of three of Mahler's most intimate musical friends, two—Rott and Wolf—died insane, while Krisper's mind was, at least, clouded. Mahler himself was by no means the most stable of characters but the resilience of his personality, his capacity for organizing his nerves in the service of himself, his art and large musical organizations—one tends to forget that even the most inspired opera-house routine requires an administrative talent that runs counter to the normal conception of the artistic temperament—stands in marked contrast to the personal disabilities of his companions.

Before we leave Rott we must touch once more upon the topic of Brahms. Dr. Redlich writes that "Fate chose Brahms as an instrument to crush Rott's promising life—Brahms, who played an equally sinister part in the early struggles of Wolf and Mahler".[56] We have seen, in an earlier chapter, something of the violent cross-currents that distinguished Viennese musical life in the latter half of the nineteenth century: the whirlpools were, so to say, centred upon Brahms, Bruckner and Wagner. Wagner, we know, declined to visit the Conservatoire in the autumn of 1875 because he thought it hostile to his music: so it was, from one point of view, though he would have been assured of a warm welcome from the pro-Wagner (and thus pro-Bruckner) student group; and there were members of staff (Hellmesberger, not least) who had a foot in either camp. As we have seen, Epstein, Mahler's piano teacher and, to a degree, patron, was an intimate of the Brahms circle; but his adherence to Brahms did not sour his relations with his impetuous and revolutionary pupil.

Brahms's dissatisfaction with the Conservatoire was stimulated, as I have said, by "the pupils and their work"; and Redlich is doubtless correct in observing that "pupils" in this context means Wolf and the unhappy Rott, who, like Wolf, visited Brahms in search of advice.[57] "Brahms, completely out of sympathy with the influence of Bruckner on the young conservatory students, told Rott that he had no talent and advised him to give up music. Mortally wounded by this blow, the young man, his constitution already severely undermined by the privations of poverty, went insane and died shortly thereafter."[58] At about the same time Mahler, too, was to meet Brahms's stubborn antipathy to

97

the kind of music he was writing as a youth and to suffer materially as a result of the great man's lack of sympathy, though not so disastrously as Rott. There can be no denying that Brahms was a power in the land and used his power, where he might, to block developments of which he disapproved. It is significant and consistent that the Mahler circle should thrice have borne the weight of Brahms's displeasure. One may doubt, however, whether his interventions, as uncivil, insensitive and wrong-headed as they often were, may justly be termed "sinister". Brahms simply did not like these young men's music, and told them so. After all, Wolf—who gave as good as he got—was driven mad not by Brahms, but by syphilis. Rott, one may presume, would have ended up in an asylum even had Brahms recognized him as a genius: that his dismissive verdict set Rott's lunacy in action, was no more than an unhappy accident, for which Brahms can scarcely be held responsible. He was aware, it seems, of the tragedy of the affair—possibly even guilty at the rôle he had played in it: for Brahms attended Rott's funeral, as did Bruckner. Their joint presence crowns this episode—which contains in essence, a slice of Vienna's musical history—with an almost classically proportioned, ironic *dénouement* that is only capped by Mahler's own rôle, at a later period, as the unwitting agent who finally brought down in ruins Wolf's, his old friend's, toppling sanity.

Another important friend of this early period was the poet, dramatist and translator of Mickiewicz, Siegfried Lipiner (1856–1911). Lipiner was known to Nietzsche, who wrote to Erwin Rohde in 1877:

> "Quite recently, a truly consecrated day was vouchsafed to me by 'Prometheus Unbound' [Entfesselten Prometheus]. If the poet is not a veritable genius, I have forgotten the meaning of the word. Everything in it is wonderful, and I was made to feel as if I were face to face with an exalted and deified self. I bow low before one who was able to experience and produce such a thing."

Wagner, too, was impressed by the young Lipiner's gifts.[59]
Mahler, no less; and on the whole he retained his admiration

for Lipiner's talent and pungent personality throughout the years.
What undoubtedly brought Lipiner and Mahler close together
when students was a mutual regard for Nietzsche. Dika Newlin
is right to point to the Nietzschean overtones of correspondence
between Lipiner and Mahler about the former's plays.[60] She is
right again in suggesting that "Nietzsche's influence affected not
only his literary tastes and, perhaps, his manner of literary expression, but also, and far more significantly, the very heart of his
music".[61] She quotes part of a letter from Mahler to Dr. Richard
Batka which discusses his conception of Nature in relation to his
Symphony III, the most obviously Nietzschean-inspired of his
compositions. Mahler was annoyed that the work's second movement, the Minuet, was so often performed as a separate item:

"That this little piece (more of an intermezzo in the whole thing)
must create misunderstandings when detached from its connection
with the complete work, my most significant and vastest creation,
can't keep me from letting it be performed alone. I have no choice;
if I ever want to be heard, I can't be too fussy, and so this modest
little piece will doubtless . . . present me to the public as the
'sensuous', perfumed 'singer of nature'.—That this nature hides
within itself everything that is frightful, great, and also lovely (which
is exactly what I wanted to express in the entire work, in a sort of
evolutionary development)—of course no one ever understands
that. It always strikes me as odd that most people, when they speak
of 'nature', think only of flowers, little birds, and woodsy smells.
No one knows the god Dionysus, the great Pan. There now! You
have a sort of program—that is, a sample of how I make music.
Everywhere and always, it is only the voice of nature! . . . Now it is
the world, Nature in its totality, which is, so to speak, awakened
from fathomless silence that it may ring and resound."[62]

That highly interesting document fills out our picture of Mahler's comprehensive approach to "Nature in its totality", his
celebration of both the fearful and the beautiful, through the
affirmation and acceptance of which one may transcend what
one accepts. It is, of course, a Nietzschean attitude, one that lies
close to the centre of the philosopher's reasoning—his acceptance

of the world *whole*, both its joy and suffering. Professor Erich Heller puts it thus:

> "... Nietzsche discovers the fountainhead of joy in the very heart of the land of sorrow. Happiness ... is not, as it was for Schopenhauer, in the absence of pain; it is the fruit of so radical an acceptance of suffering that abundant delight springs from its very affirmation. For the denial of pain means the denial of existence. Existence is pain, and joy lies not in non-existence, as Schopenhauer would have it, but in its tragic transfiguration. ... From the darkest night of the soul rises Zarathustra's 'Trunkenes Lied', his Dionysian song of the deep suffering of the world, which is yet surpassed in depth by that rapture of delight which wills, not that the world with its pain should pass away, but that it should last for ever ... an eternity not of joy (as Nietzsche is so often misunderstood to mean) but of the world *with* all its sorrow, transfigured in the act of willing it."[63]

We cannot, I think, expect to find in music didactic confirmation that a composer has assimilated, or is attempting to expound, a philosophical system. In any event what betrays Mahler's enthusiasm for, or identity with, Nietzsche, are not so much the outward portents—in Symphony III, his setting, as the fourth movement, of part of Zarathustra's *Trunkenes Lied* (the very words, in fact, which Professor Heller reckons crucial), or his idea, eventually abandoned, of subtitling the symphony *Meine fröhliche Wissenschaft* ('My Joyful Science'),[64] which can be nothing else but a clear reference to Nietzsche's *Die fröhliche Wissenschaft* of 1882; what, rather, is Nietzschean about the work is its Dionysian intoxication, in the immense first movement in particular, where we find Mahler's concept of Nature given its broadest, most elemental, most comprehensive, expression: and we may be sure that it was above all Mahler's instinctive self-identification with Nietzsche's cosmic affirmations, not an intellectual sympathy, that promoted the 'philosophical' content of Symphony III. (It is significant, perhaps, that Mahler, according to Bruno Walter in his autobiography, was "deeply occupied" with *Also sprach Zarathustra* (1883-91) at a time when he was deeply occupied with Symphony III; and *Zarathustra* is certainly

the most rhapsodical, the most poetical, the least didactic, of
Nietzsche's works. Elsewhere, Walter writes that Mahler "was
attracted by the poetic fire of *Zarathustra*, but repelled by the
core of its intellectual content".[65])

Nietzsche, of course, was in the air of the 1890s: he caught the
attention of other composers, of Delius, for example, in his
A Mass of Life (1904-5; but his setting of Zarathustra's *Trunkenes
Lied*—the same text that Mahler had used in his Symphony III—
was composed in 1898). Then there was the ever-opportune
Richard Strauss with his symphonic poem, *Also sprach Zarathustra*,
written in 1896. Delius's *Mass*, only intermittently inspired, is
most successful in conveying an atmosphere of pessimism and
nostalgia; it does not so memorably communicate the rapturous
affirmation, the will to perpetuate the world's joy and sorrow,
which is the more important part of Nietzsche's creed. Delius,
as his whole artistic character reveals, was obviously more
attracted by the nihilism than the Dionysian means of its trans-
figuration. Strauss, in his work, was neither pessimistic nor
Dionysiac, but very much his customary self, publishing yet
another chapter of symphonic autobiography. Nietzsche's Hero
was a fashionable peg upon which a symphonic poem might be
hung, which is not to deny the work its many highly original
inspirations but to suggest that its specifically Nietzschean affiliations were no more than skin deep. It was left to Mahler to dispense with elaborate literary, quasi-philosophical props and
plunge well below the surface of a fashionable thinker: the epic
properties of Symphony III, its yea-saying to "Nature in its
totality", are indicative of Mahler's profound comprehension of
Nietzschean doctrine. There were, no doubt, good reasons why
Mahler felt strongly for Nietzsche: indeed, it is perhaps not too
far-fetched to see a real relation between an essential feature of
Mahler's music—the width and depth of its contrasts, the juxtaposition of opposed moods and materials—and the active acceptance of opposites, pain and happiness, explicit in Nietzsche's
philosophy: in the one case, the Will is the means of transfigura-
tion, of unification; in the other, the work of art, through the
organization of which Mahler unifies *his* contrasts.

We have seen earlier that certain psychologically determined conflicts were rooted deep in Mahler's personality, that one basic conflict was manifest in a situation characterized by the starkness of its contrasts. Mahler, as both man and artist, had to reconcile his contrasts, to accept his conflicts, and it may well have been that the very structure of his personality disposed him in favour of a mode of thought which accommodated joy and suffering within one system—more than that, which taught him that suffering was to be assimilated rather than rejected, when it would prove not merely negatively subdued but positively redeeming. (We may note, in passing, how closely Nietzsche's ideas, stripped of their rhetoric, approach modern psychology, which would have us resolve our tensions by learning to live with them.) Suffering was a problem for Mahler, and those absolutists who would spurn the association of so subjective a topic with the objective work of art are likely to overlook the brilliance with which, in fact, he deployed his suffering as an original expressive means, and, by affirming it in art, objectified it and transformed it into a valid, communicative experience. The parallel with Nietzsche's thought is not, of course, strict; but it would not surprise me if Mahler's early absorption of Nietzsche did not facilitate his uninhibited use of what one might call regions of painful feeling as sources of inspiration: if Nietzsche's prophetically scientific and functional approach to suffering did not shape Mahler's own approach to his painful inner reality.

If, in very subtle ways, Mahler's music continued to reflect the impress of Nietzsche long after he had written his most clearly Nietzschean-influenced symphony, his outward attitude to the philosopher underwent a radical change. Mrs. Mahler records an incident from 1901 when, upon inspecting her books, Mahler discovered a complete edition of Nietzsche, "at which his eyebrows went up in horror. He demanded abruptly that it should be cast then and there into the fire."[66] His antagonism, it seems, persisted, for in 1903 he wrote to his wife from Lvov censuring "flat-heads" who "devour the whole of Nietzsche for breakfast and follow it up by Maeterlinck for supper, and have never digested a word of sense from any source whatever".[67]

This is indeed an altered tone from the Nietzsche enthusiast of earlier years; but we have already seen how changeable Mahler could be from his judgments of composers. Bruno Walter writes: "Nietzsche's anti-Wagnerism made him indignant, and later he turned against him."[68]

It was when Mahler was first making the acquaintance of his future wife, that "a certain estrangement"[69] set in between him and Lipiner (thus not only was Nietzsche lost to Mahler, but also the friend of his youth most intimately connected with his Nietzschean indoctrination). Mrs. Mahler frankly avows her dislike of Lipiner[70] (as of most of the friends of Mahler's youth), and it was doubtless in these unfavourable circumstances that the old friendship wilted: as Newlin puts it, ". . . under his wife's influence Mahler broke with [Lipiner] on personal grounds".[71] The bonds, however, were never quite broken; it was Lipiner who edited the text of Mahler's defence of his re-touchings of Beethoven's Symphony IX,[72] and for Mahler's fiftieth birthday he contributed, at Bruno Walter's suggestion, a poem, *Der Musiker spricht*, to a volume of tributes. The poem effected a kind of reconciliation between the two friends who were to die within a few months of each other.[73]

We left Mahler, chronologically, teaching the piano throughout the summer of 1879, on an estate in Hungary. In a letter to Freund, written from Hungary, in June, Mahler hopes to see his friend in August in Seelau—the Mahler family would be holiday-making in Nordeney, which would leave him "as free as a finch".[74] In September he was back in Vienna again: so much is told us by a letter to Anton Krisper, dated the 22nd. His address then was Rennweg 3, *Parterre*, 'Tür 10b'. Later, Mahler appears to have moved out to Währing, where he stayed until it was time to go home for the Christmas holidays. We know from Wolf's letter of 17 December 1879[75] that although Mahler had paid the rent for his Währing lodging up to 1 January he was leaving early—"tomorrow", writes Wolf, that is, 18 December; and this information of Wolf's confirms a letter of Mahler's written to Krisper from Währing on 14 December,[76] in which he announces his imminent departure for Jihlava.

Mahler's life in Vienna must have continued in this autumn and winter of 1879 in very much the same manner as before, perhaps rather depressingly so; on the other hand, he was doubt-less working hard at his composing, with *Das klagende Lied* taking shape under his hands, the work which Mahler seems to have regarded as a bid for recognition of his creative talent.

For the Christmas vacation he returned home, as we have seen, to Jihlava, as was his custom. A letter to Krisper, of 18 February 1880, reveals that he has changed his Vienna address again (he is now living in the Windmühlgasse, No. 39): in his journeyings from lodging to lodging he compares himself to Ahasuerus, the Wandering Jew.[77] These letters to Krisper are particularly valuable documents, because they record in sequence some of Mahler's movements during these last months of 1879 and first months of 1880, and now and again offer a glimpse of his feelings. On 3 March 1880 he writes again to Krisper, a letter in which occurs that moving sentence about the spring—"Der Frühling ist über Nacht gekommen und mit ihm die alte Sehnsucht und Wehmut" —which anticipates the spirit of *Das Lied*.[78] The spring of 1880 must have weighed on Mahler's mind: "with the coming of spring" is exultantly scrawled on the last page of the first short score of *Der Spielmann*, what we know now as Part I of *Das klagende Lied,* together with the day and date, "Sunday, 21 March 1880". It is odd, perhaps, that Mahler makes no mention of the progress of his work in his letters to his friend, especially since Krisper had been sent part of the cantata's text. None the less, March 1880 was a significant month in Mahler's calendar. An important section of his cantata was committed to paper, and the spring was a memorable one.

In his letter of 3 March, Mahler suggested plans to Krisper for a summer holiday that was typical of his circle, and, as a project alone, gives us a picture of the character of his, and his friends', leisure. The brothers Krzyzanowski were to be included, and the party of four was to travel on foot (Mahler was ever a keen walker), through the Bohemian Forest and Bavarian *Fichtelgebirge*, through Eger (the birthplace of R. Krzyanowski), Bayreuth, Nuremberg, and on to Oberammergau for the famous passion play: three weeks' holiday, and then back home, with a day in Jihlava *en route*, in Krisper's company.

It is doubtful whether this holiday came to anything. (Mahler, ten days later, was downcast and lonely because Krisper had not replied to his invitation.) Summer, in fact, witnessed a quite new situation—Mahler's first professional engagement as a conductor.

There is no doubt that Mahler habitually thought of his career as a conductor as a "hell of theatrical life", a trenchant description noted down by Bauer-Lechner in 1898.[79] (Once, on the note-paper of the Vienna Opera, he crossed out *Direktor* in the printed heading, *Der Direktor des k. k. Hof-Operntheaters*, and substituted *Sklave* ('Slave').)[80] What is curious, indeed, is that the "hell" was so little prepared. There are no signs that Mahler was ever practically interested in conducting when a student. I have pointed out that it was his piano playing that was the much admired manifestation of his gifts as an executant.

It was, in any event, Epstein, his piano teacher, who advised him to accept a post for the summer of 1880 at the theatre of a health resort, [Bad] Hall in Upper Austria. Mahler himself, though his economic position must have been as precarious as ever, seems to have taken no decisive steps to secure employment for himself other than, one presumes, his piano pupils. We have no reason to believe that conducting was suddenly revealed to him as the answer to all his problems. It is likely, moreover, that the thought of *Das klagende Lied*, the work in progress soon to reach completion, buoyed up his hopes for the future.

If Stefan is correct, it was the publisher, Rättig—he had already had dealings with Mahler over the piano-duet arrangement of Bruckner's Symphony III—who

"persuaded [Mahler], as he saw its necessity, to pay a visit to the inevitable Agent. And Mahler was offered an 'engagement' at Hall, in Austria, then not even Hall Spa [i.e., Bad Hall]. The enthusiastic disciple of Wagner and friend of Bruckner—and a summer theatre! His parents and a few others opposed; but Prof. Epstein advised Mahler to accept, in order to make a start somewhere. 'You will soon find other places,' he said consolingly."[81]

Epstein's encouragement and Rättig's perception of the necessity to act—to approach the "inevitable Agent"—suggest that these senior well-wishers thought it advisable to stop Mahler's drift, in fact, "to make a start somewhere". Doubtless their intentions were impeccable, their advice sound. Had Rättig or Epstein left Mahler to his own devices, or his family's opposition carried more weight, would his career have followed a very different path? Might he have avoided the "hell" of the opera house?

We have no means of useful speculation. Mahler himself thought that early success with *Das klagende Lied*—a success denied him—might have saved him from entering upon the treadmill of the conductor's life. We can only be certain that there was no thought of permanency in Mahler's head when he embarked upon what was, in any case, a distinctly temporary conducting appointment; and we must remember, too, that the organization of music in Austria and Germany, with its multitude of opera houses and theatres, allowed the young musician an education as a *Kapellmeister* as part of his training, which was at the same time a recognized method of keeping the wolf from one's door while nourishing other artistic ambitions. There was no need for Mahler to feel that he was committing himself irrevocably to a specific course of action by accepting the Bad Hall engagement.

On the other hand, it was just as if the irrevocable decision *were* taken; for Mahler's career as a conductor pursued an unbroken line of development, if not quite from Bad Hall onwards, then at least from 1882 onwards, the outward shape of which—culminating in the Vienna period 1897-1907—was a success story of impressive proportions. (Had we known that Mahler, from the cradle, had cherished a burning ambition to capture the Vienna *Hofoper* as the final prize in a life dedicated to conducting, his meteoric achievement would somehow seem less lacking a history, a motive, than it does at first sight.)

But though we may concede chance a big share in effecting Mahler's introduction to the conductor's desk, it was no accident that he was a great conductor, one of a handful of interpreters of genius: this gift was rooted deep in his musical personality. His apprenticeship in the provinces may have taught him how to conduct, but it could not have made him a great conductor. What it did do—and for this we must be grateful to Rättig and Epstein for their persuasiveness, as little as they can have foreseen the results of it—was to release the potentially great conductor in Mahler: thereafter his conducting career and the success of it are immediately explicable.

From this point of view we can, I think, discount a good deal of Mahler's grumbling at the "hell" he was obliged to endure. I have no doubt that the grumbling was honest, that Mahler would have preferred to have his time free for composition; and yet I am convinced that in his conducting Mahler was as much in the grip of his genius as when composing, that he was com- pelled to conduct for this reason rather than for those superficial reasons advanced as more obvious explanations, e.g., his economic situation; his need to succeed, to wield power (all the more so in view of his confessed insecurity, "Everywhere an intruder, never welcomed"); to assert his emancipation and affirm his superiority (all the more urgent where one is, as Mahler was, the possessor of superior talents); even to counteract his markedly slight and short (i.e., 'inferior') physique (he was not much over five feet in height)—this category of motives, each of which contains a grain of truth, could be endlessly extended and yet still overlook the central motivation of his conducting: his very interpretative genius, which, once unleashed, was as demanding of nurture as was his creative inspiration. In short, although I recognize the practical difficulties made for Mahler by his twin activities as composer and conductor, I contend in the teeth, as it were, of his own testimony—that his conducting complemented his composing in the sense that it was not an obligation foisted upon him by cruel fate (by chance, rather), but a basic, dynamic component of his musical character, as irrepressible as his invention. I believe that the secret of the fascination conducting held for Mahler is partly revealed in famous sentences he wrote in a letter to Bruno Walter, from New York, early in 1909:

> "Strange—when I hear music—even when I am myself conducting it—I hear quite definite answers to all my questions, and am wholly clear and sure. Or, in reality, I seem to feel quite clearly that they are not questions at all."[82]

No less worthy of being set in isolation is a significant sentence which occurs in a letter addressed to Guido Adler from New York in 1910:

> "I must have some practical outlet for my musical abilities to balance the tremendous inner experiences of creative work; and the leadership [Leitung] of a concert-orchestra [Mahler had been offered an appointment as conductor of an orchestra of his own, of what is today the New York Philharmonic-Symphony Orchestra] was exactly what I've always longed for once in my life."[83]

The relief of conducting to a personality as relentlessly questing and probing as Mahler's (qualities he carried over into his music) —of hearing "quite definite answers" to all his questions—must have been intense, relaxing (despite the ferocious concentration Mahler brought to his performances) and healing to his spirit; for the kind of problems that challenged him when composing (not to speak of the problems that beset him personally) were absent from the task of conducting, where, indeed, he was faced in other men's music with decisions that had to be executed, not taken, a not inconsiderable distinction in responsibility. Mahler, however, never abandoned his hostility to the drudgery of the opera house: "If you want to compose, you must not get mixed up with the theatre"—that was his advice to the young Alban Berg.[84] Here the wheel has turned full circle and in the reverse direction: the senior musician again advises the young composer, but Mahler proffers Berg advice the opposite of that which he received in 1880! None the less, I am willing to back my paradox:

that his conducting, the activity he scorned most, played a major rôle in making his life bearable.

There is, of course, much yet to be said of Mahler's conducting, in particular of what one might term his composing approach to the *Kapellmeister*'s art, where one sees most clearly that identical artistic characteristics and ideals endowed both spheres of his musicality with an unmistakable unity; but this was an aspect of Mahler's maturity as a conductor. For the time being, there is the *Kapellmeister* of Bad Hall—as Baedeker (1896) describes it, "a watering-place with springs impregnated with iodine. New Kurhaus, baths, and colonnade, and a theatre and fine park."

Stefan has little to say of Mahler's Hall engagement except that he conducted "operettas, farces and stage [incidental] music" and acquired his first *claque*.[85] Something is known of the history of the theatre itself. It was, first and foremost, only a summer theatre, designed as an additional attraction for the Spa's visitors. (Of such bad construction, it was said, that in wet weather the theatre was unfit for occupation.)[86] Its capacity was tiny: sixteen boxes, each with six chairs, sixty-six seats in the gallery, sixteen in the *Parterre*, and some folding chairs in the balcony. Since the theatre was built of wood, artificial light was ruled out (as was smoking) and performances took place in the late afternoon. The company was small: for the seasons of 1875-6 it consisted of eight ladies and eleven gentlemen, who appeared in a repertory which included Millöcker's *Drei Paar Schuhe*, Offenbach's *Barbebleue, Orphée aux enfers* and *Princesse de Trébizonde*. We have no precise records for 1880, but no doubt the character of the repertory would have been much the same. We do know, however, what Mahler earned as Bad Hall's *Kapellmeister*: thirty gulden a month plus a fee of fifty kreutzer for each performance he conducted—less, of course, the commission due to his "inevitable Agent".[87]

Some of Mahler's own pungent memories of Bad Hall have come down to us through his wife. She writes that the theatre's(?) director, Carl Ludwig Zwerenz ("a man whose excellent reputation in connection with operetta may still be known to many today"[88] and father of the operetta singer), appointed Mahler "conductor of the summer-theatre orchestra in a sense which must be unique":

> "His duties were to put out the music on the music-stands before each performance, to dust the piano and to collect the music again after the performance. During the intervals he had to wheel the baby, Mizzi Zwerenz, round the theatre in her pram. He drew the line, however, when he was required to deputize on the stage. He regretted later that his pride had stood in the way, as the lost opportunity would have brought him much that was never likely to come his way again.
>
> "While there he got into what—for him—was very strange company. The painter, Angeli, was surrounded by an admiring circle of young men of fashion, who invited Mahler to join their gatherings. He was flattered by the attentions of the first persons of birth and breeding he had encountered. He blossomed forth. They went long expeditions together, which of course withdrew him more and more from his duties, until one day he was so late for the performance that he was dismissed. His new friends escorted him in a body to the station and he parted from them with the promise to look them all up in Vienna."[89]

This account is an amusing commentary on Mahler's Bad Hall experiences. Perhaps not all of it (e.g., dusting the piano, wheeling the pram) should be taken too literally or too seriously: there are too many marks of the good story about it. That Mahler was dismissed for absenteeism seems unlikely—out of character on the one hand, and contrary to his own immediate interests on the other: an unpublished letter of his, written from Bad Hall on 21 June 1880 to his agent, Lewy,[90] in Vienna, tells us that he was already anxious to secure a further engagement for the coming winter season. He would give Lewy an additional honorarium of fifty gulden if he might be obtained a really good engagement, preferably in Germany, as second conductor in a large theatre, as a conductor of opera, moreover. So we see that even from the very modest beginnings at Bad Hall, Mahler's ambitions took flight, already with considerable certainty of aim. Of course, it was some years before he achieved a post which measured up to the specification in this early letter, and Bad Hall, far from leading to another appointment, simply petered out—either the season came to its natural end or Mahler was sent packing: whatever the reason, the autumn found Mahler back in Vienna again, unemployed but for his piano pupils.

(The unpublished letter divulges an interesting reference to Iglau (Jihlava), Mahler's home town. It seems that he might have become *Kapellmeister* there, but was unable to accept the engagement, he told Lewy, "because of my family". ("Director Zwerenz" is mentioned in this context as a collaborator in the enterprise— a good reason, one would have thought, for Mahler not getting himself dismissed: if he was busy thinking of his next appointment, as he was, would he have been so careless as to lose the goodwill of his only referee?) The remark about his family is ambiguous. It might mean that being a Jew precluded him from filling the position; such an interpretation is not, alas, at all improbable. On the other hand, since Mahler's parents were opposed to his accepting the Bad Hall engagement—probably because they thought their son deserved better—he may have thought it impossible to move on to Jihlava where he would, as it were, flourish the humbleness of his occupation on the family threshold. None the less, Jihlava did hear Mahler as a conductor, in 1882.)[91]

". . . In autumn", Stefan writes, "the great doings at Hall came to an end, and nothing similar was to be found. The alternative was Vienna, piano-lessons, and composition."[92] Bad Hall, none the less, had made its impact, partly painful, but also, as Adler points out, partly stimulating:

"While working in the narrow cultural back-alleys of small Austrian provincial towns, he had to produce operas by lamplight, to arrange the parts, to transcribe, to adapt, with only a third of the required instrumental resources at his disposal and faced with the complete absence of any instrument that was at all out of the ordinary; whereupon his inner ear yearned for perfection and the well-proportioned performance, as a thirsty man yearns for water."

It was these "deprivations" of his early days, continues Adler—

and there were many others after Bad Hall—that intensified Mahler's zeal and ardour when at last he found himself in charge of a theatre whose resources matched his artistic ideals.[93]

It seems that when back in Vienna Mahler tried to keep up with his smart friends from the summer but found "every door . . . closed to him. He felt at once that he was rebuffed as a Jew and, avoiding new acquaintances for the future, fell back on his boyhood friends. (The slight may have been not for the Jew but the holiday acquaintance [*Sommerbekanntschaft*].)"[94] But if there were personal disappointments, artistic disappointments—no further engagements in sight—and the endless struggle to keep afloat in Vienna, there were also compensations: old friends and the completion of *Das klagende Lied*, which news Mahler conveyed to Freund in a letter dated 1 November 1880:

> "My fairytale is at last finished—a real child of sorrow at which I've worked for over a year. As a result it's in good shape. My next aim: to bring about its performance by any means I can think of."[95]

This same letter, in an odd mixture of events and information, tells us of the onset of Rott's madness and Krisper's impending insanity, occurrences that inspire Mahler to gloomy thoughts, e.g., "If you know of a single happy creature on earth tell me his name lest I lose the little desire I still have for life".[96] But a paragraph later he bursts into rhapsody at the regenerative effects of vegetarianism, the new mode of life Mahler adopted in the autumn of this year:

> "To-morrow [i.e., 2 November, the day of the Catholic festival] is the first All Souls' Day of my life! Now I too must lay a wreath on a grave. I have become, since a month ago, a complete vegetarian."[97]

Such is the resilience of youth.

From a mass of facts about Mahler, certain conclusions about his personality, taste, and inclinations emerge of their own accord: we can assemble a partial portrait of the young man from the evidence of his actions, letters, the few public documents, the witness of his friends. It is clear that the outline of the character of later years, of the man who is, so to speak, part of our history, is present in essentials in these formative years. Stefan, writing of these early times, does round out our knowledge with a few *personalia*; he mentions Mahler's "fiery manner of speech, his lightning-like readiness of mind, his daemonic force of perception and absolutely amazing power of clearing up any situation with one word"—qualities of his maturity that "were remarked even then", in his student days.[98] We hear that his

"kindly and divinatory nature brought him near to animals. He understood much of their language, and could pass hours playing with dogs. In the same way, he was devoted to children, who have the candid seriousness of animals."[99]

(Mahler's attitude to Nature's creatures was, in fact, rather more realistic—though perhaps not the less divinatory for all that—than Stefan's words suggest. For example, Dika Newlin writes of the "symbolic significance" in Mahler's work of "bird-song", and continues:

"Oddly enough, its value for him was only symbolic; actually, he found the singing of birds around his *Komponierhäuschen* in the summertime so disturbing as to be intolerable, and even used to shoot some of them to discourage their fellows."[100]

Perhaps it was in the light of an incident of this character that Mrs. Mahler remarks that her husband's "love of animals was theoretical only".)[101]

"At this period", writes Stefan,

"[Mahler] also laid the foundations of the proud edifice of his general knowledge. He became acquainted with the philosophers, especially Kant and Schopenhauer; later [G. T.] Fechner [1801–87], [R. H.] Lotze [1817–81], and [H. L .F. von] Helmholtz [1821–94] were added. In Nietzsche he admired the hymnic vein. Philosophy, in particular the boundaries that touch the natural sciences, always attracted him; how attentively, for instance, he . . . followed the researches of [J.] Reinke [1849–1931], to whom he was led, as to Fechner, by his religious instinct. Goethe, Schiller and the Romantic School were already his precious possessions, his favourites being E. T. A. Hoffmann and Jean Paul [Richter], especially the latter's [novel] 'Titan'. History, biology and psychology held his attention always. As psychologist and poet, Dostoieffsky was for Mahler a discovery."[102]

We have here literary tastes and a bent for philosophical enquiry that remained, for the most part, constant throughout Mahler's life; he had, indeed, already revealed the strength of these inclinations at school and university. Bruno Walter writes:

". . . he was interested mainly in those phenomena of natural history that furnished philosophy with new material for thought. Friends of his, professionally occupied with natural science, were hard pressed by his deeply penetrating questions. An eminent physicist whom he met frequently could not tell me enough about Mahler's intuitive understanding of the ultimate theories of physics [cf. Freud's observation on Mahler's intuitive understanding of psychoanalysis!] and about the logical keenness of his conclusions or counterarguments."[103]

It is of interest to note that the "philosophers" mentioned by Stefan above were also, almost exclusively, men of science. Such was certainly the case of Helmholtz: Fechner was both experimental psychologist and animistic philosopher, while Lotze's aim was "the reconciliation of science with art, literature and religion".[104] Reinke was a philosophically inclined botanist. All these men, however diversely, pursued lines of investigation which—to put it very crudely—tried to knit the universe together, to demonstrate its unity (Fechner, for example, believed that even plants and stars were animated); some of these thinkers, moreover, were marked by strong religious susceptibilities. That Mahler was so interested in philosophy of this character, which, as it were, took rational, scientific account of intangibles and attempted a comprehensive explanation of the cosmos, throws light on his own philosophy, one never defined, to be sure, but implicit in many a word and deed—and, perhaps, not altogether absent as a formative influence in his music. I have suggested already that Mahler was attracted by the comprehensiveness explicit in Nietzsche's thought; one sees, I think, a similar basis for attraction in these scientist-philosophers. Mahler himself was, above all, a mixture of patent contrasts, a sceptic on the one hand, a believer on the other, a rationalist and a mystic: it is obvious why inclusive systems of philosophy, inclusive in the sense that they accommodated material phenomena, absorbed Mahler's intelligence. It may not be possible to draw effective parallels between philosophy and music, but I believe it might be held that a characteristic choice of philosophy may have its equivalents in musical characteristics; or at least one might say that when one knows both Mahler's music and his *Weltanschauung* one senses very strongly in the music the mind that was drawn to Fechner or Lotze, that esteemed both knowledge and intuition. Is there not something distinctly relevant to the point at issue in the wide scope of Mahler's music—whereupon, perhaps, his famous remark to Sibelius: ". . . symphony must be like the world. It must embrace everything",[105] assumes fresh significance—or the well-nigh laboratory-passion which he brought to the textural clarification of his invention, however uninhibited and tumultuous? Mahler's instrumental science served to expose, not combat, his imagination: it is the kind of reconciliation central to the philosophical enquiries he favoured, and in accord with the structure and dominant inclinations of his personality.

With the close of 1880—the autumn of which was punctuated by intermittent sojourns at home in Jihlava[106]—this part of Mahler's biography comes to a natural conclusion. For in a very real sense Mahler, in 1880, had his early years behind him. At the same time, with *Das klagende Lied* completed, and conducting revealed as a possible means of living, his feet were set on the double track of activity that was to be thenceforth his life's unchanging pattern.

IV

The Early Works

—1875   (a) Compositions for piano?

1876   (b) Sonata for violin and piano. [First public (?) performance, Jihlava, 12 September 1876, Mahler at the piano.]

1876   (c) First movement of Quartet for piano and strings in A minor. [Performed at Vienna Conservatoire (?) on 10 July 1876. First public (?) performance, Jihlava, 12 September 1876; Mahler at the piano on both (?) occasions.]

1876   Fragment of movement for piano Quartet; in G minor (about 36 [?] bars).

1876–1879??   Two songs [fragments]:

     (i) Unidentified text; in D minor (about 23 bars).

     (ii) *Im wunderschönen Monat Mai* (Heine); in C [?] (about 18 bars).

    Unpublished autographs in the possession of Mrs. Alma Mahler (New York).[1]

1879?   (d) Quartet for piano and strings.

1875????   (e) Quintet for piano and strings. [First movement
1878   ????. Scherzo: performed at Vienna Conservatoire on 11 July 1878, Mahler at the piano.]

1877?–1878?   (f) *Herzog Ernst von Schwaben*, opera. Libretto: Josef Steiner [after Uhland?].

1878[2]   (g) *Das klagende Lied*, text: G. Mahler, after a folk-
Completed (?)
18 March   tale collected by Ludwig Bechstein [1801–1860].

116

1875–1878?? (h) Suite for piano.

1877?? (i) 'Conservatoire' Symphony. [One? movement rehearsed at Conservatoire under Hellmesberger.]

1882–1883??? (j) Symphony in A minor. [First three movements in MS.]

1879?–1883 (k) *Rübezahl*, fairy-tale opera; text: G. Mahler. [Text completed? Music composed only for the first act?]

1879??? (l) *Quartettsatz*. [For piano quartet?? string quartet???]

Begun 1878? (m) *Das klagende Lied*, music: a cantata for soprano, contralto and tenor soloists, mixed chorus and large orchestra.

ORIGINAL VERSION

1880
Completed
1 November

(i) *Waldmärchen* (70 pp.)
(ii) *Der Spielmann* (44 pp.)
(iii) *Hochzeitsstück* (60 pp.)

Complete autograph of text and music of this version "with quite a number of corrections and instrumentation remarks", in the possession of Mr. Alfred Rosé (Canada). Other autographs connected with the original version are:

(a) a first (?) sketch (short score) of (ii) above, entitled *Spielmann* and dated Sunday, 21 March 1880. [See Plates VIII and XI.]

(b) a first (?) full score of (ii)—the first few pages of the orchestral prelude missing—entitled 2. *Stück. Spielmann*, and dated "the month of March, 1880". [See Plate IX.]

(b) would seem to be the first full score of (ii); Mr. Rosé thinks his complete autograph may be "the first full score", but in view of (b) it seems probable that (i), (ii) and (iii) represent

117

the first *fair* full score. The autographs of (a) and (b) are located in the *Stadtbibliothek*, Vienna.

The first performance of (i)—the part that was excluded from the Revised Version (see below)—took place on Radio Brno on 28 November 1934 under Mr. Rosé's direction. On this occasion (i) was sung in Czech; on 2 December it was repeated, in German. On 8 April 1935 Mr. Rosé directed the first complete performance of the Original Version on the Vienna radio (*Ravag*). (i) remains to date unpublished.

⇨

REVISED VERSION

Revised Version published: 1899 [1900?], Weinberger.[3]

The titles were dropped, but: Part I=(ii) and Part II=(iii). (i) was abandoned. This Revised Version was published in 1899(?); the revisions that preceded the work's publication were numerous and spread out over a broad span of years. The established dates of revision are: 1888,[4] 1898–9,[5] between 1891–7 (in Hamburg),[6] and post-1900 (afterthoughts upon the instrumentation).[7]

⇨

An autograph full score of *Das klagende Lied* [of the Revised Version, Hamburg] is in the possession of Mrs. Alma Mahler, together with three leaves of sketches. (Albrecht, p. 177: see II/n. 21.)

⇨

The Revised Version was given its first performance (the Original Version, of course, had no performance in Mahler's lifetime) in Vienna (*Singakademie*) on 17 February 1901, the composer conducting.[8] The first performance in England took place at the Royal Festival Hall, London, on 13 May 1956, when the conductor was Walter Goehr.

1880? (n) *Die Argonauten*, opera. Libretto: G. Mahler [after Grillparzer?]. Only the prelude composed??

(o) Early songs for tenor voice and piano. Autograph in the possession of Mr. Alfred Rosé (Canada):

19 February 1880   (i) *Im Lenz* (text: G. Mahler)
27 February 1880   (ii) *Winterlied* (G. Mahler)
5 March 1880   (iii) *Maitanz im Grünen* (G. Mahler)
Unpublished,   (See (iii) below.)
but for (iii).   "Sung for the first (and only) time on 'Radio Brno' on 30 September 1934 by Zdenek Knittl (tenor) with me accompanying at the piano". (Note from Alfred Rosé.)

1880–1883??   Fragment of Scherzo of Symphony I for piano-duet, four hands. [In A major: represents perhaps first conception of movement??? Or an intended arrangement? The character of the calligraphy suggests an earlier rather than a later date.]

1880–1883   *Lieder und Gesänge [aus der Jugendzeit]*—I:
    (i) *Frühlingsmorgen* (text: R. Leander)
    (ii) *Erinnerung* (R. Leander)
    (iii) *Hans und Grethe* (G. Mahler)
        (See (iii) above.)
    (iv) *Serenade* (Tirso de Molina's *Don Juan*)
    (v) *Phantasie* (Tirso de Molina's *Don Juan*)

Published: An autograph, '5 Gedichte componiert von
1885, Schott.   Gustav Mahler', is in the possession of Mr. Alfred Rosé. The first performance of (iii), *Hans und Grethe*, was given at Prague in April 1886; the soloist was Fräulein Frank, a member of the Prague *Deutsches Theater*. The accompanist was probably Mahler. [Two other songs from the *Lieder und Gesänge*, Book I, also performed for the first time on this occasion?]

1882?? (p) *Nordische Symphonie* [or *Suite?*], for orchestra.

June, 1884 (q) Incidental music to 'living pictures' from *Der
Unpublished; *Trompeter von Säkkingen*, a poem by Joseph
MS. lost or Viktor von Scheffel; for orchestra. [First per-
destroyed. formed at Cassel, *Hoftheater*, Mahler conducting, on 23 June 1884.]

Dec. 1883– (r) *Lieder eines fahrenden Gesellen*, song-cycle for
1 Jan. 1885 low voice and piano/voice and orchestra.
Published: Texts: G. Mahler. First performance of
1897, Wein- orchestral version,[9] Berlin, 16 March 1896,
berger. Mahler conducting the Berlin Philharmonic
Orchestra, with Sistermans as soloist. An
earlier *première* (voice and piano?) is not
known.[10]

The preceding list—or at least its many question marks, the
number of which (i.e., ?, ??, ???) indicates the intensity of each
query—makes its own comment. Mahler's youthful compositions
are as ill-documented as the biography of his early years; and ill-
documented here has a very special sense, since the documents
themselves, the compositions, have been lost, destroyed (by the
composer himself), or are inaccessible, though, one hopes, only
temporarily so. For a long while it has been assumed that none
of Mahler's *juvenilia* survived his censorship: "Unfortunately,
the mature Mahler destroyed every bit of his work which struck
him as unworthy, leaving posterity no definite idea of the quality
of his efforts during these early years."[11]

The very existence of items (*c*), (*m*) [O.V.], and (*o*), therefore,
is a surprise. When we are fortunate enough to possess facsimiles
of the autographs of all these works, or the comments of responsible analysts, we shall be in a better position to estimate the
character of Mahler's first compositions, to determine the trends
that influenced him in and outside the Conservatoire (from this
point of view, acquaintance with (*m*) [O.V.] would be of particular interest). For the time being, however, we have to content
ourselves with a list of works many of which are lost, while some
that are extant are not open to inspection; on the other hand, the

list also includes Mahler's published *juvenilia* (i.e., items (*m*) [R.V.] and (*o*) [*Lieder und Gesänge*]: (*r*) is added as pointer to the possible accomplishment of lost works from roughly the same period), which means that we have, if my conjectures about (*m*) [O.V.] are correct, two contributions from Mahler's early years which can be examined in detail and from which certain general conclusions may be drawn. Item (*c*), too, is enlightening.

As for the lost or inaccessible autographs, I have gathered together such information as is available and relevant, and something of musical value can be deduced, perhaps, from Mahler's choice of media, from what he or others said of his own first steps in composing.

My list comprises all the youthful works mentioned by any biographer and by Mahler himself. About the existence of some of them, all commentators are agreed; other works are referred to only in one source and nowhere confirmed; others may, through the years, have undergone slight variations in title (e.g., *Nordische Symphonie* or *Nordische Suite*?); or an error in documentation may have converted one work into two, e.g., a piano quartet is misdescribed as a quintet, whereupon both the work itself and the wrong description of it live on as independent compositions. Again, there is no means of knowing with a work destroyed or lost to what stage of completion it developed.

The case of (*k*), *Rübezahl*, where we have precise information about the libretto, and even about one of the opera's choruses, is rare. I suspect that many of these youthful pieces, especially the operas, were abandoned long before they were complete: the texts may have been finished (Mahler was a fluent versifier), but I doubt whether the music was; indeed, what does seem to emerge as a feature of Mahler's early works is their general incompleteness—a movement of a quartet, three movements of a symphony, fragments of an opera, three songs of a cycle of five, but few projects carried through. Where Mahler did commit an entire work to paper, i.e., *Das klagende Lied*, it has survived. So while we may regret that many of Mahler's *juvenilia* are lost to us, I think we regret torsos rather than completed compositions.

How uncertain and subject to qualification and reservation is my list of works soon becomes apparent when the explanatory notes are tackled. It is clear from them that my placing of the works represents the best possible compromise between often contradictory—not just conflicting—opinions. Dates, as is their habit, wear question marks almost throughout; only occasionally, as in (*m*) and (*o*), has it been possible to establish a date from MS. sources. If nothing else, the chronic vagaries of the list are proof of the impossibility to knit into the biography of Mahler's early years a consecutive account of his early compositions.

(*a*)

Stefan tells us that at Mahler's first interview with Epstein, the latter "invited the young unknown to play something either *of his own* or otherwise" (my italics).[12] This remark reminds us of Mahler's statement that he composed industriously from his very early years onwards;[13] it was an obvious step to take along some of his own 'works' upon the momentous occasion of his visit to Vienna in 1875.

(*b*)

We know that this sonata had some sort of authentic life, since it was one of the works played at Jihlava in September 1876. It is mentioned by a number of biographers. Stefan tells us that it "enjoyed a certain celebrity amongst [Mahler's] friends".[14] Mahler, according to Bauer-Lechner, claimed that the work won a prize (which? almost all his *juvenilia* seem to have won prizes, if Mahler is to be believed); more interestingly, he stated that he had never entirely committed the sonata to paper. He explained that the sonata was not written out because his mind at this time was too restless and unsettled; he wrote, rather, one sketch after another, and kept the complete concept only in his head. Since he had every note in his mind, he was always able to play the sonata. But the day did eventually come when he had forgotten it. Not before the work had received a rehearsal at the *Musikverein* one winter.[15] (Mahler does not specify the year but it was probably 1876, when his sonata appears to have been the object of a certain amount of attention; it is odd, however, that he did not recall its

Jihlava *début*.) One wonders, incidentally, how the sonata was entered for a prize when some of it, at least, existed only in Mahler's head? It seems probable that his memory may have presented him with more prizes than he actually won. We may also wonder how, if Mahler simply forgot the work, it was later destroyed, as Adler claims, between 1877–9.[16]

(*c*)

I think it may be assumed that this first movement was the work played at the same Jihlava concert (1876) in which the violin Sonata, (*b*), was performed. As I have suggested already, I think this movement was the prize-winning composition which concluded Mahler's first year at the Conservatoire, that the records err in describing it as a quintet.

The autograph of the Quartet's first movement is contained within a portfolio, or folder, on the outside leaf of which is inscribed: *frühe Compositionen*. The title page reads: *Clavier-quartett*: *Erster Satz*: *Gustav Mahler*: *1876*. (The bottom of this page is rubber-stamped: *Th. Rättig, Wien*—the publisher, it will be remembered, who printed the piano-duet arrangement of Bruckner's Symphony III, in which Mahler had a hand. The significance of this imprint is not clear to me.)

Two features of the MS. are met with again in the MSS. of *Das klagende Lied*; they are detailed at some length in (*m*) below: the curious marginal whorls and squiggles in which Mahler seems to test his penmanship, and, towards the end of the movement, the signs of mounting haste which similarly mark the end of the cantata's SK★.[17] In general, this quartet movement is a fairer autograph than either *Das klagende Lied*'s SK or FS, as doubtless it was obliged to be in view of its submission as a prize-winning exercise to the Conservatoire's authorities; none the less, its last three pages (pp. 16–18) are much sketchier than those preceding; the piano part, indeed, is there only in outline—though figured now and then—while *Orgelpunkt* (on A), scrawled over the bass staff in the movement's closing bars, serves as sufficient direction to the pianist's left hand.

★i.e. SK (the sketch); FS (first full score). See p. 160.

Mahler was just sixteen years old when he completed this movement. It shows no great individuality of manner, but its technical proficiency—not dazzling, but not by any means lacking in accomplishment—is proof that he was quick to learn and had, indeed, learned much in his first year; if he arrived at the Conservatoire only rudimentarily self-taught, however self-evidently talented, he had covered much ground between the date of his entry and the date of his first composing competition.

The conventionality of its invention need occasion no surprise. The movement represented Mahler's *début* as a pupil of Krenn. It was not likely that he would, in these circumstances, do anything else but his best to please his master, whose reputation, as we have seen, would scarcely lead us to expect adventurous exercises of his students. Mahler's quartet movement doubtless won a prize as much for its negative qualities as for its positive; the positive qualities of the later cantata, on the other hand, almost certainly lost the work the possibility of the prize for which it was submitted. One thing this movement confirms; how orthodox and conformist the atmosphere within the Conservatoire must have been: that it was the stimulus of musical life outside its walls which would have nourished Mahler's young genius.

Stefan's suggestion that the themes of the piano quartet movement foretell "the melodist of the symphonies"[18] has no basis in reality. (Likewise, the movement's A minor, though pointing to Mahler's feeling for the key, has little of the tragic passion about it which characterizes the A minor of his maturity.) The movement's themes, in fact, though not unshapely and not even without some genuine impulse behind their rather ordinary formulation, are innocent of gripping character, actual or potential. Which is not to say that the three principal themes are not characterized; indeed, their strongly contrasted characters—the portentousness of *A*, the rhapsody of *B* (enfeebled by a vein of weak chromaticism), the nursery-song-like simplicity of *C*—have too little in common, to the detriment of the movement's unity. But it is not, on the whole, the movement's melody which is its prime weakness; it is, rather, its organization which is defective.

The weakness of the development section rests simply, and

perhaps expectedly, in its *over*-organization. For eighty-five bars it conscientiously and somewhat tediously shuffles interlocking combinations of short motives subtracted from the movement's principal themes. So far as they go, its little contrapuntal and variational ingenuities are—academically speaking—good work; but the patterns and formulas are relentlessly pressed home long after their interest *qua* invention has been exhausted. But this, it might be said, is part of the prize-winning game; and Mahler, in his development, shows off his familiarity with the rules with no little skill. The 'pedantry' of this part of the movement may well have earned "Old Krenn's" commendation.

Though the derivativeness of the themes themselves is striking—especially the Brahmsian sobriety of the movement's opening melodic thought (*A*, an expository paragraph of thirty-nine bars)—no less striking is their genuine musicality; they do flow, are not stiff as so often 'prentice-work is. But their formal disposition and relations are odd; and ultimately unsatisfactory.

A, marked *Nicht zu schnell*, whose three-note basic motive (I–VI–V, in A minor) is put through its paces in the development, gives way to *B*, a second theme, marked *Entschlossen* ('Resolute'), when, too, 2/2 gives way to 4/4. This settling down to a firm tempo, combined with a reiteration of the tonic, seems to suggest that *A*'s solemn function is introductory; that *A*, perhaps, has a cyclic rôle to play in the whole work; that *B* initiates the exposition proper. *B*, however (twelve bars, full in texture), is followed by a new theme (*C*), though more of a codetta theme, to be sure, than a real 'second subject'. *C*, rapidly modulating, does introduce some tonal relief, but its brevity (thirteen bars) does little to counter the *double* tonic assertion of *A* and *B*, an assertion reasserted by the development (the successor of *C*), which opens in A minor on *A*'s basic motive (I–VI–V)! Mahler, moreover, has marked the end of his exposition with a double-bar and repeat sign: hence A minor is yet further emphasized if the repeat is observed. The repeat of the exposition, which includes *A*, destroys what would appear to have been the latter's promising introductory function, and the movement's recapitulation only goes further to weaken its introductory status, though here *A* is shortened to twenty-one bars. (Is it far-fetched, however, to see here the germ of the repeated introductions which are noticeable features of the first movements of Symphonies I and III?)

At the point where, if the recapitulation were exact, one would expect *A* to flow into *B* (at the change of tempo, *Entschlossen*, of the exposition), *C* returns—in a remote key (F sharp minor)—not, however, in its original version, but as it appears in the development, i.e., combined with the basic motive of *A* (sixteen bars). After which, *B* is reached, in A minor, of course; but despite the immediately preceding splash of foreign tonal colour we do not really experience an assertion of the movement's second subject at tonic level since *B*, in fact, has never departed from it. The intervention of *C* is diversionary merely, not fundamental—or fundamental only in the sense that it attempts to conceal a weakness.

The recapitulation of *B* is exact (twelve bars); *C* ensues again, and now holds the stage until the close of the movement across its sustained tonic pedal. This closing part (thirty-three bars) falls into two clear stages: a recapitulation of *C* and a coda derived from it. These two sections are divided by a miniature cadenza, in *tempo rubato*, for the solo violin—a novel stroke.

Novel effects of this rather superficial order there are in the movement. One might view the reshuffling of themes in the recapitulation, its vivid blob of colour in a contrasted key, as tentative manifestations of an original talent not altogether at ease in circumstances in which discreet self-interest dictated subservience to orthodoxy. But the successful conformity revealed in the development makes one wonder why, elsewhere in the movement, Mahler's formal aim and tonal organization should have been so direction-less, patently flouting classical 'sonata' practice without, so it appears, a very clear intent to substitute a reasoned alternative. The exposition's concentration of tonic is enigmatic.

The quartet is smoothly written, but inclined to somewhat congested textures. The pianist is occupied throughout with a sonorously conceived rôle which demands by way of counterbalance, and receives, a more or less continuous ensemble on the part of the strings—their busy-ness makes for rich sonority but provides little possibility of individual instrumental characterization or contrasts in texture.

The MS. fragment of a further movement (some thirty bars), 6/8, in G minor, a projected Scherzo (?), obviously belongs to the work just discussed. Its brisk opening theme is again conventional in contour—though here, perhaps, something of Schumann's spirit mingles with Brahms's. The theme is 'carried' on semiquaver figuration (heard in both the piano and strings), reminiscent in its persistent revolution of similar figures which roll through the music from Mahler's maturity.

The two song fragments are widely contrasted. The incomplete setting in D minor of an unidentified text is as diatonic as the attempt at *Im wunderschönen Monat Mai* is chromatic. The latter song's home tonality, which appears to be C, is approached in a miniature piano prelude, whose elaborately chromatic crawl takes D flat as its point of departure.

The D minor fragment discloses a typically Mahlerian rhythmic structure in its melody, and though, in general, a rather indecipherable MS., it conveys a faint impression of the style of the early *Wunderhorn* songs which were to be composed after 1888.

Im wunderschönen Monat Mai—whose metre varies thus within a short section: 4/4: 3/4: 4/4: 2/4: 4/4—is a curiosity. It is evidence, no doubt, that Mahler's intense affection and admiration for Schumann's art were part of his early musical life; but this act of friendly rivalry took an odd stylistic turn, since Mahler, it is clear, when he wrote the song, was patently under the intoxicating influence of Wagner: so much is suggested by the contours of the vocal line and the character of the harmony, which place Heine's fragile lyric in an extravagant atmosphere of *Tristan*-esque yearning. Mahler's *Im wunderschönen Monat Mai* has the distinction of being not only his most Wagnerian piece but also the only one in which we can watch him completely surrender himself to the colour, sensuousness and freedom of typically Wagnerian harmonic progressions, as if fascinated by a quite new

realm of sound while unable to do more than superficially revel
in—and imitate—its sonorities.

There are no dates attached to these fragments, but I think it
probable that they belong to Mahler's early student period. They
might possibly be earlier than 1876—though their siting in the
same MS. collection as the first movement of the piano Quartet
could be chronologically significant—but I doubt if they are later
than 1879, if 1880 may be taken as the year in which Mahler's
talent for song-composition bore its first fruits, among which
these interesting but very tentative fragments cannot be counted.

We are not at the end of piano quartets as a subject of debate.
To Bauer-Lechner, Mahler reported another piano quartet,

(*d*),

which belonged to the close of his "four-year [sic]" student
period and was one of the best of his youthful compositions. It
was well received and "Graedener[19] retained it for months and
liked it so much that he performed it at Billroth's.[20] I submitted
the piece for a prize competition in Russia, where the Quartet
went astray."[21] How to take that enigmatic "four-year" student
period (it was three years) sets a problem. It may have been a slip
on Mahler's part or on Bauer-Lechner's. Or Mahler might have
been thinking of the Conservatoire years plus the one year (1879)
in which he appears to have pursued his studies at the University;
if this last supposition is correct, then the lost piano Quartet
belongs to 1879, post-dating his final exercise for the Conservatoire, the piano-quintet movement, (*e*).

(*e*)

I have suggested in (*c*) that the prize-winning work for 1876
was, in fact, the first movement of a piano Quartet. If my guess
is correct, then we must discount, or better, emend an item of
information widely disseminated among Mahler's biographies.
(If it is wrong, then we must add to the list, alongside the first
movement of the piano Quartet, the first movement of a piano
Quintet. But I think it unlikely that the addition will ever be
made.)

In any event, while the Conservatoire entry for 1876—first movement of a Quintet—is dubious, there could be nothing more precise than the entry for 1878, which establishes, as we have seen, the Scherzo of a piano Quintet without any doubt whatsoever.[22]

A piano Quintet, or parts of one, figures among Mahler's *juvenilia* in most biographies. This Scherzo of 1878, however, is the only example of the piano-quintet medium which is reliably documented. It would seem to have been written "overnight", if Stefan's description of Mahler's prizewinning labours is correct.[23] Adler specifies a piano Quintet as one of the works destroyed by Mahler between 1877–9.[24]

(*f*)

Very little is known about this work, the first of the four operatic projects Mahler started and abandoned. Neither Stefan nor Specht mentions it, and the opera is not included among the pieces listed by Bauer-Lechner. There is a reference to the opera in a letter of Mahler's that has already been quoted, a letter addressed to Josef Steiner, his librettist. (Redlich has suggested that the text of the opera might have been based upon a verse-drama of the same title by Uhland.[25]) The letter is dated 18 June 1879 and, from the tone of it, it would appear that the opera was already a thing of the past: we have no sense of work in progress. Some biographers place the opera in 1877–9, following Adler,[26] but I should be more inclined to date it earlier, perhaps 1877–8. By March 1878 Mahler had completed the text of *Das klagende Lied* and thereafter was busy with its composition. In view of this new undertaking in 1878 and the retrospective tone of the 1879 letter, it seems reasonable to conjecture that *Herzog Ernst von Schwaben* was laid aside by 1878 at the latest. Adler tells us that it was destroyed.

I have written earlier that the letter to Steiner mentioned above contains a citation of Mahler's "much loved younger brother, Ernst (d. 1874), coupled, significantly, to a memory of *Ernst von Schwaben*"—significantly, in my view, because I believe firmly in the significance of names (in the psycho-analytic sense): in their capacity, that is, to act as determining factors. They can be influential, indeed, in such matters as the choice of opera libretto or text for a song. Some students of Mahler have attributed clairvoyant powers to him on the strength of the *Kindertotenlieder*, which cycle foretold a sad event in his future. A tempting explanation; but I find Theodor Reik's commentary on the songs much more illuminating and convincing, especially the point he makes that "Mahler had certainly read in the introduction to Rückert's cycle of poems, or in biographical footnotes, that the name of the boy who had died was Ernst, which was also the name of Mahler's own brother". There is not space here to follow Dr. Reik's long elaboration of his theme, but his summing-up seems to me to be well-founded, that "It is the shadow of a past whose intense emotions were forgotten, not the forecast of the future which made Mahler choose the Rückert cycle of the *Kindertotenlieder*".[27]

(g)

Das klagende Lied is dealt with, in detail, in (*m*) below, but the completion of the text on or before 18 March 1878 seems worthy of a chronological entry since it precedes the completion of the music by two years eight months. The date derives from Mr. Alfred Rosé, who writes: "In my bound copy of the whole manuscript [of *Das klagende Lied*] the entire text was written by Mahler into the first pages before the music. After this text Mahler wrote the date: '18. März 1878 Gustav Mahler'."[28]

(h)

This Suite for piano resulted from the abortive rehearsal of a symphony specified in (*i*) below.[29] Bauer-Lechner is the only commentator who mentions the work, and she had her information from Mahler.[30] Because of the fiasco of the orchestral rehearsal, he was obliged to compose the Suite quickly; his own comment on the work implied that because it was a more careless and far weaker piece than the symphony, it received a prize (another of those mysterious prizes); whereas all his good things were not successful with the prize committee. We must suppose that the composer lost or destroyed the MS.

When we think of the mature Mahler, the symphonist, it is odd to think of him, even in his early years, as the composer of a Suite for piano. But when we remember his talents as a pianist, it becomes less surprising that the instrument played so decisive a rôle in his early works. His pianistic prowess is very much bound up with the existence of such pieces as the movements for piano quartet and quintet and the Sonata for violin and piano. For reasons given in (*i*) below, it is not possible to allot the Suite to a precise date. We can do no more than assume it belongs to somewhere between 1875–8, the Conservatoire years.

(*i*) (*j*)

If Bauer–Lechner heard Mahler aright, three movements of a youthful Symphony in A minor were extant in June 1896. She records that Mahler said:

> "Three movements exist of a Symphony in A minor; the fourth was completely finished, but only in my head, or, rather, at the piano, at which, at that time, I still used to compose (which one should not do, and which, indeed, I later did not do)."[31]

The chronological obscurity of the passage from which that remark is quoted excludes any possibility of assigning the work a date. It might, conceivably, have been written during 1875–8; as we shall see below, there is a seemingly authentic mention of a symphony, again in Bauer–Lechner, which did belong to the strict Conservatoire period. Might, in fact, the Symphony in A minor have been the work that suffered Hellmesberger's wrath? There is no telling. The situation is further complicated by a loose reference, in the same context, to "two Symphonies" which apparently do not include the A minor work; on the other hand, one of these might have been the 'Conservatoire' Symphony.

This latter work was an undertaking which ended in disappointment. We learn that Mahler sat up day and night copying out the parts. At the rehearsal, in which the students' orchestra was conducted by Hellmesberger, matters went awry, whereupon the director impatiently broke off the rehearsal, threw Mahler's score down at his feet, and cried: "Your parts are full of mistakes;

do you think I'm going to conduct a thing like that?" That was the end of the Symphony and the origin of the piano Suite, (h).[32] This unhappy occasion—Bauer-Lechner's first memory of Mahler[33]—took place close upon an end-of-term composition concourse, which lends credence to Mahler's claim that the substituted Suite for piano won a prize. But the Conservatoire's archives, which document the composition prizes he won in 1876 and 1878, make no mention of a prize for a Suite. (In any event, 1877 would be the only possibility, and we have the Conservatoire's word for it that in that year Mahler renounced his participation in the concourse. If the piano Suite is discounted as an outcome of this particular incident—it does happen that the memory unites unrelated events—Mahler's renunciation might make sense in view of the director's reception of his symphony: in which case c. 1877 could be considered a not unlikely date for the work. But all this is speculative.) It is, of course, possible, even probable, that both Mahler's and Bauer-Lechner's memories were at fault over details, but it seems reasonably well established that a symphony, or part of a symphony, was actually rehearsed at the Conservatoire when Mahler was a student there. For the sake of clarity, then, let us call this his 'Conservatoire' Symphony (1877??).

The Symphony, as I have suggested, might be the A minor Symphony still extant in 1896; the possibility of a performance (i.e., the rehearsal [plus the concourse itself?]) would have encouraged Mahler to get the work down on paper. Against this conjecture tends the testimony that evidently three movements were completed. As we have seen, the pieces Mahler wrote for Conservatoire consumption were single movements—a complete symphony (the finale in his head, as it were) somehow strikes a false note so far as a *Compositions-Concurs* was concerned. It is my feeling that the 'Conservatoire' and A minor symphonies are best listed as quite distinct entities (though one must allow for the contingency that the movement(s) intended (?) for the concourse were incorporated into a later symphonic venture).

No purely orchestral works from Mahler's youth have survived. Though we may guess at a date for the 'Conservatoire'

Symphony, we are obliged to leave the A minor work in the dark; and likewise the mysterious, additional (?) "two Symphonies" which, if they ever did exist, would bring the total of Mahler's symphonic attempts to five (I include (*p*) below). Adler refers to "various attempts at orchestral works" (1882) and "occasional compositions" (1882-3),[34] and it may well be that the Symphony in A minor was composed in the early 1880s. But we really have no means of alighting upon any particular year.

None the less, a little information of value can be deduced even from the slender facts that surround these authenticated symphonic efforts. The rehearsal of the 'Conservatoire' Symphony, for example, besides giving us a fresh glimpse of the vicissitudes of Mahler's student life, is the only incident that shows him to have been in touch with an orchestra during his student years; and against that background the achievement, in instrumentation, of the original version (1880) of the *Das klagende Lied* seems less unprepared.

There are two conclusions that may be drawn from a consideration of these first symphonic exercises, one general, the other particular. If we take as established attempts only the 'Conservatoire' and A minor symphonies (and perhaps (*p*)), it is clear that already in his youth Mahler, to quite a substantial degree, was preoccupied with the problems of organizing the large-scale orchestral composition, that the challenge of the symphony was experienced early on. This in itself—not to speak of his chamber-musical essays—acts as a useful corrective to a prevalent impression that his youthful composing consisted almost exclusively of operas which misfired, that he took on the symphony almost as compensation for operatic ambitions that came to nothing. Indeed, just as the original *Das klagende Lied* proves that Mahler certainly did not have to wait to learn the art of instrumentation from his years in the orchestra pit (a common 'explanation' of his orchestral technique: no one explains why, if this were true, he was so uncertain about the instrumentation of Symphony V in the 1900s, after almost twenty years' experience as a conductor), so does the variety of media in which he composed as a youth, and especially his symphonic sketches, appear to contain the seeds of his maturity; one can sense, in fact, in the student, the developing symphonist.

So much for generalities. A particularity arises from the A minor Symphony, its key, which inevitably calls to mind Mahler's 'Tragic' Symphony VI, in A minor (1903–5). It is without purpose, of course, to wonder whether any of the dramatic character of the later masterpiece was implicit in the student piece. One wonders, nevertheless. In his maturer works, A minor, for Mahler, represented either chilling, felling strokes of fate (Symphony VI) or a kind of desperate passion (Symphonies V/2 and IX/3, *Das Lied von der Erde*/1). It was indubitably, if one does not bestow too exclusive a sense upon the word, his most tragic key, and it is tempting to imagine that the student work may have expressed, albeit immaturely, a characteristic mood of insistent strife insistently quelled (resignation, one might add, has no rôle to play in Mahler's late A minor music). In any event, one can say that this key, potent in his maturity, attracted him in his youth; for besides the Symphony there is the sober first movement of the A minor piano Quartet (1876), and the close (catastrophic!) to Part II of *Das klagende Lied*; while among the early songs (*o*) one remembers *Erinnerung*, which progresses to a conclusion in an implacable A minor.

(*k*)

Rübezahl, of all Mahler's operatic projects, was the one that seemed most dear to him; it evidently retained a certain attraction for him—perhaps nagged at him as an incomplete ambition he would have liked to fulfil: none of his other efforts in the sphere of opera (*Das klagende Lied* excepted, of course, but there is no real evidence at all that it was ever seriously contemplated as a work for the stage) maintained a like grip on his memory.

As it happens, we know a little more about *Rübezahl* than about many of Mahler's abandoned and lost youthful compositions; and in a sense, if certain accounts are to be trusted, we hear *Rübezahl* in certain published works, e.g., Specht suggests that motives from the opera found their way in part into the first movement of Symphony I,[35] while from Stefan we learn that the theme of an early song, *Mai[en]tanz im Grünen*, for which we have a date—5 March 1880 (see (*o*) below)—was supposed to have functioned in *Rübezahl* as a chorus.[36] From Stefan again we have a hint of the character of *Rübezahl*'s music:

"... in the winter of 1882 [Mahler] ... remained in Vienna and worked at the composition of a fairy opera. ... It was not completed or published, but Mahler's friends say that it was of much importance in his development. The bright humour, and the dark, biting, perverse style *à la* Callot which we know from the lyrical and symphonic works, existed already in *Rübezahl*. Especially a March of Suitors is remembered as accompanied by music in the maddest of moods."[37]

The reference to Callot is perhaps significant; it will be remembered that his famous painting, *Des Jägers Leichenbegängnis* ('The Huntsman's Funeral'), was a stimulus to the composition of the third movement of Symphony I (also a perverse march!), whose first movement, if Specht may be relied upon,[38] incorporated material from the opera. There is no justification for attempting a strict parallel; but the few bits of information that have come to hand suggest that from Symphony I we may glean some idea of what the music for *Rübezahl* was like: the symphony and the early song are the only stylistic clues to the opera we possess. How much of the work was composed is uncertain. Specht thinks that it was the first act that reached the stage of musical sketches.[39]

We know little enough, to be sure, about the music. About the origins and chronology of the project we know less; or, rather, we are faced with the customary haul of data to which it is difficult to assign precise dates. We know that text and music were written separately, the music, indeed, in part succeeding the text at some distance. The question is: how early did Mahler start his labours at putting his libretto together?

Mahler's correspondence with his friend Krisper belongs very much to his post-student Vienna period; 1879-80 are the years that appear to cover such letters that have survived, among them a letter (unfortunately undated!) that mentions work in progress on *Rübezahl*. Mahler hopes to have the first act ready. The poem, since Krisper last saw it, has taken on quite a new shape. Some of it has turned out not badly. A date to this letter would have been most valuable. As it is, we have to guess; and my guess would place the letter in 1880 or 1881 (early, probably, since it contains New Year greetings).[40] The guess at '80 or '81—by the latter date *Das klagende Lied* was past history, by the former its musical organization would have been sufficiently determined for Mahler to tackle a new literary task—is complicated by the suggestion that it was Hugo Wolf who prompted the whole undertaking, a suggestion made in a previously quoted passage from Alma Mahler's memoirs.[41]

There are one or two minor points that require comment before the major issue of chronology is raised. First, of course, one must take leave to question the originality of the fairy-tale opera inspiration. Wolf and Mahler had no need to wait upon Humperdinck as a model:[42] they were doubtless already familiar with the precedents set by Weber and Marschner (Weber was ever a favourite composer of Mahler's, and he liked Marschner's *Hans Heiling*.)[43] *Rübezahl*, moreover, was itself a familiar East German legend, "whose protagonist is the mythical mountain spirit of the Silesian Riesengebirge, often alluded to in E. T. A. Hoffmann's writings, and hero of one of Grimms' fairy tales";[44] and if the legend itself was familiar, the idea of using it as the basis of a fairy opera was not spotlessly novel: Flotow's *Rübezahl*, first performed in 1853, of which Mahler or Wolf might conceivably have heard, had precedents in works by Würfel (1824) and J. Schuster (1789); and strangely enough, in 1904, a *Rübezahl* by Hans Sommer was staged in Brunswick, the latest opera, according to Loewenberg, in a series devoted to "this favourite German subject". It proved to be Sommer's "most popular work", and was widely produced in Germany.[45] The opera—its popularity, if not its music—can scarcely have escaped the attention of the erstwhile *Rübezahl* enthusiast.

So much for the originality of the young men's inspiration. Moreover, while it is credible that the impulsive Mahler was fired to sketch out a synopsis at speed, his letter to Krisper, in which he reveals himself patiently chipping away at his first act, warns us not to place too much reliance on the suggestion that the libretto was completed overnight.

But these minor issues aside, the main query Alma Mahler's anecdote raises is chronological. We have assumed earlier that Wolf and Mahler were at their friendliest in 1879; and there is no doubt that the *Rübezahl* episode would seem naturally to belong to that year. Its placing in Mrs. Mahler's memoirs also reinforces the likelihood of the incident belonging to the strict Wolf period. In the immediately succeeding years, the two composers' association appeared to become so desultory that it is hard to imagine the sufficiently close contact that would set in motion the event she describes.

It is possible, then, that Mahler sketched out a synopsis of *Rübezahl* in 1879—a contributory factor to his cooling relationship with Wolf—picked it up again in 1880 or 1881 (*Das klagende Lied* behind him) and worked earnestly at shaping the text (cf. the letter to Krisper quoted above), and finally tackled the music—we have a date here from Stefan who gives us the winter of 1882, though Mahler might have started his composing earlier than that. We know for certain that he had abandoned the opera by October 1883. Löhr wrote to Mahler (who was then conducting in Cassel) asking him how *Rübezahl* was progressing, "at which he [Mahler] worked with much pleasure and happy inspiration before the Cassel period";[46] to which Mahler replied, on 10 October:

> "If you can send me something to read, some time, you will satisfy an urgent need of mine. Gnomes [*Berggeister*—an indirect but clear reference to *Rübezahl*] don't come to me any longer because they know they would be sent away again."[47]

Thus one can set a limit to Mahler's active creative interest in the project—1883—suggest a flash-point for the idea—1879—assume with reasonable certainty that he worked up the text in 1880 or 1881, and tackled the music *c.* 1882; a conjectural schedule for the most part, to be sure, but the few facts support it. There is one reference to *Rübezahl* in Bauer-Lechner that Mahler made when talking about *Das klagende Lied* in April 1898.[48] He claimed then, so it is recorded by his confidante, that had the Beethoven Prize committee not rejected *Das klagende Lied*, his life would have run a very different course: "I was just working on 'Rübezahl', would not have had to go to Laibach [Ljubljana] and would thus possibly have been spared my whole cursed operatic career." These remarks, as will be seen in (*m*) below, are of most interest in relation to *Das klagende Lied*; so far as *Rübezahl* is concerned, they confirm merely, if Mahler's memory was correct, that he was seriously at work on the opera in 1881 (he conducted at Ljubljana in the winter 1881-2); whether on the text or music or both is not clear, but in any event the information favours allotting the letter to Krisper to the early part of 1881.

We do not hear more of *Rübezahl* in connection with Wolf; indeed, Mr. Walker does not mention the incident recounted by Mrs. Mahler. But we do find that Wolf, in the spring of 1882, "was full of new plans for the composition of an opera, for which he thought he would be able to write his own libretto, if he could only find a suitable subject". Heine's *Harzreise* had stimulated his imagination, in particular the stanzas dealing with the Princess Ilse. The legend of this fairy princess Wolf thought "might be the subject for which he had been searching".[49] One wonders whether Wolf's project of 1882 was perhaps a hangover from the collaboration of 1879 (?), with his interest renewed in what was, originally, his own idea, by the news that Mahler was labouring at *Rübezahl*? If not, it remains a coincidence that the rivals in fairy-tale opera of 1879 (?) were both displaying degrees of active liveliness in the matter in 1882.

The amount of history that attaches itself to *Rübezahl* is extraordinary. Long after Mahler had given up all thought of composing the opera, when the music, or part of it, had been utilized elsewhere, the topic of *Rübezahl* recurs in his letters. From Hamburg, thirteen years after he had announced to Löhr that *Berggeister* were unwelcome, he wrote to Max Marschalk, a Berlin music critic and composer:

"Don't give another thought to poor 'Rübezahl'! I have grown out of it all. My searching for it amongst my papers was only one of those momentary impulses. I can imagine that you too—who confront the matter with a detached attitude—will no longer be able to get anything out of this youthful fantasy. After all, I was chiefly guided by the wish to find a subject for you."[50]

It seems that Mahler had turned over in his mind the possibility of Marschalk setting his youthful libretto. He not only looked out the libretto but appears to have sent it to Marschalk; and then to have had second thoughts. None the less, the episode shows that Mahler had preserved his text across the years, that his "youthful fantasy", however defective when viewed dispassionately, still retained for him a certain glamour. It is impossible, despite the frustrating absence of the music, not to feel *Rübezahl* as a work of special significance in Mahler's early development. He never did, in fact, quite grow out of it.

Even though second thoughts had checked a momentary impulse they were not so condemnatory as to result in the libretto's destruction. *Rübezahl* remained among Mahler's papers; whereupon it became the object of a dispute between him and his sister Justine (then the wife of Arnold Rosé), a dispute which throws no new light on the opera but is eloquent of the uneasy atmosphere that surrounded Mahler's relation to his sister after his marriage. But it does at least tell us that the text of *Rübezahl* was still extant in 1908, though under threat of execution: that he "wished to destroy it", while Justine, who was in unauthorized possession of the MS., declined to return it to her brother, was the very essence of the quarrel. The MS. was eventually returned.[51] There is no account of its fate.

(l)

This is a very slender conjecture, arising from a single sentence of Mrs. Mahler's which refers once more to the period in Mahler's life when he was most friendly with Wolf. "Once", she writes, "Mahler composed a movement of a quartet for a competition while the other two [Wolf and R. Krzyzanowski] spent the night on a bench in the Ringstrasse."[52] There is no mention of a string-quartet movement by any other biographer.[53] (One's immediate assumption is, of course, that a movement for *string* Quartet was projected.) If the story dates from the first half of 1879, "Wolf's own String Quartet", Mr. Walker tells us, "was being written at about the same time. Was it, perhaps, originally intended for the same competition as Mahler's?"[54] But even if such were the case—and letters of Wolf's from the 1870s show how prize-conscious he was, as was Mahler—we cannot be certain that both young men would inevitably have selected the same medium.

Might it be that this account, if authentic, is related to that mysterious piano Quartet listed under (*d*)? The date, if my speculations in (*d*) are correct, could fit the circumstances related by Mrs. Mahler. The prize competition, for which the lost piano Quartet was destined, was Russian. Could Wolf's string Quartet have been initially stimulated by an identical ambition?

With this ghostly movement[55] we take leave of Mahler's youthful attempts at chamber music. He never returned to the medium, and even in these early years it is plain that his dominant regions of interests were the orchestra and the opera house. Such chamber music as he wrote almost always, it seems, included the piano, an inclusion which reflected not only his own abilities as a participant but also a liking for sonorous textures which strain at the threshold of orchestration. One feels here a dissatisfaction with the limitations of the chamber-musical medium characteristic of Mahler's period, which manifested itself plainly enough in his own later Vienna years when, as a conductor, he promoted the

> "remarkable experiment of performing Beethoven's String-quartet, Opus 95, by the whole string-orchestra, in order to enhance the effect of the 'wretched' instruments and to make it possible to perform the work in a large hall. . . ."[56]

This "experiment" took place on 15 January 1899 and was followed, Stefan writes, by "an outburst of pedantic wrath" (the choice of adjective is revealing of the confidence of Mahler's supporters). Mahler himself, it appears, had trouble with the orchestra, and was obliged to address them thus:

"Don't let yourselves be confused, gentlemen, come along with me, don't be reactionaries [sic]. This quartet screams, as it were, for orchestral sound, as indeed you were able to hear for yourselves this morning."[57]

Perhaps the assumptions bound up with this affair say all that can be said about Mahler and 'chamber music', at least in the classical sense of the term.

(m)

Das klagende Lied has presented two problems—the source of its text and the circumstances in which it was submitted for the Beethoven Prize. I have been able to settle the first point satisfactorily, but not the second. Let me take first the textual source of the cantata.

Confusion rather than obscurity has been the trouble here; or neglect, simply: Dika Newlin, for example, but for the hint that there is a "legendary background"—does not refer to the model upon which Mahler based his text.[58] Stefan is not much more helpful with his "words . . . by Mahler, after an old German story".[59] Adler takes us a step further by referring to the source as a fairy tale told by "Bechstein",[60] a lead taken up by Redlich who at the same time adds a new factor in writing that Mahler's poem was "inspired by fairy tales by Bechstein and Grimm".[61] Engel, on the other hand, drops Bechstein—an unknown quantity, it seems, to the majority of commentators—and concentrates on Grimm, i.e., "the choice of theme is reminiscent of the manner of Grimm's fairy tales".[62] Nodnagel is more particular. He writes (wrongly!) that the Grimm fairy-tale in question is *Jorinde and Joringel*.[63] Bruno Walter writes (wrongly!) "[Mahler] put Grimm's tale '*Der singende Knochen*' (The Singing Bone) into verse to form the basis for *Das klagende Lied*".[64]

Before sorting out this mass of information, it is not perhaps without interest to mention what could have been the source of the source—the event that may have introduced the young Mahler to his topic. On 3 May 1876, in the second half of a concert of "new music" given at the Conservatoire, a concert which Mahler may well have attended, an item entitled *Das klagende*

⇨   *Lied* by one Martin Greif was performed.[65] I have no information about the work, apart from its title, no knowledge whether it was a song, chorus or instrumental movement; but in view of the popular fairy tale of the same title it seems not unlikely that Greif's piece had a programme associated with the story. But all this, like Mahler's attendance at the concert, is purely speculative.

What is removed from speculation is the actual source of Mahler's text, which is bound up with the identity of "Bechstein". There were, in fact, two Bechsteins—father (Ludwig) and son (Reinhold)—engaged in collecting German folk-tales and legends. Ludwig, 1801-60, was the more important figure, and it is in one of his anthologies that we find the story out of which grew Mahler's cantata: the story, like the music, is called *Das klagende Lied*.[66] Since there are not unimportant variations between Bechstein's and Mahler's versions, it will be wise if we first acquaint ourselves with Mahler's story, in the light of which may be assessed the dramatic significance of the changes Mahler effected.

The action of the cantata (in its original version of three parts) runs as follows. A proud Queen declares that whosoever shall find a certain red flower growing in the forest shall win her hand. Two brothers go in search of the flower, the younger of a sweet disposition, the elder evil in character. The younger brother finds the flower, sticks it in his hat, and stretches out to rest. He is discovered asleep by his elder brother who, jealous of his success, strikes him dead with a sword, steals the flower, and claims the Queen as his bride. The younger brother lies buried under leaves and blossoms beneath a willow tree.

Part II introduces the Minstrel, who picks up a gleaming white bone, fashions it into a flute and plays upon it—when he is astonished to hear the flute pour forth its tale of murder, "Sorrow and woe". The Minstrel ventures forth to seek out the King and his bride.

Part III brings us to the castle. It is the Queen's wedding day and a feast is in progress. The Minstrel enters the castle hall and plays his flute: it repeats once more the story of the murder. The guilty King leaps to his feet, seizes the flute and scornfully places it to his lips: the bone sings again its sorry tale of fratricide. The Queen collapses to the ground, the guests flee, and the castle walls begin to crumble.

In Ludwig Bechstein's fairy tale, the contenders for the flower are not brothers, but brother and sister; and the prize is not marriage but succession to the Queen's throne. The Princess, the first-born, finds the flower and lies down to sleep, whereupon she is murdered by her jealous brother. In later years a peasant boy picks up a bone and makes a flute from it; he is startled when a child's voice issues forth and tells the manner of the sister's death.

A knight takes possession of the flute and appears at the castle where the guilty brother is King and his mother still mourns her lost daughter. It is to the old Queen alone that the flute reveals the terrible truth. She then takes the instrument and herself plays it to her son before a festive assembly in the castle hall. The story ends on this note of chilling catastrophe, in which the mother is the final instrument of her son's doom.

Bechstein, at the end of his *Klagende Lied*, points to similarities between his story and the Grimm brothers' *Singing Bone* and *Story of the Juniper Tree*.[67] It is the former Grimm tale that may have influenced Mahler's varying of Bechstein's text.[68] In the Grimm we find two brothers competing for a wife, a rivalry which ends in fratricide. The circumstances of the competition[69] and the murder are quite different from those we find in the cantata, but the loquacious bone flute and details of the *dénouement* are as we know them in Mahler's text. There can be no doubt, of course, that the basic structure of the story turns up in the legends of many lands; curious readers can turn up an anonymous ballad in the *Oxford Book of English Verse—Binnorie*[70]— which contains all the essentials of Bechstein's *Klagende Lied*.

It seems obvious to me that the story as Bechstein had it is much richer in dramatic and psychological content than Mahler's version, which is crude in comparison and stripped of a central source of tension—the figure of the mother who destroys the son who has offended against nature (in the Shakespearean sense).

Then there is the substitution of the pair of brothers for Bech-stein's brother-sister relation which, if nothing else, results in diminished contrast. It must be that the roots of Mahler's varia-tions of Bechstein's story lay in his own psychological make-up, that the changed relationships were conditioned by emotional attitudes of Mahler's towards members of his family.[71]

The changes are mysterious indeed if they were *not* extra-musically determined; for in almost every case they tend to reduce the text's dramatic potentialities. The mystery is deepened if it is correct that the work was first envisaged as an opera. It is obvious that Bechstein's tale untouched is more operatic in its development, above all more fruitful in the provision of well-defined male and female rôles.

But it is more than probable in my view that "the original operatic form"[72] of *Das klagende Lied* is mythical. The myth, admittedly, is widespread. Few commentators forgo a mention of Mahler's "original intention of making it an opera".[73] In our own decade, Redlich is so misled as to describe the first, tripartite, version of the cantata as if it were the cantata's original operatic draft; he even goes on to write that

> "Work on this operatic [sic] version had started in the autumn of 1879 in Vienna, and the score was completed there on 1st November 1880. . . . In a subsequent first revision, undertaken in 1888, Part I was eliminated and the whole work turned into a cantata in two sections."[74]

In so far as Redlich's data are valid they apply, not to any "operatic" version, but to the first version of the cantata in three parts, a MS. of which is in the possession of Mr. Alfred Rosé and the early sketches for which version I have examined in the *Stadtbibliothek*, Vienna. (These autographs, together with any relevant chronological information, are listed in the table that introduces this chapter.) In short, there is not a scrap of textual evidence to support a belief that any music to do with *Das klagende Lied* existed at one stage in operatic form. This is true not only of the music but also of the text, which from the outset was cast as a simple ballad—the *Ballade vom blonden und braunen Reiters-*

mann;[75] we know as much from the verses that Mahler sent to his friend, Krisper, probably before March 1878, verses that form part of the unpublished first section of the cantata. There is nothing remotely libretto-like about the shape of Mahler's book.

The confusion stems, perhaps, from a remark of Guido Adler's, that the cantata "was initially thought of as a fairy tale for the stage" (Adler even criticizes the cantata because it has not wholly renounced its original operatic destination!).[76] Taking that "thought of" in its strictest sense, the statement is probably correct. Mahler, when first turning the project over in his mind, may have considered a stage setting as a possibility. But this intention was never represented at any creative level. It is unfortunate that, presumably in the light of Adler's comment, the original version of the cantata and its subsequent revisions have been assumed to be connected with the conception of the work as an opera. In fact, *Das klagende Lied* was composed as a cantata *from the start* and was revised as such. No one can deny that the world of opera exerted an influence on the shaping of the cantata, but such theatrical elements as we find in *Das klagende Lied* are typical of Mahler's dramatic approach to his medium rather than ideas salvaged from an abandoned opera.

The subject of the Beethoven Prize gives rise to a host of chronological problems. It was first broached by Mahler himself, in a conversation with Bauer-Lechner in April 1898:

"Had the jury of the Conservatoire, which included Brahms, Goldmark, Hanslick, and Richter, given me at that time the Beethoven Prize of 600 Austrian florins for the 'Klagende Lied' my whole life would have taken a different turn. I was just working on 'Rübezahl', would not have had to go to Laibach [Ljubljana] and would thus possibly have been spared my whole cursed operatic career. Instead, however, Herr Herzfeld got the first composition prize, and Rott and I went empty-handed. Rott despaired and died soon afterwards insane, and I was (and shall always remain) condemned to the hell of theatrical life."[77]

Mahler's bitterness at the routine of the opera house is characteristic. But can the blame for his enforced pursuit of a career as a conductor be placed all that squarely on the shoulders of the prize committee? Mahler himself, in this excited and indignant outburst, seems to have overlooked that the first step on his primrose path was taken at Bad Hall in 1880, not at Ljubljana in 1881; and, as we have seen, none was more assiduous in searching for new conducting posts than the young *Kapellmeister* of Bad Hall. It does seem that Mahler attempts to make the incident bear the responsibility for too many wrongs, real or fanciful: not only for his own "hell", but for poor Rott's lunacy. There is surely a whiff of imaginary persecution here?

The jury, moreover, though not inappropriately described by Engel as "a stone wall of musical classicism" (otherwise his treatment of this event is dangerously romanticized),[78] at a later period were not entirely indifferent or hostile to Mahler's status as a musician. By 1896, his relations with Brahms were more cordial, a fact that he might have recalled in 1898. (In view of Brahms's doubtless aggressive inspection of *Das klagende Lied*, his comment after seeing the MS. of Mahler's Symphony II in the summer of 1896 is of particular interest: "It is not wholly intelligible to me why Richard Strauss is proclaimed music's Revolutionary; I find that Mahler is King of the Revolutionaries.")[79] Even Hanslick was to write a not unappreciative notice of some of Mahler's songs with orchestra when they were performed in Vienna in 1900;[80] and in 1896 and '97 the aid of Karl Goldmark (1830-1915) was sought by those intriguing to have Mahler appointed to the Vienna Opera.[81] Perhaps it was only Hans Richter (1843-1916), whom Mahler dislodged from Vienna's opera house—to Manchester's (and England's) advantage—who failed by later word or deed to modify the unfavourable verdict pronounced upon *Das klagende Lied* when its composer and the members of the jury were all younger men. In London, in 1898 (?), Richter "unburdened his heart [to Ferruccio Busoni] about Mahler:

'I say, I was sorry not to be in Vienna when you played, but I heard that Mahler gave you a lesson at the rehearsal. That puts the lid on

146

it. He can't stand any soloists because he has got no routine and can't conduct at sight; but a conductor ought to be able to do that just as much as a pianist—come!' "[82]

There is, of course, no question that *Das klagende Lied* was rejected by the Beethoven Prize committee, nor that Mahler was anxious, having completed the piece, to score a success with it. In the same letter that he announced the end of his labours, he wrote: "My next aim: to bring about its performance by any means that I can think of."[83] An obvious means to that end was to try for the Beethoven Prize which, if won, would have brought welcome publicity, financial gain, and doubtless the chance of the cantata's performance.

The Prize itself was a comparatively recent institution. It had been established by the *Gesellschaft der Musikfreunde* in 1875 and was offered yearly to present and past pupils of the Conservatoire. The problem that confronts us here is one of chronology: in—or for—which year did Mahler submit *Das klagende Lied* to the committee?

Mahler, we know, had his score ready by 1 November 1880. He declared to Bauer-Lechner that the award would have spared him the necessity of taking the appointment at Ljubljana, whence Mahler proceeded in the winter of 1881.

What was the situation of the committee between these two outside dates? We know that the jury sat on 6 December 1880, to consider their decision for that year, but it appears that, "as before", they were unable to reach an agreement as to whom the Prize should be awarded. Instead, an amendment to the rules was suggested that would open the Prize to wider competition.

It seems scarcely possible that Mahler could have put *Das klagende Lied* before this December jury. There were but five weeks between his date of completion and the final session of the committee; and even if the rules did not exclude so last-minute a submission, it is hard to imagine that the jury could have found time to circulate the score among themselves. As we have seen, moreover, no award was made, a fact which would contradict Mahler's aggrieved statement that Herr Herzfeld carried off the "first composition prize".

The probability that Mahler was concerned in this session of the Beethoven Prize committee seems slight. If he was not, however, then almost certainly the journey to Ljubljana cannot be attributed to the jury's adverse decision. The award for the next year, 1881, was made at a meeting of 15 December, by which date Mahler must be presumed to have commenced work in Yugoslavia.[84] In addition, this later jury date would seem to preclude Rott from participation, since it is thought that he died in 1881; it is known he ended his days in an asylum and it is hardly credible that the blow of failing to win the competition should have resulted in his committal to an asylum and decease within two weeks. Mahler's introduction of Rott into the context of the Beethoven Prize is a most dubious proceeding. That he was possibly concerned with one prize or another for which Mahler too was a competitor is more than probable; confused anecdotes to which I have referred earlier suggest as much; and we have by no means the amount of documentation that is desirable to place or dismiss often vague asides. Mahler himself provides the strongest reason for viewing the addition of Rott as a product of both his muddle-headedness and his anxiety to find a scapegoat, deep-dyed in villainy, for his initiation as a conductor. In 1898, to Bauer-Lechner, he implied that Rott's madness was the fault of the jury: "Rott despaired and died soon afterwards insane". But what do we find when we read the very letter in which Mahler announced the completion of his cantata, on 1 November 1880, *before* there was any possibility of the Beethoven Prize committee playing any sort of active rôle in the matter? Neither more nor less than the sad fact that "My friend Hans Rott has gone mad!—And I fear the same will befall Krisper."[85] So Rott was already mad, according to Mahler, at a time when the competition was not an issue, a time that fits the probability of his death in 1881 and supports my conjecture that Mahler was mistaken in supposing Rott to have been a candidate for the Beethoven Prize for which *Das klagende Lied* was entered.

If nothing else, this confusion about Rott must warn us not to accept Mahler's or Bauer-Lechner's testaments without caution. In other respects, too, details in Mahler's statement are not con-

148

firmed by the archives of the *Gesellschaft der Musikfreunde*.[86] I
think we may assume that it was in 1881 that Mahler submitted
his cantata for the prize, in which case the operative session of
the committee would be that of 15 December 1881. It is true
that Herzfeld was not the winner on this occasion; Robert Fuchs
was—ironically, one of Mahler's professors! But a work by
Victor R. von Herzfeld (1856–1928) was specified as "prize-
worthy" (along with an overture by H. Fink), and it may well
have been that Mahler simply mis-remembered him as the prize-
winner. Two considerations may have reinforced his mistake:
Herzfeld actually did win the Beethoven Prize in 1884, and he
had left the Conservatoire in 1880 with a first prize for composition (it is noticeable that Mahler spoke of his winning the "first
composition prize"). It could be, then, that all these memories
of a prize-winning composer were telescoped into one, and
Herzfeld promoted from an honourable mention to first place.
There can be no likelihood that *Das klagende Lied* was submitted
as late as 1884, when Herzfeld *was* the winner—in 1882 and 1883
it seems that again no award was made—and thus we are obliged
to choose the year singled out by circumstantial evidence. In
1881, Herzfeld at least makes an appearance; and he was to be
the next winner, an event that doubtless would have brought
him Mahler's renewed and perhaps hostile attention.

Then there is the jury. Its personnel in 1881 partly coincides
with Mahler's memory. Brahms was on it, Richter, and Goldmark;[87] but the records make no mention of Hanslick. The
archives are sometimes unreliable; possibly Hanslick's name was
omitted in error. If not, then Mahler's memory was playing him
false, stimulated perhaps by an unconscious desire to portray
Hanslick in an overtly hostile rôle, whose antagonism, in fact, he
strongly suspected (and resented) but had no real evidence of: the
unconscious will create facts of its own to meet an emotional need.

If the adverse judgment of 15 December 1881 had gone in
Mahler's favour perhaps he would have broken off his engagement at Ljubljana and not returned there in the new year; perhaps
it would have meant that he would not have had to undertake
his next conducting job, at Olmütz, late in 1882[88] or early in

149

➪ 1883;[89] and it was, in a very real sense, from Olmütz onwards that the continuous tyranny of conducting began. Mahler might have had some reason to feel bitter if he thought that a success with the Beethoven Prize could have spared him the years of toil that Olmütz initiated.

It may be wondered whether this incident is of sufficient importance to warrant such detailed examination—other young composers of genius have experienced a like frustration and possibly made less fuss about it than Mahler. But since it was important for him, then it is inevitably important for his biographer; and that it was important for him is borne out by the wounded-cry character of his complaint to Bauer-Lechner, the inaccuracies in which, we may note, all go to intensify the depth of the wound. Mahler was ever in opposition to the establishment of his day, above all the Viennese establishment, and in this affair of *Das klagende Lied* he ran his head for the first time against that wall which was, for a period, to give way, but only after ceaseless battering on Mahler's part. The pattern was to be repeated on many later occasions, but with Mahler emerging victorious, not vanquished. The dismissal of the cantata by the Beethoven Prize committee in 1881 was the first shot fired in Mahler's long battle with Vienna. It represented a discouraging defeat, and Mahler profoundly resented it, as he was bound to do; his resistance to his father would lead us to expect impatience of all forms of fatherly tradition or authority, whether vested in one man or a group—or a prize committee; and the committee in Mahler's estimation doubtless behaved like the stern, repressive father—hence his doubly acute sensitivity, on both artistic and psychological grounds, to their decision. None the less, if *Das klagende Lied* was a failure in this respect, it was a triumph in another; because it was in this cantata, as Mahler himself realized, that he found his own voice as a composer.[90]

Guido Adler's chronology for *Das klagende Lied* has been much quoted. It runs:

"1880. *Das klagende Lied*, poem and music, begun 1878, finished

1880 (first version). Rearranged 1898, published 1899. Orchestration revised in the years after 1900."[91]

Before we scrutinize Adler's information, we shall do well to collect together such facts as are available elsewhere about the revision(s) of the cantata, some help being given by Mahler himself. The most important revision appears to have been done in Hamburg, where Mahler conducted at the opera from 1891-7. So much seems clear from Mahler's own words to Bauer-Lechner in Vienna, in 1898-9, when he was attempting to prepare the cantata for publication but was hindered by the pressure of his activities at the opera house:

"I have to change a whole passage, that is to say, *change it back to its original version*—which alas I have lost—which once, in Hamburg, I had in another form; it is the place [Part II] where two orchestras are employed, one in the distance outside the concert hall. That, I knew, the gentlemen would not perform, so I struck the second orchestra out and put its part in with the first. Now I look at it again it strikes me strongly that the change was not for the better and *I must return the passage to its original state*—whether it can be performed or not!" [My italics.][92]

Neisser is not quite correct, then, in asserting that the final version of the cantata dates from Hamburg;[93] but the Vienna pre-publication revision of 1898-9 amounted, in fact, to no more than the restoration of the second orchestra, the return to his original conception mentioned by Mahler to Bauer-Lechner. So much is disclosed by the fair autograph score of the two-part revised version which is in Mrs. Mahler's possession. This MS. must represent the Hamburg revision; the only difference between it and the published score rests in the absence of the second orchestra from the autograph (undated, but undoubtedly belonging to the Hamburg years). Otherwise, in every particular, autograph and published version exactly coincide.[94] Thus Adler's 'revised' orchestration post-1900 does not seem to mean anything in terms of the printed music, though it may well have been that Mahler altered the instrumentation here and there for the cantata's Vienna performances. Such post-publication tinkering, we know, was his custom. Perhaps it is to this on-the-spot amending that Adler refers?

In any event we must qualify his 1900 revision in the light of the Hamburg MS. and view the Vienna 'rearrangement' as a very minor affair. The major Hamburg revision Adler does not specify at all.

When was the cantata's (original) first part abandoned? Adler—not in his chronological table but in the *text* of his book—mentions 1888 as the year in which the work's third [sic] part was omitted, the first and second parts contracted, the instrumental interludes shortened.[95] Why this important stage is not placed in the chronological table is a mystery. Moreover, Adler's descriptions of the cantata's revisions prove to be almost consistently wide of the mark. For a start, it was not the third part that was omitted but the first; and we shall find much reason to doubt Adler's intimations that abbreviation of the second and third parts (he misnumbers them first and second) was the prime characteristic of Mahler's revising. In fact, so far as the revised version's Part I is concerned, it may be said that Adler's statement is the exact opposite of the true situation.

I think the schedule of Mahler's revisions to *Das klagende Lied* might be disposed as follows:

a) *c.* 1888. Part I (original version) dropped.

b) 1891–7, Hamburg. Second orchestra's part written in with first; otherwise revision corresponds exactly with later published version.

c) *c.* 1898–9, Vienna. Second orchestra restored. Publication.

d) Post-1900. Possible instrumental revisions in performances conducted by Mahler in Vienna.

As so often happens, musicology has spread confusion where the music itself would speak clearly. I have no doubt that if the extant MS. score of the complete *original* version of *Das klagende Lied* were made available, all the current textual queries could be disposed of within the space of a short article. But I think I know enough to claim this: that the loose, inaccurate commentary on *Das klagende Lied* widely promoted by previous biographers has wrongly endowed the cantata not only with a false origin (its operatic version) but a series of revisions, from the last of which one could only imagine the emergence of a work bearing little resemblance to the composer's youthful conception.

My contention is the contrary, that Parts I and II of the cantata we know today correspond very nearly to Parts II and III of the original (1880) version: that the revisions were much less far-reaching than has been assumed hitherto. The correspondence may be demonstrated in the case of the original Part II which became the revised Part I. I have had no access to any original score for the revised Part II (first version's Part III); but, in view of Mahler's significant restoration in this section of an important feature of the first version that the Hamburg revision had deleted, I think it most probable that here too we may presume that the published Part II presents, in essentials, the physiognomy of the original Part III. But only a comparison of the printed score with Part III of the MS. in Mr. Rosé's possession can put the point beyond dispute.

Before coming to an examination of the autograph sketch and first full score of the revised version's Part I, *Der Spielmann*, it may be advisable first to dispose of the cantata's original Part I, *Waldmärchen*; if nothing else, it will obviate the irritating necessity continually to distinguish between Part I of the revised version and Part I of the original. Dispose is perhaps not the right word. Not having access to the autograph, the most, the best, I can do is to bring together what information I can of its musical character. Nothing, of course, can effectively replace the music itself, but MS. articles kindly placed at my disposal by Mr. Rosé and Dr. Holländer—articles arising from the radio performances of *Waldmärchen* for which these musicians were responsible—give us some idea of the atmosphere of the unpublished first part of *Das klagende Lied*, especially if, when reading their accounts of *Waldmärchen*, we bear in mind the music of *Der Spielmann* and *Hochzeitsstück*.

We recognize that *Waldmärchen* is much of a piece with the rest of the cantata when we encounter Mr. Rosé's references to its trumpet and horn calls (one horn passage is marked *Wie aus der Ferne*—'as though from the distance'—a favourite poetic device of Mahler's), its drum fourths, bird-song, and characteristic 'Mahler triplets'; thus this prevalent stylistic fingerprint, a fondness for triplet rhythm, especially, though not exclusively, in fanfare-like invention, makes an early appearance in *Das klagende Lied*. As in Parts II and III (subsequently I and II), the shape of the music arises from the interplay between the chorus and the solo voices, their combination or alternation; the soloists comprise a quartet: soprano, contralto, tenor and bass. (There is no rôle for a bass in the work as we have it today.)

▷   Dr. Holländer writes:

"The basic musical character of *Waldmärchen* . . . is that of a romantic tone-painting, which has its stylistic roots in the ballad (choral ballad) and symphonic poem. The brilliant and mystical timbre of the winds, which was profoundly bound up with Mahler's childhood experience, grows here into. a tremendous edifice of sound. A march-like fanfare, mainly in triplet rhythm, wavers between the major and the minor, and thereby becomes a leading musical symbol of the work, expressing moods of yearning, sorrow or jubilation, according to the harmonic shades resorted to. Side by side with passages of this kind, which evince a naïve effect aiming at the decorative, there are substantial and inspired moments—for instance, the narration of the brothers' departure: this is entrusted to different solo voices and alternates with refrain-like choral interjections. The quasi-chorale melody of the chorus which interrupts the rather folkish narration of the soloists . . . achieves an expression of fatal warning.

"That Mahler associated identical situations with identical motives is proved by the passage . . . which tells how the discoverer of the red flower 'stretched himself out to rest'. Here we have almost exactly the same blissfully voluptuous orchestral song in thirds which, at the close of the *Lieder eines fahrenden Gesellen*, accompanies the wayfarer's rest beneath the linden tree. But whereas in that work Nature acts as a redemptive agent for a suffering human heart, in

Das klagende Lied it darkens to become the tragic background to fratricide. . . .

"The murder scene is built up as a great dramatic climax. A sequential chordal motive, at the words, 'A sword of steel hangs at his side, which now he has drawn', is indicative of Wagner's influence. 'The elder man laughs under the linden tree', with its sinister, melismatic song, is very beautifully contrasted with the festive 'The youth smiles as in a dream', accompanied by harp. [Mr. Rosé, in his article, suggests that at this crucial juncture—the death of the young knight—earlier themes from *Waldmärchen* are tenderly reviewed in the various sections of the orchestra.]

"Descriptive passages, worked out in diverse pictorial detail; the sonorities of the winds, based on Mahler's characteristic march rhythms; romantic major-minor ambiguities: these form the typical palette of the youthful Mahler, which reveals itself here in *Waldmärchen*. . . . Musically, only the above-mentioned fanfare is carried over from the first part into the subsequent parts [II and III], and one gets the impression that for Mahler, composing out of the fullness of his youthful creative powers, the individual musical pictures are more important than the total effect and large-scale integration.

"The expository relationship of this first part [*Waldmärchen*] to the final [two-part] version of *Das klagende Lied* applies mainly to the lay-out of the text and scarcely to the music, which is more in the nature of a preliminary sketch, occasionally displaying isolated touches of genius."

There is one aspect of *Das klagende Lied*, its tonal structure, which cannot receive much more than casual mention; it is simply not possible to discuss in detail the overall tonal scheme of the cantata without intimate knowledge of Part I of the original version. From Mr. Rosé's descriptions of the beginning and end of *Waldmärchen* we can gain some glimpses of the tonal course pursued in Part I. He writes of the opening:

"*Langsam träumerisch*: Over a soft tremolo on A sounds the call of two horns; it is answered, echo-like, by another pair of horns. Clarinets softly give voice. A call of a fifth [*Quintenruf*], *f*, in the other high woodwinds, is accompanied by a tremolo in the violins and a harp arpeggio. The first two horns take up the clarinet figures and sing a melancholy phrase in which 'Mahler triplets' are already in evidence. The other instruments join in, *accelerando*, and the first *ff* resounds in C minor. . . ."

And of the close:

"Yet once again sounds the call of a fifth, *f*, in trumpets and trombones, and the F sharp minor triad fades away in the full orchestra, *diminuendo*, to a final *pp*."

Der Spielmann (Part II) is firmly concentric (in C minor). *Hochzeitsstück* (Part III), on the other hand, opens in a festive, glowing B flat major (but the minor cuts in at the sixth bar) and concludes in an ashen A minor—yet another example of Mahler using his 'tragic' key, in this case for the final catastrophe that engulfs the guilty monarch and his castle. I doubt whether the eventual release of the original autograph *in toto* will reveal a highly organized scheme of tonalities across the three parts, though, as I think will emerge from my remarks below, there are some subtle things of this kind within and between Parts II and III. (It is significant, perhaps, that the decapitation of the cantata did not affect the tonal disposition of the torso; the original Part II, though becoming the new Part I, retained its original key.) My impression is mainly one of lavish key contrasts serving dramatic verity. Of this point of view, Part III is a cogent illustration; it might, at the same time, be said to offer an example of progressive tonality. But in the context of the whole work—taking into account what I venture to guess about Part I—tonality progressive or concentric[96] would not appear to be a guiding principle of organization. Indeed, in this single instance of *Das klagende Lied*, it does seem to me that Hans Tischler's suggested substitute for the term 'progressive tonality' has practical relevance: his "dramatic key symbolism"[97] describes very well the cantata's loose, varied, yet strikingly apt tonal procedures, whose diversity, none the less, is an aspect of the work's immaturity. The step, in fact, from a "dramatic" to a "progressive" concept of tonality was in itself a portent, a herald, of Mahler's maturity.

Now that *Waldmärchen* is behind us, we can deal with the remaining two parts and know them by the numbers, I and II, under which they appear in the published version of the revised score. So far as Part I is concerned—which was *Der Spielmann* before Mahler decided to dispense with his titles—it is possible to compare Mahler's first intentions with his final revision, since the *Stadtbibliothek*, Vienna, possesses two vital autograph stages in the life of this part of the cantata: first, what was obviously a first sketch in short score of *Der Spielmann*; secondly, what I cannot doubt was the first full score—the autograph is much defaced, by Mahler's own hand—of the same part (the first thirty-one bars of the overture are missing: presumably these pages have been lost).

Mahler's treatment of this second manuscript is strange: it is covered with Gothic, almost Steinbergian doodles, with the names of his friends (Steiner, Kralik)[98] and the names of many others whose biographical relevance, if any, escapes me (there are examples in the right-hand margin of Plate IX, of both a mysterious name and Mahler's elaborate calligraphy); then there are names of places (*Teplitz*), stray nouns (*Punktum*), and eccentric exclamations like *Leistung[s] Fähigkeit* ('Productivity'). The only explanation I can offer is this: that Mahler, for whatever purpose, was practising his penmanship, and freely chose whatever words, phrases or names came to mind; the doodles certainly look like offshoots of Mahler's ornamental capital letters, as if he were further exploring the decorative potentialities of his nib.[99] In any event, whatever promoted his scribbling, the fact that it was done on this score of *Der Spielmann* would suggest that the MS. had become expendable; which strengthens the possibility that the copy in the possession of Mr. Rosé is a fair copy, perhaps the autograph that Mahler might have submitted to the Beethoven Prize committee.

The first sketch of *Der Spielmann*, drafted mostly on four

staves, tells us a good deal about Mahler's method of setting down his ideas on paper. The overture, even at this stage of the auto-graph, is written out in detail, with indications of the instru-mentation. We have here more or less the complete texture of the music. (One may note in passing that the instrumental specifications in this first sketch make it clear that the original conception of *Das klagende Lied* already involved a very large orchestra.) Once the overture is relinquished, however, the density of the sketch is much reduced. From the first vocal entry onwards, what bears the burden of the autograph's continuity is always the vocal line. Mahler was content to leave the sub-stance of his textures to the next stage, to confine himself, in this short score, to the lay-out of the words, though of course we find everywhere accompanying the vocal parts a kind of musical shorthand which conveys the essential harmonic context or structurally places a significant motive; indeed, one of the fascinations of comparing this early sketch of Part I with its first full score is to see in the latter how Mahler builds up and fills out a texture from a mere jotting down of the motive around which the texture is to grow. Plate VIII consolidates this picture of Mahler's procedures in his sketches. The last twenty bars of the MS. page offer us the contralto and soprano lines virtually unsupported but for those shorthand indications of texture or motives that are to be developed later. The orchestral continua-tion that follows the vocal parts is again typically sketched out, with the motive that is to sustain the interlude prominently in place and an important aspect of the instrumentation—the harp —chalked up. The first half of the page—down to the common time signature—comprises the end of one of the orchestral interludes in Part I; once again we notice that Mahler concen-trates on the bare but vital bones that prove to be the framework of the final texture. Here and there, of course, we do meet passages that are elaborated in finer detail, or at any rate where every significant constituent of the eventual texture is present in the sketch—an example is the swaggering introduction of the Minstrel (Fig. 11),[100] where the sketch reveals all the figuration (not just the motives, but their interlocking combination) that

158

goes to form the texture of the accompaniment we hear today in the concert hall. One never feels, in examining the sketch, that Mahler was hard up for ideas; on the contrary, certain passages, like this one, show how the ideas crowded in, ideas already precisely articulated in character and lay-out, and demanding of instant and precise notation. Again, it is just such a passage as this, the expertness of which suggests that it must have been worked over and written into the revised version. Yet such is not the case; and there are a hundred other examples—the highly ornamental and vividly coloured writing for woodwinds in the overture (from Fig. 7) is one of them—where one assumes that the imagination and accomplishment must belong to a year later than 1880; only to be proved wrong by the witness of the sketch.

While we have a date at the end of the sketch, we have no means of knowing exactly how long Mahler worked at *Der Spielmann*; we may assume he worked hard. Bauer-Lechner suggests that he toiled arduously at his cantata, with such intensity, in fact, that he suffered a nervous condition. (She also thinks his vegetarian diet contributed to his overwrought state of health.[101]) As it happens the latter third of the sketch (from Fig. 29 onwards) does seem to offer evidence of exceptionally concentrated, indeed, feverish labour. The sketch is often well-nigh indecipherable and confined to the barest essentials written down, it would appear, in the greatest haste. That Mahler was, so to speak, galloping towards the conclusion of this part of the cantata is borne out by a briefly-sketched coda that brings *Der Spielmann* to an end at a much earlier stage than was eventually the case. Mahler seems to have realized this himself, for an additional sheet, a more extensive coda (seventeen bars against four), replaces the first—and now deleted—idea. The first full score follows the sketch's revised coda, which is, again, the model for the coda of the revised (published) version, though here the passage undergoes a slight extension.

That extension is typical of the relation between the first full score in MS. and the published edition of the cantata. The impression of the revisions left by most commentators is one of abbreviation, the excision or reduction of youthful verbosity. In fact, however, the revisions tend to extend rather than curtail, especially in transitional passages which the mature Mahler—a master of transition—must have found abrupt in their original form (abrupt in the wrong way, that is; Mahler also mastered the art of non-transition, of which there are a few examples in *Das klagende Lied* and many in his later works). Revisory extensions are certainly evident in Part I and may well be so in Part II, no autograph material of which I have seen. But a definitive statement of the variations between the original version and published edition of the cantata cannot be made until the fair copy of the complete first score is opened to inspection.

In the main, the first full score of *Der Spielmann* faithfully executes the intentions made plain in the sketch. Such differences as exist between the three available manuscript and printed sources—that is, the sketch (SK), first full score (FS), and published edition (RV)—are, for the most part, of a minor character; but they are not without musical interest and illumine the progress of the work from one stage of development to another.

We find an example of an extension if we compare SK, p. 4, the orchestral introduction preceding *Ein Spielmann zog einst des Weges daher*, with RV, Fig. 11, where the introduction is lengthened by one bar. But this extension has already been effected in FS, p. 18, where also the final rhythmic shape of the principal ostinato accompanimental figure has been established, from Ex. 1 in SK, to Ex. 2 in FS[102] and RV:

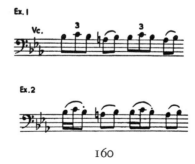

160

At the end of the foregoing *Spielmann* section (SK, p. 5) we arrive at a crucial juncture in the music, when the chorus makes its first entry in this part of the cantata. It is obvious from SK that Mahler was uncertain how to proceed, having reached (what we know as) RV, Fig. 14. Some twenty-five bars are sketched and then crossed out before we encounter a chorus that is recognizably RV, Fig. 15. The transition between RV's Figs. 14–15 is a blank so far as SK is concerned. FS, p. 22, shows signs that the difficulty of continuation was still present at the later stage. RV, Fig. 14, is once again successfully achieved, but thereafter twenty-three bars of chorus and/or orchestra precede the chorus which stands today in RV (Fig. 15). Mahler evidently found this solution unsatisfactory and struck the twenty-three bars out; the deleted passage, incidentally, called for a battery of percussion at one point—triangle, bass drum, timpani, bells, and tam-tam—which exceeds the eventual requirements of RV.

I think it is clear why Mahler excised these elaborately scored bars; not because they were not thematic—on the contrary, they were built around familiar motives—but because they did not present the chorus to striking effect; in fact, the novelty of the instrumentation in certain bars was a distraction. Thus in FS, too, the transition between RV's Figs. 14–15 was left a blank: which means that the present eight bars—unless they are to be found in the original version's fair copy—were a later addition. They are, indeed, the only bars in Part I for which neither SK nor FS offers a precedent, though, to be sure, the sustained pedal F over which the transition is suspended in RV is already present in FS. The aptness of RV's transition needs no emphasis: its austerity and economy (the transition *is*, in fact, the accompaniment to the chorus which, as it were, drops into an enveloping orchestral texture) serve perfectly to introduce the chorus as a new factor in the unfolding of *Der Spielmann*. This is the only passage, in SK or FS, which reveals uncertainty and second or third thoughts on Mahler's part.

A characteristic transitional extension between SK and FS is found if we compare the former's p. 7 with the latter's p. 33 (in both cases, the orchestral bars before RV, Fig. 21). In SK only three bars precede the entry of the voice, *O Wunder, was nun da begann!* In FS the passage has been extended by four bars, which extension is followed in RV. The broadening out was necessary to reduce the big orchestral crescendo and prepare the way for the hushed accents of the contralto, all of which Mahler in SK had attempted in too small a space. This is an instance of an abrupt transition in SK already smoothed over in FS.

In SK, p. 8, the pregnant vocal phrase, *Ach Spielmann, lieber Spielmann mein!*, appears thus (Ex. 4), imitating, in fact, the cor anglais' continuation of the melody (Ex. 3):

In FS, pp. 38–9, Ex. 4 is already transformed into the simpler and more effective contour of Ex. 5, which stands out clearly against the elaborate writing for winds (the discrepancies in the note-values of Ex. 4's bars 7 and 8 are Mahler's own).

RV follows Ex. 5 almost exactly (while further elaborating the part for first flute).

Ex.5

One often meets phrasing and scoring in RV that one imagines can only have been the result of revision by the mature composer. An instance is the phrasing of the tune associated with the Minstrel, which appears in RV (8 bars after Fig. 11) like this (Ex. 6):

Ex.6

The placing of the rests in those bars—which, if observed, automatically secures the precise phrasing Mahler wants—is typical indeed of his later scores, in which such nervous attention to detail is a commonplace (one might add that the phrasing here lends a nervous, taut quality to the Minstrel's gay melody). To be sure, the tune is not fully phrased thus in SK (e.g., pp. 2–3), but the germ of the phrasing—the abbreviating quaver rest— appears in SK, p. 5; and in FS, pp. 8–9, or 18–19, the melody is phrased virtually as we have it today in RV—the latter simply applies the principle a little more consistently.

163

An example drawn from the sphere of scoring is the use of three solo violins to characterize the texture of the theme quoted above (Ex. 6); one might say that here the detail in soloistic orchestral lay-out points up the detail of the phrasing (RV, Fig. 11 *et seq.*, Fig. 32 *et seq.*). This kind of scoring is, once again, typical of mature Mahler, and it comes as a surprise to discover it as part of his original conception of the cantata; not in SK, but in FS, p. 47, that is, not at RV's corresponding Fig. 11, but at Fig. 32. Once more, the initial idea was formed at the earliest stages in the life of *Das klagende Lied* and, presumably during one or other of the revisions, applied to the parallel passage.

We also find many other orchestral touches in the FS that we might, without the evidence of the MS. sources, too readily assume to have been the work of later years—for example, the up-beating scalar ornamentation of the first beat of the bar in RV, Fig. 29 (cf. FS, p. 42), or the chilling, prophetic scoring—harp prominent—of the surge of E flat minor that engulfs the cantata at RV, Fig. 25 (cf. FS, p. 38, an expansion of a germinal idea already explicit on p. 8 of SK, though in shorthand style: the placid F major bars that precede this striking outburst are also slightly extended in FS (and yet further in RV), doubtless to heighten the contrast when it finally arrives in the shape of the undiluted E flat minor triad; but of course the vivid juxtaposition of tonalities is already embodied in SK, p. 8, if not fully worked out there).

A feature of FS one constantly encounters when comparing the MS. with SK or RV is the incessant redistribution of vocal parts among the soloists and, on occasions, between soloists and chorus. For an example of the latter practice, see FS, pp. 15–16, and RV, eight bars after Fig. 9: FS sets the melody for male chorus, RV for tenor solo (a return to an even earlier concept in FS—deleted—that this passage might be made a baritone solo). Again, the great cry that tops the climax of *Der Spielmann*—*Was soll denn Euch mein Singen?!*—in RV is sung in unison by all three soloists (three bars after Fig. 36); in FS, pp. 54–5, the phrase is chorally envisaged, for male voices (the phrase does not appear at all in SK, p. 11).

I need only give one or two instances of the changes of mind Mahler had about which soloist should sing what. In FS, p. 19, the song of the Minstrel is marked down for soprano; in RV, Fig. 11, for tenor, then contralto; in SK, pp. 4–5, no specification at first, but soprano and contralto introduced later, to which scheme RV in principle partly returned. Again in FS, p. 31, the tenor has the rôle that in RV, five bars before Fig. 20, is allotted to the contralto. There are many variants of this kind, especially in ensemble passages: for example, the lay-out of voices (soloists and chorus) in the first choral interlude is much different in RV (Fig. 15) from the version in FS, pp. 25–7.

One extraordinarily interesting idea Mahler had at the FS stage was to have a boy's voice doubling, "from afar", the contralto's delivery of the flute's narration of the murder (RV, Fig. 26, FS, p. 38). This dramatic vocal scoring corresponds to Bechstein's fairy tale, in which the flute speaks with the murdered *child's* voice; and it is one of the very few instances in *Das klagende Lied* in which a detail from the text is faithfully matched by the musical conception. The idea, in this form, is dropped in RV.[103] Probably Mahler himself realized that, having adopted Grimm's brothers in place of Bechstein's children, his *Knabenstimme* lost much of its point; and when *Waldmärchen* (the original Part I) was omitted—which had contained the murder scene—the child's voice would have become even more of an anomaly. We need not imagine that Mahler made the deletion on any other grounds. He was to use boys' voices in Symphonies III and VIII; and the abandoned intent to employ a *Knabenstimme* in *Das klagende Lied* holds a certain interest as a precedent for later events.

Finally, there is one small detail in which RV stands alone, where we may presume that the variant (unless, of course, it is present in the fair copy of the score) is part of a revision from a later period. It centres on the textual refrain *O Leide!* (or *O Leide, weh'!*).

A recurrent exclamation in Mahler's ballad, he treats it as a musical motto. (In fact, as the coming examination of the cantata's music will show, the refrain is variously set; but one setting acquires the status of a motto proper, and all the settings of the phrase share a common—appropriately sorrowful—character.) The principal motto is, of course, established in both SK and FS—its first appearance in RV, Fig. 16, is precisely anticipated in SK, p. 6, and FS, p. 26. Indeed, the motto proper, throughout *Der Spielmann*, always has its precedent in SK or FS. Such is not the case with what might be called the motto's associates. The first of them—it actually precedes (at RV, Fig. 10) the first unfolding of the motto proper—is to be found in both SK, p. 4, and FS, pp. 16–17, which suggests that Mahler was conscious at this early stage in his composition of the possibility of introducing varied settings of the refrain. None the less, he did not proceed with the idea in FS, which thereafter reveals only the motto proper.

This means that the three associates of the motto, to be found in RV at four bars after Fig. 22, five bars after Fig. 29, four bars before Fig. 30, are additions made after completion of the FS. (In one respect I think they may be criticized: they tend to confuse for the listener the otherwise clear function of the principal motto.) But what perhaps is of greater interest is the means by which Mahler accumulates a handful of new vocal motives. Additions, in this context, proves to be the wrong word. The motto's associates in fact derive exclusively from the orchestral parts, parts already clearly outlined in FS (i.e., p. 35, p. 42, p. 43). In the first case Mahler 'vocalizes' a two-bar series of descending thirds for a pair of horns, with the result that the contralto and tenor soloists both echo and dovetail with the last phrase of the soprano: what was a purely instrumental continuation becomes a vocal one (RV, 3 bars before Fig. 23, where the original instrumentation for horns is redistributed between flutes and bassoons, in pairs). In the second and third cases, a music example (Ex. 7) makes plain the method by which Mahler extended the continuity of his vocal line and introduced the textual refrain: the 'new' voice phrases (RV, Fig. 29 *et seq.*) are contained within brackets and in both instances were simply lifted from (what is now) their orchestral accompaniment.

To sum up. In essential structure SK and FS correspond almost exactly to RV. Extension rather than abbreviation is a characteristic of RV and, in so far as Adler specifies cuts, i.e., of the instrumental interludes, these do not apply to *Der Spielmann* (RV, Part I), whose instrumental interludes do not significantly vary in length between SK, FS and RV. The close relation between sketches for the cantata and the finished product is true of later works: Mahler rarely made any major alterations in the shape or structure of his music once his conception of the work had reached a certain stage in its unfolding (i.e., the stage represented by *Der Spielmann*'s SK). Instrumentation was another matter. In this sphere, and in almost all his works, Mahler tinkered about endlessly.

Das klagende Lied is no exception to this rule; and it is here that there is most variation between FS and RV. None the less, as I have pointed out above, many of the most mature, revised-sounding orchestral textures are in fact established in FS in all their colourful and sonorous detail. Indeed, in essentials, in this department too, RV and FS coincide more often than they diverge. Re-instrumentation as extensive as the wholesale transfer of string parts to woodwinds (FS, p. 36: RV, five bars after Fig. 23, from *Più mosso* for four bars) is exceptional.[104] A characteristic move in the direction of clarity occurs in RV, five bars after

Fig. 9, where, in FS, p. 15, the clarinets' figure was reinforced by the violas. The revision has weeded out the superfluous violas. Since their part is ringed round in FS, it is probable that it was excised in the first fair score of the original version. A good deal of the polish and finish we enjoy in RV, indeed, may have been accomplished in that MS. copy; especially, perhaps, the additions of dynamics, of which FS is sometimes surprisingly nude but sometimes clad in the detail, or potential detail, we associate with Mahler's scores (cf. Plate IX).

Plates IX and X, a juxtaposition of a page from FS[105] with its published counterpart in RV, show how much of RV's instrumentation was already explicit in FS. We hear *Das klagende Lied* today very much as Mahler 'heard' it when he wrote it.

One aspect of the music of *Das klagende Lied*—its eclecticism—needs no demonstration; here, the music does the historian's work for him. Redlich writes:

> "With great skill the music manages to integrate cross-influences such as Wagner's *Ring*, Bruckner's earlier symphonies and the operatic gesture of Weber and Marschner, whose music re-echoes here and later in Mahler's work."[106]

I do not think one need quarrel with the list of names, though perhaps two others—Schumann, Schubert—should be added, and one, Marschner, taken as representative of that flourishing art of minor German opera which, though unfamiliar to many English ears, was undoubtedly part of the young Austro-German musician's education at the end of the nineteenth century. Another writer puts a different point of view. Křenek, in fact, is discussing Mahler's relation to the famous *Wunderhorn* anthology of folk poetry, but what he says, from his own standpoint, is equally applicable to Mahler's relation to his own *Klagende Lied*:

> "The landscape which [Mahler] populated with his musical characters was still the picturesque German Middle Ages as seen through the eyes of the early German romanticists. . . . The romantic scenery of *The Youth's Magic Horn* appears as embodiment of that which is

inexorably doomed to perish. Just as Mahler chooses to associate his music with the picture of an archaic stage of life, so he clings to a musical idiom which is prevailingly pre-Wagnerian—that is, to a musical material which is not yet affected by the destructive principles let loose by Wagner against tonality. . . . It is his unconscious reaction against Wagner."[107]

A comparison of Redlich's and Křenek's words reveals some common ground (certain of the former's choice of influences are strictly "pre-Wagnerian") and one basic contradiction—about the influence of Wagner himself. We see that Redlich mentions the *Ring* as a source of inspiration. Křenek, on the other hand, writes of Mahler clinging to a "prevailingly pre-Wagnerian idiom" that was "his unconscious reaction against Wagner". This contradiction seems to me to stem from the same confusion, expressed, so to speak, in opposite terms. Redlich rightly hears a Wagnerian influence in the cantata but attributes it to the wrong period of Wagner's composing; his error is part of that loose thinking—I have referred to it earlier[108]—which automatically brackets 'Wagnerian' to Wagner's later style and operas and overlooks his early but, in its day, both influential and novel period. Křenek really makes exactly the same mistake; though correctly not hearing any later Wagner in early Mahler, he wrongly interprets its idiom as "pre-Wagnerian", whereas in fact the idiom *is* often, if not prevailingly, Wagnerian; but early Wagner, not the Wagner of the *Ring* or *Tristan* or *Die Meistersinger*. Křenek joins hands with Redlich in a perverse definition of Wagnerian which excludes the early operas as a potential sphere of influence and leads both commentators to commit themselves to statements that are illusory.

Křenek, moreover, constructs a whole theory upon this fallacious assessment of Mahler's youthful style:

". . . this apparent regression [that is, his 'unconscious reaction against Wagner'] is exactly what makes Mahler a propelling force in the evolution of music. . . . In his late symphonies he succeeded in drawing the conclusions from this reaction and in laying down the foundations of the music to come."[109]

This proposition holds good only on the basis of Mahler's "pre-Wagnerian" idiom: that plank removed, the argument falls to the ground. As for such developments in later symphonies which anticipate future trends in music, it is surely forcing the facts to fit a preconceived theory to ascribe these traits to Mahler's reaction against Wagner? When he wrote *Das klagende Lied*, for example, his early enthusiasm for Wagner was undoubtedly in full flood (no room for reaction at this stage, in any event); and the language he used was exactly that which one might expect of a young, progressively-minded composer of Mahler's sympathies and inclination, a composer familiar with the sources of Wagner's early works as well as the early works themselves. This much Mahler freely inherited. Much else from, and of, Wagner he had to learn. Is it not quaint that Křenek should write of the "picturesque German Middle Ages" and their "romantic scenery" as if they were somehow alien to the composer of *Lohengrin* and *Tannhäuser*?

The fine *Wunderhorn* songs themselves represent another case altogether, one related to *Das klagende Lied* perhaps, but very different in kind because the songs are so much the later in time and thus more mature. But even if one cared to accept the songs' world—their atmosphere—as un-Wagnerian, this 'reaction', in Křenek's own terms, can have nothing to do with the late symphonies' reaction, by which, I imagine, Křenek has in mind such traits as Mahler's chamber-musical orchestral textures, i.e., a turning away from sumptuous Wagnerian sonorities (which the future was to consolidate). Here, Křenek seems to confuse two quite distinct and unrelated phenomena,[110] one of which is more literary than musical, the other a matter pertaining to technique. The course of Mahler's development as a composer, which came to march across the threshold of twentieth-century music, owes nothing to any reaction against Wagner, conscious or unconscious, and everything to the singular evolution of Mahler's unique creative personality: an evolution as consistent as Wagner's own, from *Tannhäuser* to *Tristan*, which also embraced and promoted both the old and the very new within a wide sweep. (The reaction that always emerges where a young genius is voluntarily bound to an admired model of Wagner's calibre, i.e., his assertion of a personal mode of utterance, is inevitable, indeed, obligatory, if the younger man is to swim beyond his idol, not sink beneath him. But this self-protective reaction is not, I think, what Křenek had in mind.)

Mahler's debt to—assimilation of—early Wagner has never been sufficiently stated. It is important, I think, to recognize the Wagnerian influence in his early music for what it is, to realize, for example, when in the midst of the Wagnerian prelude to the cantata's Part II, how close Mahler's idiom stands to, say, *Der fliegende Holländer*, to its overture especially. It was years later, in very different music, that Mahler fully registered the impact of the whole of Wagner's creative personality.

That said, one can scan the cantata for what it reveals of the authentic Mahlerian voice. Stefan writes of the orchestral introduction to Part I, "the themes follow one another just as in an opera overture";[111] this overture, indeed, is the one thing in *Das klagende Lied* that does smack of the theatre. Outwardly, the procession of tunes seems to place the introduction in that category of rather primitive opera overtures which are hastily assembled after the work has been composed. It may well have been that Mahler's was similarly conceived, though a feature of SK is the detailed finish of the overture and the comparatively rough filling-out of the body of the cantata's first part (one recalls the prelude to *Die Argonauten*, which was completed in advance of the opera which it presumably introduced). But whatever the history of its composition, and despite the overture's seemingly quite straightforward review of the cantata's pungent and sometimes breezy tunes, when we come to examine its motivic structure we discover an unsuspectedly subtle wealth of thematic relations and a method of motivic organization and evolution which directly, if rudimentarily, anticipate Mahler's later manner.

A small handful of music examples will show how the overture is built around the theme of the Minstrel (as Part I is, dramatically, and was so entitled in SK and FS). Ex. 8 comprises the cantata's opening bars (x is crucial; note also the 'Mahler triplet').

Ex. 8

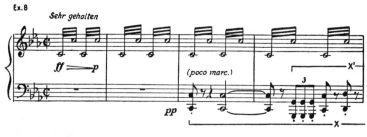

Ex. 9

In Ex. 9, we find a typically Mahlerian combination of motives, in which x accompanies the continuation (o) of another important motive (see Ex. 11 below). In bar 4 of Ex. 9, x^1, divested of its triplet, half-concealedly introduces a new motive, y—or, rather, a new continuation of x^1 itself. Though y proves to have an independent life of its own, no one can deny its derivation from x nor its patent identity with Ex. 10 to come, where indeed, the

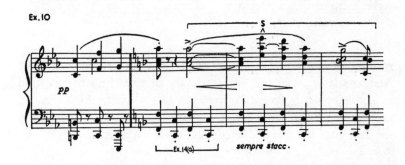

upbeat function of x^1 in Ex. 9 (in relation to y, bars 4 and 5) becomes a marked feature of the Minstrel's theme proper. Ex. 10, towards which x (Ex. 8) and y (Ex. 9) have been persistently and pervasively evolving, appears almost at the overture's close; it is in every sense a fully-fledged melody. As the overture's most compelling melodic inspiration, it stands in the strongest contrast to the brief motives out of which, for the most part, the rest of the introduction is constructed. The gradual growth of Ex. 10 from Exx. 8 and 9 is one of the unexpected subtleties that this outwardly happy-go-lucky chain of motives and melody presents.

It is not my intention to quote every motive. (The overture, in any event, does not yield every motive that is to be found in the cantata.) At the resumption of Tempo I, five bars after Fig. 3, we hear the beginning (Ex. 11) of the motive whose direct continuation (o) is included in Ex. 9 above. This characteristic horn invention, which appears again in the work,[112] represents in the overture the first real departure from C minor: it heralds, in fact, the onset of the new key, F major, established by the

Minstrel's tune (Ex. 10), a tonal centre that persists across the
contralto's entry with her first instalment of the narrative
(Fig. 8), though by this time the major has darkened to minor.
The passage that succeeds Ex. 11, part of which is quoted in
Ex. 9, offers another clear instance of Mahler's mosaic-like

Ex.11

motivic organization. The row of motives is a striking feature of
Mahler's later style. It is extraordinary that we find the method
in statu nascendi in so early a piece as *Das klagende Lied*. Ex. 12
unfolds in turn x^1 from Ex. 8, *w* from Ex. 11, and *y* from Ex. 9
(x^1 and *y* are compressed vertically: cf. Ex. 9, bars 4 and 5):

Ex.12

Another important motive emerges in the extended passage
which rounds off the overture; it might be named Mahler's 'forest

murmurs'. Against a soft background sustained in the clarinets, horns and lower strings, flute, oboe and piccolo burst, as it were, into individual bird-song. The piccolo, in particular, adds a brilliant glint to the texture. The timbre and conception of the passage (Figs. 7–8) are Mahlerian to a degree, and the handling of the woodwinds so confident and original that it is hard to believe that in essentials the sonority of these bars was determined in SK and FS. It is the continuation of the oboe's song (Ex. 13) that merits our special attention:

Ex. 13

The fantasy of this passage has its complement in an earlier passage in the overture (Figs. 1–2) in which Mahler exploits the woodwinds not for their decorativeness but their bleakness. In these two contrasted sections we have, in brief, Mahler's twin approaches to the woodwinds, which so often carry the weight of his sorrow or effervescing imagination.

There is one further general comment to be made about the overture, about its C minor part (from the beginning to Fig. 3). Ears reasonably familiar with the first movement of Mahler's Symphony II (in C minor) will be reminded of the latter at many points in the overture to *Das klagende Lied* (the textural lay-out of Ex. 8, for instance, is evocative of the symphony's opening bars). There are many spots where the timbre of the music or contour of a motive bring the symphony to mind. The chorale motive (RV, five bars before Fig. 5; Symphony II/1, eight bars before Fig. 17) and the broad climax to which the music builds up from Fig. 2 onwards to Fig. 3 offer, perhaps, the closest parallels—in rhythm (e.g., ♩♩♩ ♩♩♩ , a prominent rhythm in Symphony II/1) and the hurtling chromatic descent in the 'cellos and basses (cf. Symphony II/1, Fig. 27 to end, with RV, two bars before Fig. 3 to subsequent Tempo I: the conception and texture of this passage directly anticipate the later invention). Such parallels and similarities as exist are not, of course, evidence of *Das klagende Lied* actively influencing Symphony II; rather is it the case of characteristic C minor music revealing a certain unity of shape and sound, the kind of relation one often finds in a composer's *œuvre*: a specific key and mood can develop their own musical imagery which will cross-fertilize otherwise quite disparate works. We may also note that this climactic passage most plainly unfolds the influence of Bruckner on the young Mahler. It is one of the few places in Mahler where one can hear him make use of mannerisms unmistakably associated with his eminent senior.

The character of the vocal writing for the cantata's soloists alternates between *arioso* (which bears the burden of the narrative and ranges widely in scope between extreme tension and relaxation) and song (conserved for moments of lyric intensity, e.g., the bone-flute's tale of woe). The deployment of the soloists aims less at dramatic consistency than at variety, though one notices that Mahler has a particular liking for the contralto voice, which is favoured with many of the cantata's most compelling vocal inspirations. One feels here the sympathy which cast a contralto for the principal rôle in *Das Lied von der Erde*; furthermore, as Dr. Newlin remarks, the first narrative passage in Part I, "wherein alto and tenor alternate in the exposition of the tragic tale", is "an interesting foreshadowing of the alternative technique" in Mahler's late masterpiece.[113] Alternation of soloists and chorus, with orchestral interludes relieving the predominantly vocal textures—these are the means by which Mahler recounts his fairy tale with due contrast of effect.

Soft trills and bird-song from the piccolo and flute bridge the transition from orchestral introduction to cantata proper. The contralto begins to unwind the story of the fair knight lying buried in the forest beneath a willow tree. A stark motive of grief (minor second) emerges here (RV, Fig. 9) as an emphatic echo of the contralto's last word—*begraben* ('buried'). The tenor

picks up the narration, delivering it in a typically Mahlerian
mixture of (B flat) major and minor (the chromatic oboe part is
characteristic and already in place in FS, p. 16). Then soprano and
contralto join in uttering the refrain, *O Leide!*, but not yet in its
guise as a musical motto.

The Minstrel's jaunty tune (see Exx. 10 and 6) now emerges in
E flat; in the motivic lead is *y* from Ex. 9 (thus this first appearance
of the Minstrel's music in the cantata proper unites components
that were isolated in the overture, a characteristic process in
Mahler). The tune rolls, as it were, on the wheels of those "drum
fourths" (Ex. 14(a)) which, we have been told, are a feature of the

Ex. 14(a)

Ex. 14(b)

Ex. 14(c)

original Part I (*Waldmärchen*): this motive is certainly no stranger
to Mahler's later music (e.g., the *Lieder eines fahrenden Gesellen*,
Symphony I; we may note that the fourth is insisted on as an
interval in Ex. 8, the cantata's first bars). But there are other
wheels on which the melody rolls, two others to be exact (Exx.
14(b) and (c)). This complex of repeated figuration—a combination of three motives—is maintained almost throughout the
Minstrel's song (his discovery of the bone and shaping of it into
a flute), the vocal line of which is shared between the tenor and
contralto. Ostinato repetitions are exceptionally rare in Mahler's
music—hence the strangeness of finding a positive nest of them
in *Das klagende Lied*.

177

The song over, we pass on to the first chorus, *O Spielmann mein!*, by way of a short passage of conventional orchestral rhetoric and (at Fig. 13) a triumphant restatement of Ex. 9, now in G flat major. Insistently repeated G flats, decreasing in dynamic intensity, suddenly drop a semitone to F (Fig. 14, double-basses)— a most striking, tense effect—which note becomes the long-sustained pedal over which the 'new' transition to the chorus and the chorus itself are delivered. The pianissimo build-up to the chorus is very well managed, and the hushed, choral entry, if anything, more than fulfils the expectations aroused by its preparation in the orchestra: we hold our breath, as it were, along with the chorus, while the unsuspecting Minstrel fashions his flute from the bone.

The tenor soloist utters the warning that the flute will sing a strange song; he follows it up with the refrain, *O Leide, weh'!*, in which he is joined by the contralto, and on this occasion the lament appears in its (almost always two-part) motto version (Ex. 15):

Ex. 15

A brief orchestral coda rounds off the motto. Descending D flat (melodic) minor scales (oboe and bass clarinet, five bars before Fig. 17: their stepwise movement is prophetic of Mahler's late melodic style) bridge the gap to the start of the first orchestral interlude, a development, in D flat major and minor, of the Minstrel's tune (Ex. 10). The tune is accompanied by two of its associate ostinato figures, Exx. 14(a) and (b). It is highly significant, of course, that already in this early work Mahler felt himself obliged to develop—and I use the word advisedly—his material in a purely orchestral section; or, to put it another way, that his material would allow of such development, even, to a degree, demand it. We have here, in fact, the germ of the principle which motivates the great symphonic development for orchestra alone in *Der Abschied* from *Das Lied von der Erde*. This example in the cantata is, naturally, very rudimentary; yet it is more than a vividly coloured recapitulation of the Minstrel's tune. A segment (*s*) of Ex. 10 provides the pattern for the main substance of the interlude's development. There is also a splendid instance (Ex. 16) of Mahler's motivic counterpoint. The familiar ostinato figure Ex. 14(b) and ubiquitous x^1 from Ex. 8 combine with a new motive (*z*, in Ex. 16), a thrusting gesture in the trombones. What is exciting about the new motive, *z*, is its reappearance, this

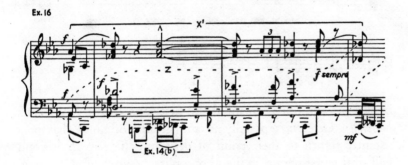

Ex. 16

time towards the close of the interlude and transferred from the trombones to the contralto voice (Ex. 17): it carries, moreover, a crucial text, the placing of the flute to the Minstrel's lips. We realize retrospectively that the placing of Ex. 17 in the trombones

Ex. 17

Der Spiel - mann setzt die Flö - te an,

is an anticipation of the vital moment when the flute is played upon, the crisis towards which the interlude develops; thus the organic assimilation of the motive within the interlude's first bars is most appropriate.

It was a clever stroke of Mahler's to reintroduce Ex. 17 across the closing section of the interlude. The sudden intervention of the voice is most telling in effect, and dramatically economical—the inevitable closing section is made use of as a vehicle for narrative. When we reach Fig. 21, the way, musically and textually, has been prepared for a new stage. Here we meet a new song (Ex. 18), in which the contralto and, later, the soprano, describe the flute's narration. The character of the vocal writing

in this passage brings to mind the first song of the *Lieder eines fahrenden Gesellen*, especially in the groups of notes that persistently return to their point of departure (i.e., in the second half of the first phrase, in the second phrase complete). One may, I think, write of 'song' quite specifically, because it seems that the whole of this passage originally formed part of the early song *Im Lenz*, the MS. of which is in the possession of Mr. Alfred Rosé. Mr. Rosé has kindly sent me this description of the autograph:

"In *Im Lenz* a section (*Noch einmal so langsam*) shares a theme with *Das klagende Lied*. . . . From Fig. 21, *Noch einmal so langsam* [until 5 measures after] Fig. 22 the music [of the song] is identical [with the cantata], only instead of the printed words . . . the words in *Im Lenz* read: "Ich bin nicht blind und sehe doch nicht—Im Dunkel wach' ich und träume im Licht—Könnt' lachen und könnte weinen, doch sagen könnt' ich es keinem."

The refrain—text, not musical motto—concludes this song-like section, which is followed by the second orchestral interlude. It is much shorter than the first and more decorative than developmental, though it has its own combinations of motives and its own sound. It is very much a forest piece, glitteringly, shimmeringly orchestrated (harp, piccolo). We hear the bird-calls from the overture (including Ex. 13) and the pastoral horn theme (Ex. 11). A solo violin injects a lyrical, chromatic counterpoint into the texture, which is softly taken up by the strings. The interlude subsides in a solid, gently-rocking F major, redolent of woodland peace.

It is at this juncture (two bars before Fig. 25) that Mahler brings off one of his most dramatic strokes of colour, the parallel, in orchestral terms, to the chilling effect upon its listeners of the flute's tale of fratricide. For there could be nothing more unexpected than the contrast offered to the somnolent F major of the second interlude's close by the acrid E flat minor triad projected in three flutes and four horns (see Ex. 19; the dynamic scoring of the chord is worth detailed examination in full score).

Ex.19

There is something very typically Mahlerian in the sound of this passage, in the boldness of the juxtaposition. In his later works there are many like examples of these abrupt tonal dislocations whose violence never seems arbitrary, however unprecedented. Strangely enough, it is a passage in Mahler's Symphony X that this part of *Das klagende Lied* brings to my mind. Mahler consolidates the pungent statement of the minor triad in Ex. 19 with four bars of E flat minor (Fig. 25), the chord sustained across the full orchestra, the harps rippling the surface of the texture with steely, ascending arpeggios. For an almost exactly similar texture

181

and sonority and, again, a situation in which the element of surprise is paramount, see the *Andante-Adagio* first movement of Symphony X, at bar 194,[114] where a bleak wave of A flat minor engulfs the work—and the listener: one finds that in essentials Mahler achieves his end in Symphony X by much the same means as he employed in his youthful cantata, and one cannot but help hear the early work echoing on in the later. It might be said that one minor triad is bound to sound like another, but in fact context, instrumentation, and sonority all combine to offer patent idiosyncrasies of treatment in either case which lend to both a unity of style whose common source was the idiomatic consistency of Mahler's genius, from his early period to his very last.

There can be no doubt that the outbreak of E flat minor in the cantata is directly associated with the horrid surprise of the singing bone, of the murderous tale it recounts; for it is in E flat minor that the flute sings (Fig. 26; see Ex. 5 above). This is a vital moment in the development of the cantata and Mahler has found an inspiration for it of a most memorable and immediately impressive kind. Dr. Newlin is right to draw attention to "the delicate nuances of metrical structure" of this "mournful phrase".[115]

The flute proceeds to unfold the tragic story:

> "O minstrel, dear minstrel,
> I must tell you my sad tale:
> For a brightly coloured flower
> My brother murdered me.
>
> "In the woods my young bones whiten.
> My brother woos a fair bride.
> O sorrow, woe, O sorrow!"

Mahler treats each stage in the narration quite differently. E flat minor and Ex. 5 serve the flute's warning of impending sorrow. A brief transition on a dominant pedal A leads to D (Fig. 28), where tender textures, and a flexible, ecstatic vocal line—already one senses that free vocal writing, unimpeded by barring, which is so characteristic of the radiant arches of song in *Das Lied von der Erde*—carry the image of the flower. The news of the murder revives the grief motive in the flutes, four bars before Fig. 29 (cf. Fig. 9), at which point the music plunges into an agitated and indignant C minor as the contralto continues the flute's indictment. (It was the vocal line in this passage which Mahler filled in with exclamations of passionate sorrow: see Ex. 7 above. Strangely enough, something of the sort seems to have happened in the case of the *Lieder eines fahrenden Gesellen*. Compare the miniature score (Philharmonia), two bars before Fig. 20, with the parallel passage in the vocal score (Weinberger), p. 13; in the latter, the orchestral part is vocalized—*Es schneid't so weh und tief!* The procedure is as we have met it in the cantata, but since we have no MS. sources for the song-cycle (and it is not certain which version of the score unfolds Mahler's first (or last) intentions),[116] we must allow for the possibility of an excision in the orchestral score, at a later stage, accounting for the filled-in bars of the vocal score, which may represent the original conception. That the piano and orchestral versions of the *Lieder eines fahrenden Gesellen* should differ in this fashion—and it is not the only example—is typical of the many textual ambiguities which abound in Mahler's published music.)

The transition (Fig. 30) to the third and last orchestral interlude is largely effected with the aid of Ex. 13 which builds up to a big climax in a fateful E flat minor and continues agitatedly in the same key—this tail-piece to the transition is especially Mahlerian in the sound and shape of its restless figuration. We are then launched upon the interlude (in A flat, then E flat) which again concentrates upon the Minstrel's tune (Exx. 6 and 10). This is a jaunty piece, the Minstrel, it seems, setting out on his travels not unduly depressed by the flute's history. There is nothing very developmental about the interlude, though we may note that the tune newly extends itself upon its E flat repetition by exploiting a continuation derived from a segment of the tune other than that which was the main concern of the first interlude (*p* in Ex. 6).

But if the third orchestral interlude is a disappointment as a developer, the immediately ensuing chorus (Fig. 33) fully compensates—its orchestral accompaniment follows the sinewy example of the first interlude, while the vocal parts comprise Ex. 17 and the first vocal appearance (Ex. 20) of the Minstrel's tune itself, in a shape that has been divulged orchestrally in the first interlude (six bars after Fig. 18). Ex. 20 spotlights the segment, s, of Ex. 10 which was prominently elaborated in the first orchestral interlude; thus, doubtless, the third interlude's abstention takes heed of the

coming chorus. From this vantage point it is interesting to look back to Fig. 11, where the tenor and contralto soloists keep company with the Minstrel's tune, but not, we must notice, with s (on the contrary, they vocalize to y from Ex. 9); whereby this choral setting of a derivation from s is all the more refreshing.

This powerful chorus is soon over—having thrown off one further pungent derivative of the segment (Fig. 34, *Ach weh, ach weh*)—but it is ingeniously linked to what is, in fact, the choral finale, by the contralto's cry, *Was soll denn Euch mein Singen?!* (Ex. 21):

Ex. 21 has not been heard since the overture, where it occurs as a bleak motive in the woodwinds (eight bars before Fig. 2). It proves to be a link in more ways than one: from the contralto's vocalization of it to Fig. 35, the music—but, of course, for the choral additions—is identical with the overture. This satisfying recapitulation re-establishes the home-key, C minor—a pedal on

C takes root at Fig. 36 and does not significantly shift for the forty-one bars that remain of Part I—and (from Fig. 35 onwards) expansively develops the rhythmic figure, | ♪♪♪ ♪♪♪ | ♪ etc., which was prominent in the overture seven bars after Fig. 2 but has not been heard before in the body of the cantata.

The mood of foreboding—what can come of the flute's strange song?—is maintained with splendid fervour by this choral realization of the overture's dramatic potentialities; the mood of the finale, indeed, does something to counter the perhaps rather too easy-going, relaxed atmosphere of the third orchestral interlude. At the height of the climax, when the Minstrel has announced his intention of making his way to the King's hall, to the King's bride (a burst of C major!), the three soloists, in unison,[117] and fortissimo, cut across the texture with another, almost desperate, setting of *Was soll denn Euch mein Singen?!* After which the tumult subsides, and Part I ends in C minor with a soft, augmented elaboration for chorus of the motto (Ex. 15)—*O Leide, Leide! weh'! O weh'!*

It is not my intention to go into Part II of the cantata in quite such detail. The method by which Mahler shapes his music here differs scarcely at all from that of Part I. We encounter the same combination-of-motives technique and, of course, much of the same thematic material. It would be tedious to describe what, given a reasonably full account of Part I, must be immediately apparent to the listener to Part II. On the other hand, Part II has its own originalities; to these, and to points where it differs from Part I or represents a new departure, I shall confine my commentary.

In outward form Part II is more simply designed than Part I. Part I comprised a succession of rather short, contrasted vocal (solo or choral) sections interspersed with orchestral interludes: the whole framed by the overture and choral finale (the latter, in part, recapitulating the overture). Of Part II, a broad outline divulges six clear developments in the drama which are matched by six main divisions in the music: (1) An extensive choral *tableau* which sets the scene in the King's hall. It is his wedding-day and a feast is in progress (Figs. 39-53). (2) The guilt-ridden King is pale and silent, neither hearing the sounds of jubilation nor seeing his bride or his guests (Figs. 53-60). (3) The Minstrel appears (in Part II's only orchestral interlude) and his flute sings its song of woe (Figs. 60-68). (4) The King leaps to his feet and scornfully places the flute to his own lips (Figs. 68-72), whereupon (5), the instrument repeats its charge (Figs. 72-78). (6) The Queen falls to the ground, the sounds of festivity are extinguished, the guests vanished; the old walls of the castle begin to crumble: only darkness, sorrow and woe remain (Fig. 78 to end).

The prelude to Part II opens in a brilliant B flat, with a festive rhythm, § | ♪♩♩♩ ♩.♪♩ |, festive instrumentation (brass dominant, trills in strings and woodwinds), and a pounding, pouncing main tune (Ex. 22) first thundered out by the trumpets—as the example reveals, by the time this tune has been ejected by

Ex. 22

its four introductory bars, B flat major has already given way to the minor; the festivity, it seems, is not altogether without a potential flaw. At Fig. 40 appears the prelude's second main tune (Ex. 23), the continuation of which becomes combined with familiar motives from Part I—Exx. 11 and 13—and then develops into a chain of hectic fanfares, which alternate minor with major,

Ex. 23

to reinforce, perhaps, the impression of doomed gaiety. At Fig. 41, Ex. 23 achieves the major mode and brings the prelude

to a rousing conclusion on C flat major. But this does not mean
that the immediately resumed festal first bars of the prelude
appear in anything other than their brazen B flat major—we
have simply slipped back to the home key by way of the flattened
supertonic (whose relation to the second main theme's E flat
minor—i.e., the minor third of E flat minor's subdominant, A
flat—is obvious).

When the voices enter and set about Ex. 22 with the zest that
characterizes Mahler's choral writing throughout the cantata
(he may have written more weightily and imaginatively for
chorus in later works but never again with the exhilaration and
impetuousness that he reveals here), we find the successive entries
of bass and tenor (Ex. 24) present, in amusingly concentrated
form, the major-minor dichotomy of the prelude. If one wanted
to parody Mahler's major-minor predilection, this passage would
provide an eminently serviceable model.

Ex. 24

The big choral *tableau* which forms the first main section of
Part II (its point of departure is Ex. 24) is built around Exx. 22
and 23; its clearly defined subsidiary sections range through
widely contrasted keys. The first big climax culminates on
C major, with shouts of joy from the chorus—*Heiah! Freude!*—
which are distinctly Wagnerian in tone. The chorus is broken off,

and we move on (four bars before Fig. 47) to a new plane, both dramatic and musical, with the employment of those resources—the supplementary off-stage band—which Mahler thought at one time he could do without and then found he could not.

The wind band—to be placed in the distance—comprises piccolo, two flutes (D flat instruments, where possible), two oboes, four clarinets (two of them Mahler's favourite E flat clarinets), four horns, two trumpets (or, better, *Flügelhörner*, i.e., a kind of valved bugle), triangle, cymbals and timpani. The constitution of the band—e.g., shrill, military E flat clarinets, vulgar bugles rather than trumpets—is evidence of Mahler's taste for the authentic sonority of the wind band, a taste undoubtedly conditioned by his familiarity with the piercing, plangent timbre of the military band in his childhood days. (In Mahler's symphonies, the 'military' influence persists, especially in his writing for woodwinds: Symphony III/1 is an obvious example. Symphony IX/3 assimilates an E flat clarinet in the pursuit of ideally audible counterpoint; by this late stage, the instrument has been wholly purged of its wind-band associations—an interesting metamorphosis.)

⇨ Of course, the very importation into the cantata of what is, more or less, a full-dress military band, is of no little significance for our understanding of the development of Mahler's style. It speaks volumes for that fascination with the potentialities of winds and percussion which is so prominent a feature of his scoring (e.g., the wind-band enclave in Symphony V/1, Figs. 12-14), while his (eventually ironic) use of the band in *Das klagende Lied* is more than prophetic of certain developments in the idiom and artistic method of his maturity; but more of this topic later. It is sufficient for the moment to realize that there is more to the presence of the band in the cantata than its dramatic justification, i.e., functioning on a realistic level as festive noises-off.

It is, however, simply as straightforward noises-off that the wind band first appears. Ex. 13, in a new form (Ex. 25), is part of the band's repertory (note the "drum fourths"). On its heels comes the band's principal tune (Ex. 26), whose character and rhythmic structure suggest immediate comparison with the famous parodizing melody (Ex. 27) which disrupts the slow movement of Symphony I; the validity of the comparison is itself suggestive of the potentialities of Ex. 26. In any event, Ex. 26 is the earliest known appearance in Mahler's works of the musically mundane, of that deliberate banality of which he was to make such subtle and complex use in later years. In *Das klagende Lied* the intrusion of popular elements is, of course, 'justified' by the needs of the drama. (Likewise, in Symphony I/3, Ex. 27 was justified by the movement's programme—a band of gypsies and animal musicians process with the dead huntsman's coffin.)

In time, Mahler was able to dispense with such props. Probably in these early stages of the development of this highly personal and innovatory departure Mahler had need to justify the procedure to himself, to lend it respectability by binding it up with the obligations imposed by a drama or a programme. By such means he even placed it a convenient distance from himself, i.e., the programme becomes responsible for the possibly disturbing and hostility-arousing 'banal' inventions. One cannot blame composers for thus attempting to protect themselves from the consequences of their own audacity. Audiences take even longer to accustom themselves to new modes of expression.

The full orchestra breaks in violently two bars before Fig. 48—to remind us, as it were, that there are two levels of dramatic aural experience—and thereafter orchestra (in part) and wind band combine in accompanying the soloists (soprano and contralto, then contralto and tenor, then a trio), who mellifluously dwell upon the joy of the Queen's wedding; the orchestras, meanwhile, dwell upon Exx. 23, 25 and 26. (The very sparse contribution of the orchestra proper is, in fact, determined by purely technical considerations. Mahler was much too experienced in matters of practical performance to leave his soloists on the platform supported only by an off-stage band; and so he supplied them with a framework closer at hand which would afford a reasonable chance of successful ensemble between all the vocal and instrumental participants.)

The wind band fades out with the soloists, and chorus and orchestra return in full strength at Fig. 50, where the final part of this first main division opens in a brisk F♯ minor. Ex. 23 is much worked at, as are the ubiquitous Exx. 11 and 13, and this vigorous chorus ends on the major to those repeated cries of *Heiah! Freude!* that we have encountered before (cf. Fig. 46 *et seq.*; one is also reminded that the harmonic progress of this whole division (B♭→C♭) parallels the prelude's similar progression). In fact, the culminating assertion of *Freude!* is very short-lived—it is cut across by an ominous diminished seventh, and the ensuing bars for orchestra (Fig. 53), in which a muted, spectral version of Ex. 22 emerges (for four horns on stopped notes: a favourite Mahlerian colour, cf. Symphony IX/1, Fig. 7), leave one in no doubt that something untoward is waiting round the corner.

The second main division—itself comprising three subsections—mainly concerns itself with the strange reluctance of the King to participate in the wedding festivities. First the contralto queries the King's pallid dumbness in an opulently scored E major-minor passage (Fig. 54) whose invention is not always the equal of its imaginative instrumentation; the chorus which follows is more strikingly contrived, especially at Fig. 58, where the sopranos and tenors express their astonishment at the King's indifference to his bride's wondrous beauty: their sustained, awed, pianissimo E's, dropping an octave on the last syllable of *Schö-ne!*, are combined with simultaneously down- and up-climbing E major scales to singular textural effect. A descending minor scale unwinds us into the most pungent putting of the question we have yet met—*Was ist der König so bleich und stumm?*, asked by the contralto and set to the haunting song from Part I (see Ex. 18). The melody and its accompaniment run a course identical with their first appearance in Part I (though here the whole section is transposed down a semitone): the only difference is the addition of the textual refrain *Leide, Leide!*, achieved once again by realizing an orchestral part in vocal terms (cf. bars 2-4 after Fig. 59 with bars 2-4 after Fig. 21).

Since it is the Minstrel who is the instrument of the King's doom, it is dramatically appropriate that the orchestral interlude which brings him to the King's door should open with (his) motive *y* from Ex. 9, in an A flat whose brightness, one need hardly add, is soon dimmed. Thereafter, the interlude continues with the customary row of motives—customary in method, that is, not in the order of the motives themselves. But students of the work can sort out the mosaic pattern for themselves; they will notice, no doubt, that Mahler uses material which has not been heard since the overture to Part I, in particular (at Fig. 61), the fateful chorale theme (trumpets and trombones); it stands complete, with its contrasted middle section for woodwinds (Fig. 5) now more elaborately scored (six bars after Fig. 61). This interlude is not of the same substance as, say, the first orchestral interlude in Part I; and despite its skilful adherence to Mahler's established motival principle, the procession of motives gives the impression of scissors-and-paste contrivance, the very opposite of that natural spontaneity which underlies the most complex of the motival combinations or associations elsewhere in the cantata.

At Fig. 63, the second main division of Part II ends and we

embark upon the three divisions which contain the kernel of the drama. In (3), the flute speaks through the Minstrel; in (4), the King puts it to his own lips; in (5), the flute addresses the King as "brother, dear brother mine". Section (4) is an exciting choral outburst based upon Part II's principal tune, Ex. 22. (Mahler makes some contrapuntal play with the tune, in both the chorus and orchestra (cf. Fig. 43 *et seq.*).) Sections (3) and (5), which frame the chorus, comprise the flute's narrations: they are, of course, related to one another through mutual dependence upon the flute's song from Part I (Ex. 5). Section (3), in fact, is a free development of Ex. 5 and its continuations (Part I, Figs. 26-30). Ex. 5 remains the point of departure, though slightly varied— its final phrase, on *klagen*, is more melismatic than before (the character of this variant is prophetic)—and now in C sharp minor, as against E flat minor in Part I. (The *pp* end of the interlude, which immediately precedes (3), abruptly vouchsafes—*ff*— a sustained D flat minor triad, spread through the orchestra. It functions not only as the introducer of the flute song's C sharp minor across the tail of the interlude but also as the parallel in this passage to the fierce minor triad which heralded Ex. 5 in Part I (Fig. 25). The effect on this occasion is more subdued since D flat-C sharp minor grows naturally out of the harmonic context of the interlude instead of—as before—dislocating an established tonality (i.e., E flat minor disrupting F major). But this kind of strong contrast is reserved for the second, intensified appearance of Ex. 5 in (5), for which reason, no doubt, it is absent here.) The story of the murder in (3) is textually the same as we heard it in Part I from Ex. 5 onwards, but the music is newly conceived. The narration is pitched more passionately and feverishly than previously and thrice discharges (once for soloist, twice for divided chorus) into the motto proper (Ex. 15).

Section (5), like (3), departs from Ex. 5; and (5), again like (3), represents a development and intensification—in this instance not only of the precedent in Part I, but of (3), some of whose new material is driven through to a frenzied climax (cf. Fig. 75 *et seq.* with Fig. 65 preceding). In (5) the vocal line is marked by extravagant melismas (thus fulfilling the promise of the earlier emphasized *klagen* in (3)) and wide leaps. It is, of course, the moment of high drama, when the flute accuses the King *in the voice of the slain brother*—for this is the significance which we must read into the *soprano* undertaking this crucial narration (here the casting even harks back to Bechstein's conception).[118] At this juncture one would expect music of strain and tension, but, as Dr. Newlin remarks (who quotes the whole passage), part of the eccentricity of this exacting soprano solo is due "partly, at least, . . . to youthful inexperience, for such [vocal] lines as these are not found in Mahler's later choral works". On the other hand, she is aware that there is another side to the seeming flaws in the passage, commenting upon it: "Plainly, the immense range and mobility demanded of the female voice by Schoenberg, in such a composition as *Herzgewächse* [op. 20, 1911], are not without precedents in the Viennese school!"[119]

We witness here, in fact, what might be called a conflict between immaturity and inexperience on the one hand and, on the other, the struggle of a highly original talent to create a vocal expressiveness adequate to a tense dramatic situation—to that friction we may perhaps ascribe these two flute narrations' defects and virtues. Neither is quite convincing, though both are often characteristic, especially in the common whipping up of an impressively frenzied climax by means of an agent (Ex. 28) first disclosed in the accompaniment to (3): this kind of rhetoric has

its parallels in later works. But there is no doubt that sections (3) and (5) are not as achieved as are other parts of the cantata; and since they bear the weight of the dramatic development in Part II, Part II is so much the weaker for their failings, as is the whole piece, indeed. None the less, if certain unvocal traits contribute to the slight disappointment and discomfort we experience upon listening to (5), there can be little doubt that had we heard the music when it was first composed, much more than strikes us today would have struck us then as bizarre of conception and written against the voice; in short, the residue of immaturity and inexperience should not blind us to the adventurous imagination behind Mahler's brave attempt to float a soprano line which would express—literally ex-press—the horror and terror of the flute's climactic indictment. His imaginative vocal shapes which, at the time they were written, would have been condemned as cruelly unnatural, are a measure of the pioneering originality of his invention, in which he anticipated the fresh exploration by his successors of the potentialities of the voice as an expressive instrument. (It is clear to me that Mahler could not have ironed the inexperience out of his soprano rôle without damaging its originality, for which reason I believe he preferred to let it stand rather than attempt revision.)

This big soprano narration, which soon leaves Ex. 5 far behind, is prefaced by a cold douche of A minor (Fig. 72)—a transposed replica of what was heard in E flat minor in Part I, two bars before Fig. 25 (see Ex. 19; but now the first appearance of the triad is scored for three trumpets and three oboes). It is A minor which, in this context, is the key of catastrophe, and it is the cantata's tonal centre from this point onwards; it carries us through the soprano solo and the last, choral statement of the motto (Fig. 77), through a final, gloomy revival of Ex. 10 (*Am Boden liegt die Königin!*), through (6), the last, sombre chorus (Fig. 79), which describes the dark, crumbling scene within the castle, to the quiet epilogue (Fig. 83)—based on a pedal E—in which the tenor announces that the lights are out in the King's hall, using a motive which first emerged in instrumental guise in (3), at Fig. 74 (horn). Then the soprano breathes *Ach Leide!* across an octave span and across what is, in fact, a filled-out version of the octave motive; i.e., the unwinding minor scales we met in Part I, five bars before Fig. 17. And the cantata ends with two bars of the A minor triad, a sustained pianissimo that is abruptly cut off by a savage, fortissimo tonic chord on the first beat of the last bar, a passage that was surely (the doubtless unconscious) model for the concluding (A minor!) bars of the first song in *Das Lied von der Erde*? Redlich is sensitive to the inspiration of these closing pages, rightly suggesting that the "spectral contours" of their counterpoint, "bereft of any supporting harmony, anticipate the lean and ascetic part-writing of the mature Mahler".[120]

It is A minor, then, which represents the catastrophe that overwhelms the festivities; and since the unblemished festive key has been C major (i.e., not the flawed, major-minor B flat of Part II's prelude and opening chorus, etc.), the heart of the drama is contained within the close relation of these two keys. C major, moreover, did make a fleeting but significant appearance in the finale to Part I, at Fig. 36, where it is associated with the King's radiant bride. In Part II, it is again the Queen and the festivities surrounding her and the event of her marriage which are characterized in C major (e.g., Fig. 45 *et seq.*). Thus the primary components of the tragic unfolding of the tale in Part II can be concisely summed up in the related tonal progression, C major→A minor.

C major, of course, is the key in which the wind band first enters, as the middle section of (1). The band, always with the same motive and tune (Exx. 25 and 26), makes two further entries at critical turning-points in the drama. On the first occasion (Fig. 66), it actually breaks in on, and for six bars is mingled with, the motto O *Leide, weh'!* (Ex. 15), with which the male chorus rounds off the contralto's flute narrative (3). The second occasion (six bars after Fig. 70) is similarly placed, at the end of the choral section (4), where the horror of what the King hears when he puts the flute to his own lips is forcefully realized. "Hear the fearful story!", sings the chorus (Fig. 70; to the accompaniment of Ex. 23). The chorus cuts off and we hear, in textural isolation, the wind band's Ex. 25 (in a D flat major-minor built into the chorus's C sharp minor context). At Fig. 71, after only four bars, the wind band is silenced by the full orchestra, which, fortissimo and accelerando, picks up the popular tune continuation to Ex. 25 (Ex. 26), distorts it, and hurtles it to a tumultous, break-neck finish on G sharp. After which there follow two bars of general pause; and then (Fig. 72) the cold onset of A minor and Ex. 5, the beginning, as it were, of the end.

It is impossible not to quote Freud's testament again: "In

Mahler's opinion the conjunction of high tragedy and light amusement was . . . inextricably fixed in his mind, and the one mood inevitably brought the other with it."[121] The two wind-band entries discussed above could hardly illustrate the conjunction more clearly; and while the first intensifies and ironizes the drama by injecting a massive contrast into the very texture of the tragedy (Figs. 66 to 68), the second approaches an even more developed stage in Mahler's unique bending of popular materials to his own artistic ends: the festive noises not only provide an ironic contrast (four bars before Fig. 71), but are actually converted into an agent of fear and terror, into the very opposite of what they were at the outset. Such is the transformation that Ex. 26 undergoes between Figs. 71-2.

In the deployment of the off-stage band in *Das klagende Lied*, we find in principle—and in achievement—one of the most singular traits in Mahler's idiom, one that creeps up continuously in the music of his later years and is, in a very intimate sense, part of his genius. (One might almost say that the now by no means uncommon ironic use of popular music—the off-stage military band in Berg's *Wozzeck* (Act I/3) is a famous example—was fathered historically, if not practically (though Berg very probably knew Mahler's cantata), by the wind band in *Das klagende Lied*, where Mahler's treatment of the device is at once idiosyncratic and peculiarly modern.) There was good reason, then, why he thought of his "real child of sorrow"[122] as his "opus I", the "first work in which I found myself as 'Mahler' ".[123] The "child" may have grown up, but the features of his maturity were already brilliantly etched and apparent—even to a mysteriously comprehensive degree—in the youthful composition. Among cantatas—a form in which the mortality rate is high—the originality and promise of *Das klagende Lied* must earn it a secure and prominent position. It is not, of course, a wholly achieved work; but there is no mistaking the genius that is to come.

(*n*)

Die Argonauten was another operatic project, to a text devised by Mahler himself in alliterative verse (*Stabreimen*), a technique which suggests to Redlich that "Mahler must already have been fairly familiar with the libretto of Wagner's *Ring*". Redlich is also of the opinion that the opera was "probably based on Grillparzer's dramatic trilogy *Das goldene Vliess*, of which *Die Argonauten* forms the middle portion".[124]

In order to assign the work a date we have to rely upon Adler, who places *Die Argonauten* ("unfinished, destroyed") in 1880.[125] This is a possibility, I suppose; *Ernst von Schwaben* yielded to *Das klagende Lied*: perhaps *Die Argonauten* was a momentary idea intervening between termination of the cantata and serious labour at *Rübezahl*.

I doubt very much whether either text or music of *Die Argonauten* reached an advanced stage. There is a single reference to the project in Bauer-Lechner, who writes of a prelude to the opera that Mahler "had composed earlier on".[126] It would not surprise me if the prelude, lost or destroyed, was as far as Mahler progressed with the music. (Stefan writes vaguely that the work's composition was "partly executed".)[127]

It is inexplicable that "fragments" from the opera should have been included in the list of works published in Riemann's *Musik-Lexikon*.[128]

(*o*)

Mahler made only one comment about his early songs—without, of course, specifying what early songs he had in mind. The comment runs:

> "Quite inadequate were my songs of that time [i.e., his student period], for which my imagination was too wild and undisciplined; all the more so, since to pour a large content into a small form is really the most difficult thing and requires the greatest art and the most thorough capability."[129]

Most of these "inadequate" songs—whenever they were composed—were presumably destroyed by Mahler. But the two song fragments specified in (*c*) above and a projected set of songs from 1880 apparently escaped destruction; the set was preserved, perhaps because one of the songs in the series Mahler thought worthy of publication (more than that: as a source for Symphony I and *Rübezahl* (cf. (*k*) above)). For knowledge of this autograph I am indebted to Mr. Alfred Rosé, whose description of it runs as follows:

Josephinen zugeeignet
5 Lieder (für Tenorstimme)

Im Lenz	19. Februar 1880
Winterlied	27. Februar 1880
Maitanz im Grünen	5. März 1880

Mr. Rosé remarks, "As far as I know, only these three songs of the five Mahler intended to write in this series, exist".[130] The tempo markings for *Im Lenz: Sehr lebhaft—Noch einmal so langsam—Wie im Anfang—Noch einmal so langsam*—seem to disclose the song's structure; the theme of the second section, *Noch einmal so langsam*, appears, as we have seen, in *Das klagende Lied*.[131] A comparison of the dates of *Im Lenz* and the (original) second part of *Das klagende Lied* in short and full scores (respectively, February and March 1880) shows how song and cantata rubbed chronological shoulders. Was the song an offshoot of the cantata? Or was the incorporation of material from *Im Lenz* into *Das klagende Lied* the first instance of the frequent thematic relations between Mahler's songs and his large-scale compositions?

The third song in this abandoned set of five is none other than the song placed third in the first book of the published *Lieder und Gesänge aus der Jugendzeit—Hans und Grethe*. (Stefan also records the early version of this song, with a slight variation in title, i.e., *Mai[en]tanz im Grünen*.)[132] Thus there is a link between the abandoned set and Book I of the *Jugendzeit* songs. In *Maitanz*, the tempo indication reads: *Lustig und keck. Im Zeitmass eines Ländlers.* In *Hans und Grethe*, it has become: *Im gemächlichen Walzertempo.*

Book I of the *Jugendzeit* songs was published by Schott in 1885.[133] An undated autograph MS. of the five songs that went to make up this volume is in Mr. Rosé's possession. The titles of the songs coincide with the published edition, but the collection itself is headed *5 Gedichte componiert von Gustav Mahler*. In the Schott edition current today the comprehensive title is

Lieder und Gesänge, Books I, II, or III, as the case may be. (We may note that this title introduces a distinction between the *Lied*, the art song, on the one hand, and the *Gesang*, the unsophisticated air, on the other; e.g., *Frühlingsmorgen* as contrasted with *Hans und Grethe*. In Books II and III there are really no *Lieder*, though many of the songs (to *Wunderhorn* texts) are too complex in feeling to bear description as *Gesänge*: it is not surprising that for the mature *Wunderhorn* songs Mahler was at first driven to use a title altogether new to vocal music, i.e., the (five) *Humoresken*[134] of 1892.) There is yet a further query in connection with these songs' collective title. On two Schott editions in my possession—one earlier than the other—the words *aus der Jugendzeit* do not appear. But at a later—post-1900—stage in the rather involved story of Mahler's copyrights, the three volumes of the Schott publication were obtainable bound up in Universal Edition covers; and it is in this edition that the additional words form part of the title (in brackets, beneath *Lieder und Gesänge*). ◁

It does not seem that Mahler's first biographers knew the songs as specifically *aus der Jugendzeit*. Adler, whose book was written shortly after Mahler's death, gives the title in full in his chronological list; and commentators since have followed suit. Not so the printed music: a later Schott edition, which post-dates the songs' temporary accommodation within the U.E. catalogue, bears no trace of *aus der Jugendzeit*.

We must remember that a gap of seven years separates Books II ◁ and III of the *Jugendzeit* songs from Book I, that the collection was not conceived as a whole. It is hard to believe that Book I was entitled *aus der Jugendzeit* (or *Jugendlieder* as Adler has it in his text),[135] in 1885, when it was in fact a young composer's ◁ first published work, not an established composer salvaging worthy pieces from his immaturity (indeed, the volume might have been issued under the title of the autograph owned by Mr. Rosé). It seems to me probable that the collective title—*Lieder und Gesänge*—may have been imposed in order to relate Book I to Books II and III—that is, when Books II and III were published (1892); while *aus der Jugendzeit* was added later, at the wish of the composer, perhaps,[136] or U.E., his publishers, in order to

199

make it quite clear that the three books of *Lieder und Gesänge* were early compositions and not to be confused with his later *Lieder* or *Wunderhorn* songs.[137] One may note, in this context, the not insignificant title-category of the *Sieben Lieder aus letzter Zeit*,[138] published in 1905 (but not then thus entitled).

It is a pity that the only precise date we have for Book I of the *Jugendzeit* songs is 5 March 1880, for *Hans und Grethe*. But Mahler himself, for once, proves of chronological assistance. He said to Bauer-Lechner, in 1900, that *Hans und Grethe* was "the first song he thought of any worth, which he held on to and later permitted publication".[139] Therefore we have a date, March 1880, which none of the four remaining songs of the *Jugendzeit* set, Book I, can precede. Adler helps us to put a boundary to the songs' chronology, promoting 1883 as the year before and about which Book I was completed;[140] since the *Lieder eines fahrenden Gesellen* were almost certainly begun towards the end of that year, there is some reason for believing that ⇨ 1880-3 is a just estimate of the *Jugendzeit* songs' period.

Guido Adler, in the text of his book, points out that it is these songs and *Das klagende Lied* that represent "the period of [Mahler's] youth", but only to emphasize that in the presence of so little extant material "the historian cannot treat the first period, although he has to assume that it existed".[141]

This judgment underestimates the value of both the songs and cantata as authentic guides to the style of Mahler's first period which may, in fact, be treated with reasonable confidence despite the many missing autographs; and, as my chronological table shows, there is additional material extant—the first part of *Das klagende Lied*, for example, and the early songs in the possession of Mr. Rosé—which will, when open to inspection, widen our knowledge of these crucial years. The period which cannot be treated very extensively is the strict student period, from which few compositions remain and the probability of discovering further MSS. small indeed.

Adler omits, moreover, what is perhaps the most important work of all when writing of Mahler's first period, the *Lieder eines fahrenden Gesellen*, composed in 1883-5 *before* Books II and III of the *Jugendzeit* (!) songs. The cycle is the masterpiece that crowns his first period and would be considered here were the work not so intimately bound up with Symphony I, discussion of which necessarily comes within the scope of my later volume.

In any event, first period, it seems to me, is a misleading classification for the works from 1880-5. The 'early works' is preferable, since it leaves free for application to the symphonies, and later songs and song-cycles, the conventional, but useful and appropriate, three periods, the first of which, Mahler himself considered, was represented by his first four symphonies.[142] The *Lieder eines fahrenden Gesellen*, of which there are many anticipations in *Das klagende Lied*, are the songs with which Mahler quitted his early works and embarked upon his first period. (The pivotal composition is met with again in Mahler's *œuvre*, e.g., Symphony IV, in which he writes himself into his middle period, neither entirely relinquishing characteristic features of the earlier symphonies nor completely committing himself to the new style that was to be unfolded in Symphony V.)

The five songs that go to make up Book I of the *Lieder und Gesänge aus der Jugendzeit* are not of equal importance. The two songs to texts from Tirso de Molina's *Don Juan*, the *Serenade* and *Phantasie*, are the slightest. The texts, F. E. Pamer tells us, were substantially re-modelled by Mahler himself, an approach to his poets which did not change across the years. Both songs are like folk-songs. *Phantasie* (Ex. 1) is the simpler. The second half of the song is a straight repetition of the first. Throughout *Phantasie*, an oscillation is maintained between F sharp major and B minor. Since the introductory refrain in the accompaniment persistently reposes upon the former, it comes as something of a surprise when, in the guise of a tail-piece, the refrain settles for the tonic minor. It is the song's only surprise.

Dika Newlin remarks of a later song in the *Jugendzeit* collection, "It is interesting to see how in the accompaniment of this simple song [*Zu Strassburg auf der Schanz*] the piano is always reaching out for orchestral effects."[143] The accompaniment of *Phantasie* is marked *Der Klang einer Harfe nachzuahmen* ('Imitate

the sound of a harp'), and in a footnote, one of the very first of the many footnotes that abound in Mahler's scores (*Das klagende Lied* may contain the first footnote of all), we are informed: "For this song one might perhaps recommend the accompaniment of a harp."

Serenade is even more explicitly instrumental—its sub-title runs *mit Begleitung von Blaseninstrumenten* ('with the accompaniment of wind instruments'). But the instrumentation begins and ends with the sub-title: no score exists.[144]

The song itself (Ex. 2) is more complex than *Phantasie*, of

greater musical interest, and not without character, though the debt to Brahms is plain. The structure of the song evolves from two repetitions of its warm, flowing melody (Ex. 3), each statement of which encompasses a verse. The shape of the melody is extremely natural—homely

Ex. 3

almost; it is, none the less, very deftly composed: the sequence of its phrases offers a nice example of varied accent, of rhythmic repetition mitigated by melodic variation, of a steady ascent to a late point of climax in the final bar. One broad impulse carries the melody through, from first bar to last. Though the essential shape of the melody does not change throughout the song, fresh modulations enliven its second and third statements; and while the first two verses have cadenced on the dominant seventh—the D major of the immediately ensuing verse functioning as dove-tailed resolution and recapitulation—the third and last cadences firmly on the tonic. *Serenade* is no major inspiration, but it is a very well-made song, evidence of a neat and polished technique.

In the yearning, appoggiatura-formation of some of *Serenade*'s phrases, there is an anticipation of the style of Mahler's later songs, a breath of things to come, a little at variance, perhaps, with the popular status of the song. (Another interesting feature of Ex. 3 is its tendency, as it progresses, to convert itself from a *Gesang* into a *Lied*.) But there is nothing in *Serenade* as characteristic as the principal features of *Hans und Grethe* which, indeed, is characteristic as a whole, not in parts, and characteristic not so much of Mahler's songs (its links with the world of the *Wunderhorn* songs are, of course, obvious) as of his *Ländler* movements, which are so striking and novel a feature of his symphonies. Redlich is quite correct when he writes that *Hans und Grethe* "clearly foreshadows the manner of Mahler's later *Ländler* scherzo (still camouflaged here under the direction 'Gemächliches Walzertempo')";[145] the camouflage, however, was a later thought: as we learn from Mr. Rosé's autograph, the song was *originally* marked *Im Zeitmass eines Ländlers. Hans und Grethe* is, then, the first *Ländler* of Mahler's that we possess, and as such, is of particular interest, though it be no more than a very simple song (Ex. 4). Mahler, as we have seen, was especi-

Ex. 4

ally fond of the song, used it in other contexts, and gave it an early performance; he was also author of the anonymous text, which has the authentic feel of folk-poetry about it (we must remember that Mahler was an accomplished versifier: he also wrote the texts, it seems, for *Im Lenz* and *Winterlied*).[146]

Bauer-Lechner has something to say of the composition of *Hans und Grethe*, in which Mahler's 'second self' took a hand in helping the song along; having worked at one part of it in the evening, he woke up during the night with further substantial sections of the song completed in his head. He wrote them down and found in the morning that nothing had to be altered.[147]

It is unlikely that we shall ever know how *Hans und Grethe* was employed in *Rübezahl*. With both Symphony I and the song before us, it is plain that *Hans und Grethe* was much in Mahler's mind when he wrote his first symphonic Scherzo. (In (c) above is to be found a fragment of a four-handed duet version for the piano of Symphony I's Scherzo, marked *Fröhlich bewegt*: the existence of this arrangement [?] among the autograph collection of *Frühe Compositionen* suggests that the Scherzo, in one guise or another, was the first movement of the symphony to achieve a clear shape in Mahler's mind, possibly at a date well in advance of the composition of the rest of the work.) For a start, the song's *Ringel, ringel Reih'n!* motive (see Ex. 4, voice part and accompaniment's bass) is the Scherzo's—not only the Scherzo's, but also the symphony's—basic motive (interval of a fourth): see Ex. 5 (from Symphony I/2), in which, moreover,

Ex.5

we find that exuberant, upbeating octave leap (*x*) which is a pronounced feature of the song (cf. also *z* in Ex. 5 with *z* in Ex. 6 (a)). The difference between Scherzo and song lies in what follows the upbeats—the main tunes of both works are quite distinct. In one instance, however, the continuation of an upbeat in the song (y, in Ex. 6 (a)) finds a place in the Scherzo (Ex. 6 (b))—less its upbeat. This characteristic *Ländler* figure has a not insignificant rôle to play in the movement, especially in the second section of the trio, e.g., as a counterpoint in the flutes to the 'cellos' broad melody (Symphony I/2, Fig. 22 *et seq.*). The motive itself (Ex. 6 (a))—a typical *Ländler* figure—may well

have been handed down to Mahler through the trio of the Scherzo in Bruckner's Symphony III, in which very similar figuration appears: it was a work with which Mahler was exceptionally familiar by the time he wrote *Hans und Grethe*.[148] On the other hand, it may equally well have been mutual use of a convenient cliché.[149]

There were, of course, many composers before Mahler who had paid attention to the *Ländler*, not only Schubert and Bruckner but also Mozart and Haydn. One does not, it is true, often think of Mahler in relation to an eighteenth-century master, but now and again in Haydn's minuets (e.g., from Symphonies 96 and 97), in their exuberant rusticity, their humour or shaft of melancholy, one is brought to sudden realization that Mahler's scherzos may be construed as part of a classical symphonic tradition. It was, perhaps, Haydn's symphonic minuet that was most strongly penetrated by popular components, especially the trio, which thus stood in effective contrast to the minuet proper.[150] Mozart's symphonic minuet, on the other hand, tended in general to cling to its breeding, and his trios retained their character as second minuets though there was, on occasions, a marked relaxation of atmosphere. None the less, Mozart was not always averse to the fashion of introducing popular materials into his serious compositions, even in the sphere of chamber music: the second trio of the minuet from his clarinet Quintet (K.581) is surely an example, and the most sublime one, of a Mozartean *Ländler*? (It is characteristic of Mozart that his sets of popular dances, expressly composed for social occasions, should be yet more refined—I do not use the word evaluatively—than Haydn's symphonic minuet.) One does not wish to father Haydn with more innovations than he is obliged to father already, but I must confess to discerning a line, thin but clear, between Haydn's minuets and Mahler's *Ländler*. (I would also, had I the space, suggest a parallel between Haydn's assimilation of popular and folk melodies and Mahler's.)

In a limited sense, then, the symphonic *Ländler* has a respectable classical pedigree (though respectable is not the adjective that flies to the lips when describing Mahler's scherzos). As innovatory as, at one time, the practice of incorporating popular tunes and rhythms into the symphony may have been, at the stage when Mahler entered the lists as a composer the practice was sanctioned by custom and tradition, and facilitated, even in Mahler's case, who was not moved to express himself in terms of musical patriotism, by the wave of nineteenth-century nationalism which swept Europe, especially those regions which cherished independence but had not yet won it. (Mahler's provinces, Bohemia and Moravia, were among them. While I would not suggest that Mahler's artistic passport was anything but Austrian, I am convinced that what one might call his musical sense of locality was sensitive to his early environment, a sensitivity which in his first period, at least, could colour his music with—to state it crudely but starkly—village rather than Viennese culture, an aspect of style which brings Mahler into the orbit of nationalism. Of course, the creative use to which he puts his "sense of locality" was far removed from the more explicit patriotism of such figures as Dvořák and Smetana.)[151]

Mahler, in short, inherited an established and still prevailing language of which the *Ländler* formed an integral part. Personal predilection aside, there was valid historical reason why, in the most dance-like movement of the symphony, he should have continued to call upon the *Ländler* as a source of inspiration. On the other hand, it may well have been his very familiarity with the work his predecessors had already done in this field, Schubert's and Bruckner's in particular, that encouraged him to strike off on a new line of his own; one must always bear in mind that Mahler lived at the end of a great musical tradition and was obliged to innovate, to assert his originality, if he was to survive as an independent voice. There can be no doubt that he did ruthlessly transform the *Ländler*. Indeed, from the day he took it up, the days of its pastoral innocence and sweet nostalgia were numbered. Mahler, in a sense, murdered the *Ländler*, but in so doing lent it a new life.

One cannot, outside the context of the symphonies, launch out on a detailed examination of Mahler's scherzos and their relation to the *Ländler*, but one can make a mental note of the two features that distinguish Mahler's mature treatment of the *Ländler* from any other composer's: its savage transformation of musical character—possibly the most macabre example is the Scherzo of Symphony VI—and its scale. The first point is self-explanatory; the second is clarified the moment we compare a Bruckner scherzo with a Mahler scherzo (say, from either composer's Symphony V). In Bruckner's case the *Ländler* character—one must not fail to mark his own wonderfully subtle handling of the style—is still concentrated in the trio (a maintenance of the classical procedure); the Scherzo proper sustains the Beethovenian scherzo tradition, of which Bruckner and Schubert were masters but which Mahler never seriously attempted. When one comes to the Scherzo of Mahler's Symphony V, the contrast with Bruckner is immediately striking: the *Ländler* has engulfed the entire Scherzo. The scale of Mahler's adoption of the *Ländler* is, then, a principal innovation in his development of the scherzo.

The process of development towards the scherzos of his maturity, in which character and scale were fully unfolded, was gradual. In his first period Mahler seemed not completely certain to what to commit himself in the field of the scherzo, at times offering, as it were, alternatives side by side (in the guise of character pieces). We encounter this curious situation in Symphony III, upon which Hans Keller makes a most penetrating and stimulating comment, that the work is

"probably the only symphony which projects, as it were, a crucial *space* of historical time against a musical *plane*, by juxtaposing the scherzo and its historical forerunner, the minuet".[152]

Symphony III is the only symphony of Mahler's in which Minuet and Scherzo are juxtaposed (III/2 and 3), but in Symphony II we have a rather similar succession: except that on this occasion it is a *Ländler* which is juxtaposed with the Scherzo (II/2 and 3). Here we have an early stage in the evolution of the Mahlerian scherzo; the *Wunderhorn* character-Scherzo (II/3) is preceded by the dance which, from Mahler's middle period onwards, was to furnish the substance of his scherzos; as yet—despite the undoubted *Ländler*-like physiognomy of the Scherzo of Symphony I—*Ländler* and Scherzo are kept apart. The Scherzo of Symphony I, moreover, is something of a special case. It plays to perfection its appointed rôle within the frame of the symphony, but the movement is not required to bear that crucial weight of emotion which, in later Mahler, is demanded of the scherzo. Thus, though the Scherzo in Symphony I is not without its moments of stress and self-regarding scepticism—the Scherzo is already less innocent than the germinal song, *Hans und Grethe*—it is content for the most part to confine itself to a defined bucolic convention, to follow in Schubert's and Bruckner's footsteps (the latter composer's scherzo style was obviously a model for this movement).

It is plain, I think, from the example of Symphony I, that Mahler was fascinated by the potentialities of the *Ländler*, and sensed its musical possibilities; but had not yet evolved his singular approach to the *Ländler* which both created his unique type of scherzo and represented a sharp break with tradition. In Symphonies II and III, as I have suggested, he experiments with the juxtaposition of *Ländler* with Scherzo (a completely guileless *Ländler*, be it noted) and Minuet with Scherzo. The work in which we first find Scherzo and *Ländler* combined is Symphony IV/2, a movement whose structure (not style!) is distinctly prophetic of later scherzos, e.g., Symphony IX/2. It is appropriate that the Scherzo-*Ländler* alliance—or the precedent for it—should have been achieved in Symphony IV, a pivotal work, as I have mentioned above.

Symphony IV/2 brings Scherzo and *Ländler* together; the juxtaposition (e.g., Symphony II) now occurs, as it were, under one roof. A like procedure distinguishes the Scherzo of Symphony IX, except that here the juxtapositions are more complex and include Mr. Keller's projection of "a crucial *space* of historical time against a musical *plane*"—all within one movement; for, as Erwin Stein remarks, the characters of the three dances that make up the symphony's Scherzo may be described, "with due exaggeration", as "*Ländler*, Waltz and Minuet" (respectively, Tempo I, II and III).[153] In this sequence of events, the waltz rubs shoulders with the *Ländler*, the dance that was its historical predecessor; while the minuet is placed in a formal situation of considerable piquancy: it now functions as a subsidiary episode (trio) within the outward form (the scherzo) to which it gave birth, while its dominant partners comprise the dance by which it was superseded, the waltz, and the dance, the *Ländler*, to which at one time and in certain composers (cf. Haydn) the minuet's relation had been that of principal section to contrasting trio. There is, then, as this remarkable Scherzo shows, a great deal of history bound up with Mahler's development of the *Ländler*. Indeed, in the case of the Scherzo from Symphony IX, the very history of a dance form seems to be anthologized; perhaps this kind of new, cumulative form is a characteristic manifestation of a very late stage in the growth of a musical tradition.

We may note, before leaving this subject—and an understanding of Mahler's *Ländler* is central to our understanding of him as a composer—that the juxtaposition of the *Ländler* with its derivative, the waltz, gave rise to one of the most inspired of Mahler's scherzos, the third movement of Symphony V; the contrast—conflict—between the two styles, one the primitive, peasant forerunner, the other, its brilliant, worldly successor, of the city, and sophisticated to a degree, presented the kind of dialectical complex which attracted Mahler's synthesizing musical intelligence; and from the attempted synthesis emerges part at least of the Scherzo's hectic tension.

Tension—if we now return to the song which provoked this digression—has no rôle to play in *Hans und Grethe*. The strongest contrast offered to Ex. 4 is the tender, interrogatory phrase of Ex. 7—and the consequent to that is a robust *Ländler* figure (a derivative of *γ* in Ex. 6(a)).

The song falls into two main sections, each of which comprises Ex. 4 plus Ex. 7 (and its continuation); we approach the latter by way of the 'saucy' (*keck*) piano interlude Ex. 6(a): Redlich's comment on the "somewhat orchestral aspect of the piano part" of the song is perceptive (the accompaniment is certainly not pianistic).[154] The repetition of the first section brings only minor variations, but the yodelling shouts, *Juch-he! Juch-he!*, ejected by the upbeat to Ex. 6(a), are extended; gradually diminishing in volume, they merge into the coda—perhaps the song's prettiest and most original stroke—softly reiterated, spaced-out whispers of *Ringel, ringel Reih'n* (see Ex. 4), the song's basic motive.

There is no denying the strong character which pervades *Hans und Grethe*—it is not sham peasant ware, but felt through to its bones. Equally, there is no denying its primitivity, part of the song's charm, no doubt—as are, for instance, the accompaniment's horn fifths—and certainly insisted upon by the young composer with a stubbornness that is altogether typical of the mature artist: his faithfulness to the heavy boots of the accompaniment's bass (see Exx. 4 and 6(a)) ties the song to an almost unbroken F major. But one can see why Mahler liked his *Hans und Grethe*. Though his approach to the *Ländler* altered radically —but for the idyllic Andante of Symphony II he never repeated the spontaneous geniality of *Hans und Grethe*—it was in his early song that he declared his affection for the dance in terms that are both endearingly idiosyncratic in manner and authentic in spirit: perhaps an indication of the latter, of the song's inconnexion with the 'art' folk-song, of the composer's curiously successful identification with the *Ländler*'s world, is the by no means unimaginable or laughable thought that *Hans und Grethe* might not only be sung but danced, especially in those piano interludes where the stamping *Ländler* (Ex. 6(a)) whirls us on to the next vocal phrase (Ex. 7).

One is inclined loosely to imagine that Austrian or German composers turn out songs like *Hans und Grethe* by the dozen. But they do not. What are widespread are amiable exercises in the folkish style like Mahler's *Serenade*, a pleasing stereotype in its kind. A comparison of *Hans und Grethe* and *Serenade* exposes very forcefully how rare, refreshing and original in this over-crowded sphere of vocal composition is the former song's deliberate crudity.

I have already mentioned, when earlier discussing *Serenade*, that the song's melody (Ex. 3) unfolds as a *Gesang* and develops momentarily as a *Lied*. The contrast—in reverse—is momentarily encountered in *Frühlingsmorgen*, which is, none the less, together with *Erinnerung*, the most *Lied*-like of this book of *Jugendzeit* songs (if the division has to be made between the *Lieder und Gesänge* of the title, *Frühlingsmorgen* and *Erinnerung* fall into the first category, the rest of the songs into the second). The calmly

rippling opening bars for piano (Ex. 8) suggest the almost Schu-
mannesque atmosphere of the song, though the yearning ninth
in the treble part is perhaps more Mahler than Schumann (cf., for
instance, the cor anglais melody in Symphony II/1, Fig. 8 *et seq.*).

Mahler's admiration for Schumann was intense (his own early
attempt at setting *Im wunderschönen Monat Mai* in his Conservatoire years was doubtless provoked by Schumann's incomparable
song). He remarked to Bauer-Lechner in 1901:

"Schumann is one of the greatest song-composers, worthy of being
named in the same breath with Schubert. No one is a more consum-
mate master of the rounded song-form, complete in itself, than he;
his conception never exceeds the bounds of lyricism, and he does
not demand anything beyond its realm. Suppressed emotion, true
lyricism, and deep melancholy fill his songs. . . ."[155]

The vocal line of *Frühlingsmorgen* (Ex. 9) is as placidly lyrical as
the accompaniment's introductory bars lead us to expect, though

it becomes more animated when the sleeper, dreaming his way
through the beauties of a spring morning, is exhorted to get up

(*Steh' auf! Steh' auf!*). The second part of the song continues
with the first notes of Ex. 9 but then pursues both a fresh harmonic
region (E flat) and a varied melodic course (but consistency of
figuration unifies the new developments): after further appeals
to the sleeper to rouse himself, *Frühlingsmorgen*, for a couple of
bars, breaks into music of a decisively dance character—the singer
reminds the dormant sluggard, 'I have also seen your lively love
already abroad'—music whose heartiness, as descriptively appropriate as it is, echoes *Hans und Grethe* in a context from which,
so the style of the song would seem to suggest from the outset,
such robust stuff as the *Ländler* must needs be excluded. But there
is, of course, almost a programmatic justification here for the
introduction of dancing steps or stamps, to contrast the sprightli-
ness of the loved one with the somnolence of the lover. This little
in-break of rusticity modulates as swiftly as it sets one's feet
tapping: E flat is relinquished and, as the song broadens out into
its closing phase, we return to G major, on the flow of a new
motive (Ex. 10) which presents the injunction *Steh' auf!* in the
accents of a lullaby—an original fancy, the charming irony of
which requires no demonstration. Two statements of *Steh' auf!*,
delivered across the accompanimental figuration derived from the
first half of the first bar of Ex. 8, bring *Frühlingsmorgen* to a hushed
 conclusion.

Ex. 10

Steh' auf, Lang - - - schlä - fer!

The closing section of the song, in lay-out, melodic shape and
rhythm, is particularly characteristic of Mahler's early style;
and, moreover, though the piano part of *Frühlingsmorgen* is, for
the most part, almost stressedly civilized and pianistic, the
accompaniment to Ex. 10 tends towards a Mahlerian orchestral
texture typical of his first period. Which is not to suggest that
the rest of the song wants in personal flavour; on the contrary,
this youthful spring piece already hints at a later inspiration which

celebrates the season in quite another spirit—*Der Trunkene im Frühling (Das Lied von der Erde/5)*. But in the latter song's more relaxed middle section—*Was hör' ich beim Erwachen?*, etc.—we are reminded of the bird-song trills and scales from *Frühlings-morgen* (and, perhaps, of the middle part of the *Lieder eines fahrenden Gesellen/1*), despite the fact that in *Das Lied* the intoxica-tion of spring appears in a new and desperate guise.

Erinnerung (Ex. 11), again, is a *Lied*, not a *Gesang*. It strikes

Ex.11

much deeper than *Frühlingsmorgen*. *Erinnerung*, indeed, is the first manifestation of that intense melancholy with which Mahler's later works have made us familiar. As we have seen, there were signs of characteristic anguish in *Das klagende Lied*; but in the cantata the accents of sorrow were dramatized, objectified, kept at a distance; *Erinnerung*, on the other hand, is the setting of an intimate lyric, the central thought of which is contained within its last line: *Es weckt das Lied die Liebe! Die Liebe weckt die Lieder!* ('Song arouses Love! Love arouses Songs!'): disappointed love and a sad song, it must be added. It was a lyric born for musicalization, one might say, and it released in Mahler a mood that lies very close to the heart of his music. In a very real sense, Mahler's *Erinnerung* is his *Klagende Lied*, more so than the cantata. The climax to which the melody ascends (Ex. 11, bar 9) insists

upon the doleful minor second, in a melody in which semitonal pressure is prominent.

The melody is stated twice; but its repetition (Ex. 12), while rhythmically a replica of the original (Ex. 11), is varied melodically—there is a parallel here with the structure of the melody in *Serenade* (Ex. 3), though in that song rhythmic repetition, allied to melodic variation, with the rhythmic unit changing after each repetition, was the means by which the melody extended itself. In Exx. 11 and 12 one rhythmic unit, exceptionally, serves the unfolding of the melody—its obsessive repetition, in fact, is very much part of the frustrated, compulsive character of the song, which faithfully reflects the predicament explicit in the text: pain and sorrow emerging from an inescapable coalition of experiences.

In Exx. 11 and 12, the constructive principle which yielded Ex. 3, which is self-contained therein, divides to form two melodic sentences, of which Ex. 12 is one big variation of Ex. 11: their relation, in fact, is much the same as are, *within* the single melodic span, bars 6 (from obliques) to 10 of Ex. 3, which comprise one segment of melody, its rhythmic repetition and melodic variation.

Thus, while Ex. 12 carries the second verse of the poem, and unfolds an immediate unity with Ex. 11, this second statement of the melody is, at the same time, felt as a fresh continuation (the song's harmonic movement—with the onset of Ex. 12 we first encounter the dominant seventh and move thence into a warmer (relative major) climate—aids this impression); or, to put it a little differently, Ex. 12, in complementing—answering— Ex. 11, says something new.

The next stage, which reasserts the tonic, is altogether freer in conception than the earlier verses. The voice, after four bars of continuation founded in the pattern of Ex. 11—one assumes that this third verse will be a further case of Ex. 12, i.e., another variation—breaks off; and when the melody is resumed (Ex. 13),

Ex. 13

So kom - men mei-ne Lie - der zu mir mit Lie - - bes - kla - - - - - . gen!

the prevailing rhythmic model has been abandoned; but only to build up to a climax of sorrow (to *klagen* in the text!) whose despairing diminuendo is maintained in the accompaniment across eight transitional bars (see Ex. 15). The dolorous chromatic descent (the characteristically wide skip by which it is approached is, of course, a feature of Ex. 11, bars 8-9) is reminiscent, a little, of the extravagant soprano shriek that is the climax of the second part of *Das klagende Lied*.[156]

This third verse of *Erinnerung* brings to a head the passionate sorrow which is the song's characterizing mood. The section, as I have suggested, is freer; but nowhere, not even here, does Mahler relinquish his accompanimental triplets (see Ex. 11), which throb insistently from first bar to very near the last—a second rhythmic pattern whose monotony is functional; and, although the vocal line for a short while (see Ex. 13) loses touch with Exx. 11 and 12, the accompaniment does not: its treble figuration (Ex. 14) alludes to the missing melody—it is an early instance of Mahler's intense thematic conscience (cf. *q* in Ex. 11):

Ex. 14

The cry of grief (Ex. 13) forms the substance of the lengthy accompanimental transition which slides us into the song's final verse (in earlier transitions the accompaniment has briefly extended the minor second motive on which the voice closes). The transition combines our return to the familiar melody (Ex. 11), with a mid-stream introduction, into the very flow of the transition, of a pedal E as the dominant of A minor, the key in which the old melody is to reappear, entering on the dominant seventh (Ex. 15: the entry of the voice is marked by square brackets).

The final statement of the melody brilliantly recapitulates both Exx. 11 and 12, their contrasted harmonic texture and melodic shapes—its first two phrases follow the pattern of Ex. 12, and its last two follow Ex. 11, with but a minor adjustment of the ultimate (vocal) bar to match the now resigned character of the singer's final cadence; it is not, however, the final cadence of the whole song: the latter (Ex. 16) is first preceded by a sonorous little coda for piano, in which the regular triplet pulse of the song is broadened out in syncopation, as if the frustrated lover's heartbeats were slowing down. Ex. 16 applies the chilly closure.

As Ex. 16 indicates, *Erinnerung*, having set out in G minor, finally arrives in A minor, by way of the dominant seventh on E referred to in Ex. 15 above. A striking feature, one would have

thought, that this song ends in the 'wrong' key; but only one commentator on Mahler's music, to the best of my knowledge, remarks upon it; which is all the odder since there is little doubt that *Erinnerung* is the earliest example known to us in print[157] of progressive tonality[158] in Mahler's music, a principle which plays so important a rôle in his symphonies and song-cycles. It is astonishing enough to uncover a quite unequivocal use of progressive tonality—if on a small scale—in so early a piece. It is even more astonishing that the innovation should have been continually overlooked.

The topic of progressive tonality has already been broached in (*m*) above, where I suggested that our as yet partial knowledge of *Das klagende Lied* in its original version did not permit us to come to rounded conclusions about the work's tonal scheme—though the dramatic sequence of keys in Part II is obviously germane.

It is not surprising that we meet progressive tonality at this early stage—it was Mahler himself who did much to develop it as a constructive principle in absolute music—in the song (and cantata, if we come to include *Das klagende Lied*). What Mr. Keller writes, in his article on Mozart's *Entführung*, of the relation between opera and progressive tonality holds good for the song, i.e.,

> "the dramatic element [in the case of a song, its lyric] may help to achieve, within a new musical unity, a newly expressive disintegration which might not, to start with, be readily comprehensible in absolute musical terms, though as soon as it has lost some of its frightening newness, absolute music assimilates it".[159]

This is a very pertinent comment. One sees the process of assimilation in Mahler's own works. First the dramatic approach (in cantata (?), song and song-cycle), then the principle applied (though this is too self-conscious a word) to the symphony, tentatively, half-concealedly in Symphony I/4, confidently, openly, in Symphony II. In *Erinnerung*, as orthodox as, comparatively, the song's tonal progress is—up the spiral of fifths, thus strictly progressive in Mr. Keller's use of the word—we feel the plot of the text as a co-ordinating factor, a thread which helps to bind the structure together. Not that the thread is arbitrary; on the contrary, tonal progress and dramatic evolution are inter-twined: what more telling, more natural—indeed, more *truthful*—than Ex. 16, which announces that the point at which we have arrived at the end of the song is not the point from which we departed, a progress that has kept in step with the emotional development of the text (but differentiating its varied levels of feeling more precisely than words could ever do in so short a space)?

The text of *Erinnerung*, in fact, opens and ends with an expression of the same basic thought, the mutual involvement of 'Song and Love'. Superficially, this would seem to be simply no more than a neat recapitulation, one that lends itself to conventional musicalization—tonic harmony plus original melody, the components which served the exposition of the sentiment. We have seen that Mahler does recapitulate his melody; but the song's assertion, at this crucial stage, of a new region of tonality faithfully realizes the new element present in the verbal recapitulation: what was, as it were, a conceit at the start of the poem, a romantic exaggeration that is well characterized in G minor, becomes a reality—'Song and Love' *are* inextricable—in terms of what one might call a factual A minor. Thus does progressive tonality in *Erinnerung* illuminate the dramatic structure of even so slight a lyric as Leander's.

Mahler was one of the first composers[160] to adopt progressive tonality as a constructive principle: he helped to create the term, so to speak. But there were, of course, classical precedents, among them, as Dr. Newlin is rightly aware, the tonal organization of nineteenth-century opera, a sphere which would undoubtedly have been influential in Mahler's case. Mr. Keller offers a particular precedent, Schumann, a composer for whom Mahler's admiration, as is clear from his comments on Schumann's songs and his instrumental revisions of the symphonies, was explicit in word and deed. "It seems to have remained unobserved", writes Mr. Keller,

"that Schumann was the first who succeeded in 'disintegrating' absolute music by way of progressive tonality: in what we might call the 'schizophrenic' String Quartet in A minor [op. 41, no. 1,

1842], the first movement stands in F major. I would submit that Schumann is the father of Mahler's progressive tonalities, and one of the grandparents of Schoenberg's dis- and re-integration of tonality."[161]

This is an important precedent; especially important, because it is an instrumental one, which accomplishes the transfer of progressive tonality into the field of absolute music.

It has been noted above that progressive tonality's assimilation by absolute music represents a later historical development. Mahler, an early exponent of the principle, wrote its history into his own music—into his own development as an artist—by successively juxtaposing therein both stages, the dramatic and absolute, the former in *Erinnerung*, the *Lieder eines fahrenden Gesellen*, and possibly *Das klagende Lied*, the latter in the symphonies; and it is significant that Schumann's instrumental innovation of 1842 was preceded by at least one work, a song-cycle, in which the principle of progressive tonality was plainly foreshadowed, if not even more precisely anticipated. The 'father' too, it seems, approached absolute progressive tonality in his own music by way of a song-cycle, in which the continuity of the "dramatic element" helps to unify its "newly expressive disintegration"; the 'son', in following suit, put Schumann's audacities to the test, assured himself of their validity and then proceeded to make them his own. It is, I think, suggestive of the "frightening newness" of progressive tonality that Mahler was obliged to begin, as it were, from the beginning, to demonstrate the natural growth of the procedure in terms of his own creativity before progressing with progressive tonality into hitherto uncharted territory.

If we look through Schumann's songs we shall not, I think,[162] find any single song as straightforwardly progressive in tonal structure as Mahler's *Erinnerung*. (Indeed, this early song, in its tradition,[163] seems to be a unique achievement.) But we do find in and *within* the *Dichterliebe* cycle (op. 48, 1840) the most striking anticipations of progressive tonality. The cycle, in any case, is progressively conceived, starting in A major and ending in D flat.

This is not novel in itself—Schubert's *Winterreise* (D minor→A ◁
minor) and *Die schöne Mullerin* (B flat→E major) are both progressive—though we may note that by no means all Schumann's
cycles follow the *Dichterliebe*'s example: for example, *Myrten*,
Frauen-Liebe und Leben and *Liederkreis* (as its title would suggest)
are all concentric, and in this respect, at least, follow the precedent
set in an earlier cycle (the earliest?) by another composer, Beethoven's *An die ferne Geliebte*. One wonders, of course, whether
or no the loose sequence of the *Dichterliebe*'s lyrics did not contribute to the character of its tonal organization, but in. fact
similarly loose cycles like *Myrten* or *Liederkreis* cling to a tonal
centre; whereupon one may surely presume that the sense of tonal
direction in the *Dichterliebe*—despite the absence of a compelling
narrative—is very much part of the work's structure? (Here,
indeed, one feels a progressive tonality supplying an integration
lacking in the succession of lyric texts.)

But in any event, when one comes to examine the *Dichterliebe*,
one finds the tonal relation between song and song organized so
minutely—e.g., through the spiral of fifths, relative keys, or
Schumann's much-favoured *Terzverwandtschaft* (the relation
between keys a third apart)—that one cannot entertain for a
moment the thought that D flat is arrived at by chance. The final
sequence of songs well illustrates the dramatic progression to the
piano's epilogue; the penultimate song's E major (*Aus alten
Märchen*)—the only E major in the cycle—suggests that we may,
after all, return to the tonic A major from which we departed;
but the bitter character of the last number, *Die alten, bösen Lieder*,
dictates instead a stormy C sharp minor which is soothed enharmonically into the epilogue's D flat major. Here, already, we ◁
glimpse a foreshadowing of the methodical dramatic organization
of keys which was to be a feature of Mahler's *Lieder eines fahrenden
Gesellen*.

There is, however, a finer detail, an even more telling progressive parallel. Compare, from the tonal point of view, the first two
songs in the Mahler cycle with the first two in the *Dichterliebe*:
Mahler's no. 1 moves from D minor to G minor, with G minor
acting, in Dr. Newlin's words, as "the logical upbeat to the begin-

ning . . . of the next song".[164] Schumann's no. 1—the exquisite *Im wunderschönen Monat Mai*—starts in A major and ends, expectantly, on the dominant of F sharp, which comprises, no less in this case, the upbeat to no. 2, *Aus meinen Tränen spriessen*; for the latter song, although it re-establishes the previous tonic, A major, within its first phrase, momentarily allows for the possible establishment of F sharp minor as the tonic of the new song. (Its first chord is virtually neutral so far as the two tonics are concerned: it contains neither F sharp nor E, and the expectation aroused by the end of no. 1 counters the tonic assertion of the A at the beginning of no. 2.)

When regarded within the context of the harmonic organization of the whole cycle, this aspect of the *Dichterliebe*'s first two songs wears a most prophetic face.[165] Confronted with it, one can hardly doubt that the link between Schumann's progressive tonalities and Mahler's is direct. (Mahler's own attempt at *Im wunderschönen Monat Mai* suggests that this very song of Schumann's, central to the point at issue, haunted his early youth.) Whether the influence was received unconsciously or consciously we cannot be certain, though the latter seems likely in view of Mahler's enthusiasm for Schumann's music, music which, I am convinced, if deeply excavated, would throw up many a bridge between the practices of romanticism and the very recent past—if not the present, indeed. Schumann, moreover, stands at the back of Mahler's music not only in this tonal respect: the precedent for *Hans und Grethe*'s remarkable vocal-*Ländler* style will be found in the first song of Schumann's triptych, *Der arme Peter* (op. 53, no. 3, 1840), the first line of which runs, *Der Hans und die Grete tanzen herum!* They dance, needless to add, in the true *Ländler* manner.

To sum up: Book I of the *Lieder und Gesänge aus der Jugendzeit* yields two songs, *Hans und Grethe* and *Erinnerung*, both of them rich in characteristic traits and both of them heralds of the future: *Hans und Grethe* in its *Ländler* style, *Erinnerung* in its progressive tonal structure. In short, major elements of Mahler's maturity are bound up with this first *Jugendzeit* volume. There could hardly be better evidence of the early stage at which Mahler's musical personality revealed certain of the most pronounced features which we recognize today as uniquely Mahlerian.

(p)

Little is known of the *Nordische Symphonie*, or *Suite*, as Specht describes it.[166] Adler places the work ("destroyed") in 1882, among the attempts at various (unspecified) orchestral works he supposes Mahler to have made at this time.[167] Stefan writes of the piece as if it were written earlier than 1882,[168] while Specht unambiguously includes it among the compositions of 1875–8. There is no saying which is the right, or righter, date. A clue—but a very tenuous one—rests in a letter addressed to Krisper in which Mahler refers to "a mythical Nordic king" whose "heroes and drinking carousals" would put an end to his peace (i.e., drive him into creative activity). Holländer takes this to be a reference to the *Nordische Symphonie*, and he may well be correct.[169] As we have seen, a date for this letter has now been established, i.e., 14 December 1879. We cannot, of course, exclude the possibility that the germinal idea of 1879 only bore fruit in 1882; on the other hand it is no less possible that Adler's date is wrong and that the *Nordische Symphonie* belongs more nearly to Specht's chronology. If the letter is a genuine guide, the symphony must have been programmatic, inspired perhaps by Norse sagas and mythologies.

(q)

It may come as a surprise that Mahler the symphonist once tried his hand at some incidental music to a play and scored a great success with it. The origins of the practice have been neatly summed up by Eric Blom, writing of Lortzing,

"much of [whose] gift was wasted on incidental music for plays. German theatres with mixed repertories of drama, opera and operetta were disinclined to keep their orchestras idle on certain days of the week and therefore often commissioned music to adorn spoken plays, sometimes from more or less distinguished composers who happened to be on the spot, but at the minor houses usually from the conductor, who would hastily concoct something he knew would not outlast a particular production."[170]

In 1884, Mahler was second conductor at Cassel—a minor house; and there he was invited (or required) to provide incidental music to what was not strictly a play but a dramatic adaptation of a widely popular narrative poem by J. V. von Scheffel (1826–86) entitled *Der Trompeter von Säkkingen* (*Ein Sang vom Oberrhein*). Scheffel was both a poet and a novelist. He wrote his *Trompeter* in 1853, "a romantic and humorous tale" which soon ran into over two hundred and fifty editions.[171] Its literary style is not exacting:

> *Blauer Himmel, warmer Sonnschein,*
> *Bienensummen, Lerchenjubel,*
> *Spiegelklar des Rheines Fluth.*
> *Von den Bergen flieht der Schnee weg,*
> *In dem Thale blüht der Obstbaum,*
> *Mai zog über's Land herein.*[172]

The poem is divided into sixteen sections, each with a title (e.g., No. 6: *Wie jung Werner beim Freiherrn Trompeter ward*; No. 12: *Jung Werner und Margaretha*), and it was doubtless a selection of the most theatrically effective which comprised the "living pictures after Scheffel's *Trompeter*"[173] for which Mahler wrote his music. Exactly what shape these "living pictures" took is not clear. Did they combine dialogue and mime? And what function had Mahler's music? Did it illustrate the illustrations, link them together, or act as a musical backcloth?

Mahler wrote about the *Trompeter* music to Löhr on 22 June 1884:

> "The other day I had to write, head over heels, incidental music for the 'Trompeter von Säkkingen', which is going to be performed tomorrow with living pictures in the theatre. The opus was ready within two days, and I have to confess that I find it a great joy. As you can imagine, it hasn't got much in common with Scheffel's affectations but, of course, goes far beyond the poet's conception."[174]

Mahler's "great joy" was shared by his public at Cassel; and his *Trompeter* music travelled to Mannheim, Wiesbaden, and Karlsruhe, and was acclaimed. But in reporting this news to Löhr in January 1885, Mahler discloses a change of heart towards the *Trompeter* score. He disclaims that he has had any hand in promoting the music's success outside Cassel, "for you know how little this, of all my works, matters to me".[175]

Despite the rather ominous tone of this remark, we have no evidence that Mahler destroyed the work, though there can be no doubt that he would have disowned it in later years and was on the verge of so doing in 1885. Destruction, in any case, would have been difficult in view of several, widely-dispersed sets of parts. We may be sure Mahler did nothing to encourage interest in the piece, that the novelty of the spectacle wore off and demand for the music simply expired. A bundle of parts—perhaps the original score—may well be awaiting discovery on a library shelf in some German provincial theatre. A start could usefully be made at those places where it is known Mahler's *Trompeter* was performed.

It could be that the quality of the music would reward a search. After all, *Der Trompeter* lies very close to Symphony I—it may, indeed, post-date the symphony's first sketches—and the *Lieder eines fahrenden Gesellen*. Mahler's initial pleasure upon completion of the music, his critical reflection that it went "far beyond the poet's conception"—not least, perhaps, the positive reception accorded it by the public—seem good reason for trying to track down *Der Trompeter*, despite Mahler's eventually sour judgment of his—to my knowledge—first and last essay in the sphere of incidental music.

One memory of the actual music itself has persisted in the shape of a music example. Stefan quotes it from an article by Max Steinitzer (who was also, it seems, of the opinion that some part of the score of *Trompeter* might survive at Cassel);[176] the tune (Ex. 1) was *Werners Trompeterlied*, beginning something like this, according to Steinitzer:

Ex. 1

The first phrase is not unpromising, but its continuation is so feeble that belief is shaken in the accuracy of Steinitzer's memory. Though we learn that Mahler himself came to angry condemnation of the tune, on the basis of Ex. 1 it is scarcely possible to imagine that there was ever a time when the tune had his confidence. None the less, while the music remains lost, Steinitzer's recollection, however faulty, retains a certain value as a curiosity.

When Mahler turned his back on his "living pictures" it was not by any means the last he had heard of Scheffel's "affectations". He was conducting in Prague at the *Deutsches Theater* in the summer and winter of 1885–6 and one of the works of which he was in charge was Viktor Nessler's (1841–90) opera, *Der Trompeter von Säkkingen*. Nessler's piece "proved very popular on German stages";[177] it reached Prague in September 1885. Its *première*, oddly enough, took place in Leipzig (a theatre to which Mahler moved upon quitting Prague) in May 1884, only a few weeks before the hurried preparation and *première* of Mahler's own *Trompeter*, at Cassel. It might have been that the success of Nessler's work at Leipzig set the wheels in motion at Cassel which resulted in the commission of Mahler's incidental music.

Needless to say, he disliked Nessler's opera. "Dreadful" is the adjective which occurs in Bauer-Lechner's passage about the piece;[178] and in Prague it seems that Mahler got so sick of conducting *Der Trompeter* that, to satisfy his mounting aggression, he performed the work with its *Leitmotiv* omitted throughout: no one noticed the loss.

(Scheffel's poem engendered a quantity of apparently inferior music. We find Wolf in 1880, thundering "against [Carl] Riedel's [1827–88] settings of poems from Scheffel's *Trompeter von Säckingen*, which were then very popular".)[179]

But for Mahler his encounter in Prague was not the end of his professional acquaintance with Nessler's "dreadful" opera. When he came to Covent Garden in 1892 with the Hamburg company, what should the repertory consist of but Wagner's *Tristan* and *Ring*, Beethoven's *Fidelio*, and—by what Mahler must have considered a singular stroke of misfortune—Nessler's *Trompeter*, which was advertised thus on the play-bills:

IN ACTIVE PREPARATION—THE
TROMPETER OF [sic] SAKKINGEN
The Great Popular Success of the last 10
Years in Germany, in which Herr REICH-
MANN will appear in the Part of "The
Trompeter", which he has played with
such striking success in the principal Ger-
man Opera Houses.

Mahler, as the company's principal conductor, was probably
expected to take charge of the work's English *première* on 8 July,
but understandably funked it and saddled his deputy with the
responsibility. As the *Morning Post* critic, commenting upon *Der
Trompeter*, remarked:

"Herr Mahler is evidently not in sympathy with this work, for he
relinquished the baton to Herr Feld. . . ."[180]

◁

(r)
The *Lieder eines fahrenden Gesellen* do not properly belong to
this list, or indeed to this book. I include the songs here simply
because they usefully round off the tally of early works with a
composition that has the advantage of physical existence, unlike
many of the entries which precede it. The *Lieder eines fahrenden
Gesellen* were Mahler's first masterpiece, and it was approached
by a series of youthful attempts at composition, of so few of which
we have any practical knowledge. But there are *Das klagende Lied*
and the first book of the *Lieder und Gesänge aus der Jugendzeit* to
act as signposts amid the obscurities of chronology; and, to a
degree, they help to fill in the steps—missing, for us—by which
Mahler eventually arrived at his maturity in the song-cycle, in
which, in a very real musical sense, he took leave of his early
years, with their long record of abandoned, half-completed, lost
or destroyed creative ventures, and smaller haul of triumphs.
Thereafter he was borne forward irresistibly on the powerful tide
of inspiration which encompassed him from young manhood
until the end of his life; and when the *Lieder eines fahrenden
Gesellen* were completed, almost half his life was lived.

229

NOTES
I (1860-1875)

[1] PS, pp. 11–12. His statement that "the papers are lost" can now be discounted.

[2] See Plate VI, p. 124. I am most grateful to Mr. Nicolas Slonimsky for allowing me to reproduce the document his diligence secured.

[3] PS, p. 11.

[4] NBL, p. 52.

[5] The photograph of Mahler's birth-house (see Plate V(a)) is suggestive of its humble character, though a certain amount of whitewashing seems to have been done by the time the picture was taken; and windows added and the puddle removed. See BGM, no. 91. TR, p. 324, n. 11, writes that "the house in Kalischt was burned down many years ago"; but it was reconstructed.

[6] GA, p. 96.

[7] AM[1], p. 109.

[8] EK, p. 158.

[9] When the Mahlers moved to Jihlava, they crossed the border into Moravia. Redlich points out (HFR, p. 111) that "both parents came from the border country between the two crown-lands [of Bohemia and Moravia]". Mahler's mother was born in Ledeč, his father in Kaliště; Kaliště is certainly in Bohemia (AM[1], p. 6), not in Moravia, as stated by Alma Mahler in AM, p. 4. See also GMB, p. 201, where Mahler writes: "[18]60, born in Bohemia."

[10] HFR, pp. 109–10.

[11] GE, p. 10.

[12] Rudolf Louis, *Die Deutsche Musik der Gegenwart*, Munich, 1909, pp. 180–5. Quoted in N. Slonimsky, *Lexicon of Musical Invective*, New York, 1953, p. 121. See also Max Graf, *Legend of a Musical City*, New York, 1945, pp. 210–11, and LK, pp. 172–4.

[13] AM¹, p. 6.

[14] HH¹, p. 452; AM¹, p. 6.

[15] NBL, pp. 52–3. Mahler was writing Symphony III at the time he made this communication to Bauer-Lechner; hence his reference to the work.

[16] AM¹, p. 6.

[17] The dates of birth and death of Mahler's parents appear in GA, p. 95. Marie was born 2 March according to HG, p. 703.

[18] AM¹, p. 6.

[19] GA, p. 95. HFR, p. III and n. I, requires correction.

[20] AM¹, p. 7.

[21] AM¹, p. 6.

[22] AM¹, pp. 6–7.

[23] EJ, II, p. 89.

[24] See pp. 20–1.

[25] AM¹, p. 8.

[26] AM¹, p. 175. See also TR, p. 343, where, in a letter to Reik (written in 1935), Freud says, "In highly interesting expeditions through his life history, we discovered his personal conditions for love, especially his Holy Mary complex (mother fixation)".

[27] AM¹, p. 8; GMB, p. 22. See also n. 101 below.

[28] AM¹, p. 6, who recounts, however, that "the man she loved did not give her a thought".

[29] See p. 5.

[30] AM¹, p. 6.

[31] AM¹, p. 6.

[32] AM¹, p. 40. See also BW¹, pp. 19–20, NBL, p. 66.

[33] BGM, p. 13, who also refers to other physical manifestations of anxiety in Mahler as a man—intense nail-biting, for instance, and facial contortion (p. 15, pp. 22–3).

[34] The word *hinkte* is used in the operative passage, AM⁰, p. 13.

[35] AM¹, p. 7.

[36] GA, p. 95.

[37] AM¹, p. 7.

[38] AM¹, p. 9.

[39] Rosé emigrated to England in 1938, and died in London in 1946. His wife, Justine, Mahler's sister, died in Vienna in August

1938. "The remains of both rest now in the *Grinzinger Friedhof* at the foot of the Vienna woods, not too far from Mahler's grave." Mr. Alfred Rosé continues, "My mother's younger sister Emma married my father's brother Eduard, the 'cellist, in 1898. . . . Aunt Emma died in May 1933 in Weimar. Uncle Eduard was deported to Theresienstadt by the Nazis in the fall of 1942 and died there of actual starvation at the age of 84 in January 1943."

[40] AM¹, p. 9.

[41] AMᴼ, p. 298; AM¹, p. 10.

[42] AM¹, p. 9.

[43] Richard Strauss, *Briefe an die Eltern, 1882–1906*, ed. Willi Schuh, Zürich, 1954, p. 148.

[44] GA, p. 95, has 1896, but the correct date was 6 February 1895 (see HG, p. 324).

[45] AM¹, p. 9.

[46] BW¹, pp. 28–9.

[47] AM¹, p. 7.

[48] AM¹, p. 175. This account of Mahler's interview with Freud is Alma Mahler's recollection of what she was told by her husband. In very many significant details it coincides with Freud's own notes.

[49] GMB, p. viii.

[50] AM¹, p. 6.

[51] GMB, p. viii.

[52] PS, p. 12. For examples of Mahler's absent-mindedness, see NBL, pp. 65–6.

[53] BW¹, p. 26.

[54] BW¹, p. 53.

[55] AM¹, p. 8. Presumably it is Anna, Mahler's second daughter, to whom Alma refers.

[56] AM¹, p. 7. Mahler later indulged his untidiness as a student, in his dress and dwelling-room, both of which were apparently disordered (NBL, p. 66).

[57] Baedeker: *Austria*, Leipzig-London, 1896, 8th edtn.; see also HH¹, p. 450.

[58] Baedeker: *Austria-Hungary*, Leipzig-London-New York, 1911, 11th edtn.

[59] GE, p. 10.

[60] AM[1], p. 6.

[61] PS, p. 12.

[62] AM[1], p. 6.

[63] AM[O], p. 13.

[64] PS, p. 12.

[65] AM[1], p. 63.

[66] BGM, Nos. 1–5. See Plates II(b) and (c).

[67] RS[1], illustrations, p. 1. See Plate II(a).

[68] This, and subsequent, information from Dr. Hans Holländer, in personal communications. See also HH[1], p. 450.

[69] GMB, p. 261.

[70] RS[3], p. 14. Hans Joachim Moser, in his *Geschichte der deutschen Musik*, Stuttgart and Berlin, 1928, Vol. III, p. 400, is almost precise in his description of Mahler as the "son of a Jewish innkeeper". But "innkeeper" is yet too exalted a status. "Publican", I think, best meets the case.

[71] Published in KB[2], p. 153.

[72] See pp. 29–30.

[73] AM[1], p. 6.

[74] AM[1], pp. 6–7; TR, p. 356.

[75] AM[1], p. 8.

[76] PS, p. 12.

[77] AM[1], p. 7.

[78] GMB, p. viii.

[79] PS, p. 12; RS[2], p. 46.

[80] GMB, p. 201.

[81] HFR, p. 113.

[82] Accordion, in other sources.

[83] In one version of the story (H. Gutmann in *Anbruch*, March 1930, p. 104), Mahler was actually found inside the barracks.

[84] PS, p. 12.

[85] GMB, p. viii.

[86] "At the age of two"(!) in GE, p. 11.

[87] RS[2], p. 46. But who counted these?!

[88] DN, p. 125, and pp. 4–5. Another view of the influence on Mahler of his military environment is expressed by Gerald

Abraham in 'An Outline of Mahler', *Music and Letters*, October 1932, p. 399:

> "If we want to make good composers of our children we should see that their minds are packed with the right sort of memories. The poor little Jewish boy who used to hang about the barracks at Iglau . . . was storing up bad material for a symphonist worried about the universe."

Professor Abraham does qualify this comment a little by adding:

> ". . . it is only fair to remember that the banality of Mahler's material was not always [sic] unintentional, a matter of bad taste, but was sometimes intended ironically . . . ," etc.

[89] EJ, II, p. 89. Dr. Jones meant, of course, 'O, du lieber Augustin'.

[90] DN, p. 125.

[91] AM¹, p. 135.

[92] Information from Holländer. Sladky, perhaps, was a member of the orchestra in Jihlava's theatre? Since *Kapellmeister* Viktorin succeeded him as Mahler's teacher, it seems likely (HG, pp. 16–18).

[93] GA, p. 96, who does not mention Sladky. Holländer (see n. 92) omits Brosch.

[94] RS², p. 46; PS, p. 12; cf. GE, p. 12, however, who informs us that "Gustav's progress was so rapid, that he was at the age of *seven* delegated to teach an *older* boy" (my italics); AN, p. 13, also offers us a pupil one year older than his teacher. HFR, p. 113, follows RS² and PS.

[95] PS, p. 12.

[96] PS, p. 12, and RS², p. 46.

[97] Information from Holländer; HH¹, p. 452.

[98] Holländer; see also HH¹, p. 453, where the journal is quoted as the *Iglauer Blatt*.

[99] Holländer. Gisela, Archduchess of Austria, daughter of Franz Josef I, married Prince Leopold of Bavaria in Vienna on 20 April 1873 ('Bavaria', in *Almanach de Gotha*, 1943). The silver wedding of the Emperor was celebrated on 24 April 1879 ('Austria', in Haydn's *Book of Dates*).

[100] HH[1], p. 454; Holländer, private communication.

[101] See pp. 82–5. At some stage or other a piano must have been introduced into the Jihlava house for Mahler's use. Alma Mahler writes how "when playing the piano as a child he used suddenly to feel there was somebody there, and it was always his mother listening at the door. . . . Then he used to stop playing and show his annoyance." This show of resistance to the tyranny of his and his mother's mutual affections "haunted him in later years". (AM[1], p. 8.)

[102] GA, p. 96. RS[2], p. 46, gives 1870 as the date of Mahler's entry into the *Gymnasium*.

[103] EK, p. 158.

[104] Holländer.

[105] HFR, p. 113.

[106] AM[1], p. 7.

[107] AM[1], pp. 7–8.

[108] GMB, p. 201.

[109] PS, p. 12; RS[2], p. 46.

[110] PS[O], p. 25.

[111] PS, p. 13. Epstein, according to Stefan, said that Bernard "had objections"; but they cannot have been very serious ones.

[112] GdM[1].

II (1875–1878)

[1] EK, p. 197.

[2] EK, p. 199.

[3] For example, GMB contains only a few letters from Mahler's student period and most, it seems, have remained unpublished. Dr. Hans Holländer published some valuable documents in *Die Musik*, Vol. XX, no. 11, 1928: 'Unbekannte Jugendbriefe Gustav Mahlers'. It seems from an article by R. Baldrian ('Gustav Mahlers erstes Engagement: Eine vergessene Sommerepisode aus Bad Hall', *Die Österreichische Furche*, 16 October 1954, no. 42, Jahrg. 10 [in *Der Krystall*, the paper's literary supplement]) that Mahler's youthful correspondence was "recently" auctioned in

Vienna "and fell into unknown foreign hands". It is probable that these letters contain much information of importance. They should be rediscovered and made public.

[4] AM[1], p. 63; PS, p. 14.

[5] GdM[1].

[6] See GMB, p. 12.

[7] PS, p. 15.

[8] HFR, pp. 113–14; RML, p. 334.

[9] GMB, p. 5.

[10] AM[1], p. 63.

[11] PS, p. 19; LS, p. 6; GA, p. 11; HH[1], p. 454.

[12] GdM[1].

[13] See n. ***, GMB, p. 8, which states that Mahler was enrolled as a private student at the Jihlava *Gymnasium* from 1875–7. Mahler began his grammar school education in 1869 (GA, p. 96); he would have completed the necessary eight years' course by 1877 and been ready to sit for the examination. In an undated letter to Epstein (GMB, p. 11, which may now be allotted to the summer of 1877), Mahler claims that he has arrived late in Jihlava for the examination and must now wait a further two months. Here Mahler seems to have been keeping the true facts of the situation from his revered teacher. He had not missed the examination. He had failed it. Holländer (HH[1], p. 454) writes:

> "As a special student at the Iglau gymnasium, he passed his final examinations with the greatest difficulty and only after reëxamination in the autumn of 1877. He received good marks only in religion and philosophical propaedeutics; in all other branches his alert mind barely met the lowest requirements for a certificate of maturity in the local preparatory-school."

(In view of Mahler's exceptional literary accomplishments it is hard indeed to believe that he failed the German language exam in his matriculation.) Mahler must have made an early start (1865) at the *Volkschule* if he was to complete the minimum course of four years necessary for acceptance at the *Gymnasium*.

[14] Mahler himself wrote in a letter (GMB, p. 201): "In my seventeenth year [i.e., 1877] frequented the University of Vienna

and instead of lectures (philosophical Faculty) industriously visited the Vienna woods." Mahler could not have enrolled at the University before his matriculation, which excludes HFR's date for the latter event, i.e., autumn of 1878 (p. 114).

[15] FW, p. 42.

[16] AM[1], pp. 63–4.

[17] PS, p. 13.

[18] Which A minor sonata is not specified; there are three.

[19] Dairy farms in the vicinity of Časlau.

[20] A MS. article from Holländer, who is, however, mistaken in describing the Quartet movement as scored for two violins, viola and piano. The string ensemble comprises, in fact, the customary trio.

[21] The autograph is in the possession of Mrs. Alma Mahler, New York. A photostat of the MS. has recently been lodged with the International Gustav Mahler Society, Vienna, and this I have been able to examine through the good offices of the Society's President, Professor Erwin Ratz, to whom I owe a special debt of gratitude for the promptness with which he sent me these important documents. (See also Chapter IV[(c), pp. 123–8.) The existence of the autograph has for some time been recorded in an invaluable compilation: O. E. Albrecht's *A Census of Autograph Music Manuscripts of European Composers in American Libraries*, Philadelphia, 1953, p. 177, which also lists certain other Mahler MSS. relevant to our study of his early years, though by no means all of those recorded in the table of early works on pp. 116–20. See also Plate VII; and n. 116 *10*, p. 300.

[22] HFR, p. 114, who was, perhaps, following Stefan's hint, PS[O], pp. 29–30.

[23] e.g., PS, p. 14 (who, however, warns us (p. 15) that the Conservatoire's annual reports "are not all too trustworthy"; and see n. 22 above); RS[2], p. 46. NBL, p. 39, refers to a piano Quintet among Mahler's early works with no specific reference to its first movement. GA, p. 96, allots no Quintet first movement to 1876 and mentions no prize. GE, p. 17, on the other hand, writes of a "piano quartet and quintet, both awarded prizes by the faculty", but gives no sources.

[24] Though HFR may be right in assuming the Quintet of 1876 to be a piano Quartet, he is mistaken in deducing from this speculative conclusion that the Scherzo, too, belonged to a piano Quartet (p. 114); as the Conservatoire records show, this movement, without doubt, was designed for piano Quintet. Pamer (Vol. XVI, p. 116, see IV/n. 146 below) makes the opposite mistake when he writes that a piano Quintet earned the prizes in both 1876 and 1878.

[25] PS, p. 14.

[26] Adolfo Salazar, *Music in Our Time*, trans. Isabel Pope, London, 1948, p. 54.

[27] GA, p. 96.

[28] LK, pp. 99-100; for further on Hirschfeld, see Paul Stefan, *Gustav Mahlers Erbe: Ein Beitrag zur Neuesten Geschichte der deutschen Bühne und des Herrn Felix von Weingartner*, Munich, 1908, pp. 6-7, 45-9; AM, p. 360, note to p. 49, and preface p. xxxv.

[29] GMB, p. 11.

[30] *Grove*, 4th edtn., Vol. IV, p. 547.

[31] See PS, pp. 14-15. Perhaps the fact of attending lectures on the history of music at the University obviated Mahler's attendance at lectures on the same subject at the Conservatoire. A mistranslation in PS, p. 14, obscures Stefan's meaning. For: "he also heard lectures on the history of music", read: "he is also said to have heard lectures on the history of music, but . . ." (see PS°, p. 27.)

[32] GA, p. 96.

[33] PS, p. 14; and see n. 14, above.

[34] FW, p. 19.

[35] *The Memoirs of Carl Flesch*, trans. Hans Keller, London, 1956, p. 22.

[36] Flesch, *op. cit.*, pp. 23-4.

[37] Flesch, *op. cit.*, p. 24.

[38] GA, p. 11.

[39] Flesch, *op. cit.*, p. 24.

[40] See pp. 131-4.

[41] GAWW, p. 8.

[42] PS, p. 13.

[43] PS, p. 13.

[44] FW, pp. 43-4.

[45] Stefan, evidently without knowledge of the GdM letter, writes correctly (PS, p. 13), "Mahler, too [like Hugo Wolf], once conducted himself 'insubordinately', and the same punishment [i.e., expulsion] was not so far distant for him". The letter, however, suggests that Mahler, so to say, expelled himself and was afterwards repentant, though it may well have been that Hellmesberger did not react favourably to Mahler's threat; perhaps the director seriously considered taking Mahler at his word. Engel's statement (GE, p. 16) that Mahler was never in "open conflict with the authorities" is a little misleading in view of Mahler's implied resignation and the apologetic recantation which presumably earned him his reinstatement.

[46] The letter is undated but ascribed to a qualified 1876 by an archivist's hand. There is no documentary reason to connect Mahler's and Wolf's acts of rebellion, though it is tempting to try so to do.

[47] HFR, p. 278; hence Mahler's prize-winning performance of a Schubert sonata in 1876 doubtless mirrored the taste of his teacher.

[48] GMB, p. 11; see n. 13, above.

[49] GMB, p. 12.

[50] PS, p. 15; Stefan writes in the present tense because Epstein was still alive. Epstein did not die until 1926; it is odd to think that Mahler was long outlived by two of his teachers at the Conservatoire (Epstein and Fuchs).

[51] Flesch, *op. cit.*, p. 27 (see n. 35, above).

[52] PS, p. 13.

[53] GA, p. 96.

[54] HFR, p. 280, and RML, pp. 680-1.

[55] FW, p. 41.

[56] PS, p. 15.

[57] FW, pp. 43-4.

[58] R. Specht, *Johannes Brahms*, Dresden, 1928, trans. E. Blom, London, 1930; quoted in FW, p. 85. HH[1], p. 459.

[59] GA, pp. 10-11.

[60] PS, p. 18.

[61] AM¹, pp. 140-1.

[62] FW, pp. 22-3. See, however, pp. 62-3, p. 146, for further thoughts on this topic.

[63] FW, p. 121. See also Ernest Newman, *The Life of Richard Wagner*, London, 1947, Vol. IV, pp. 591-3, for a lengthy *précis* of the views unfolded by Wagner in this essay and its various pendants.

[64] GMB, pp. 14-15; trans. in FW, p. 121.

[65] FW, p. 121. See also Newman, *op. cit.*, pp. 592-3, who, condensing Wagner, writes:

> "There is no virtue in, no hope for, any but a 'pure' race, of which the German could be the shining exemplar if it would only rid itself of the Jews. . . . He [Wagner] had been appalled by the 'levity', the 'frivolity', of the so-called statesmen who, in 1871, had decreed 'the equalization of all German citizens, without regard to differences of "confession"'. This 'conferment of full right upon the Jews to regard themselves in every conceivable respect as Germans' seems to Wagner on a par with the rule in Mexico that the possession of a blanket authorizes a black to consider himself a white.
>
> "The Germans, of course, are by nature the flower of humankind: to fulfil their great destiny they have only to restore their sullied racial purity, or at all events to achieve 'a real rebirth of racial feeling'."

And so on. Mahler, naturally, could not be expected to have swallowed this non-vegetarian part of Wagner's programme.

[66] FW, p. 23.

[67] Newman, *op. cit.*, p. 426.

[68] FW, p. 25.

[69] Newman, *op. cit.*, p. 426.

[70] FW, p. 27.

[71] Salvatore Marchesi (1822-1908) and his wife (1821-1913) taught at the Vienna Conservatoire from 1869-81.

[72] Newman, *op. cit.*, pp. 444-6.

[73] Newman, *op. cit.*, p. 448.

[74] Mahler, then, *c.* 1879, could hardly have been regretting "a

fine performance" of *Tristan* that he was unable to attend, as is suggested in GE, p. 27.

[75] These Wagner statistics for Vienna may prove of interest. They come from Alfred Loewenberg, *Annals of Opera, 1597–1940,* Cambridge, 1943.

Tristan: 1st Vienna perf. 4.x.1883 (c. Richter).
Die Meistersinger: 1st Vienna perf. 27.ii.1870.

Das Rheingold: 1st Vienna perf. 24.i.1878.
Die Walküre: 1st Vienna perf. 5.iii.1877.
Siegfried: 1st Vienna perf. 9.xi.1878.
Götterdämmerung: 1st Vienna perf. 14.ii.1879.
   1st Vienna perf. of the *Ring* as a cycle: 26.30/v.1879.

Der fliegende Holländer: 1st Vienna perf. 2.xi.1860.
Tannhäuser: 1st Vienna perf. 28.viii.1857. 1st perf. Paris version
   in Vienna 22.xi.1875.
Lohengrin: 1st Vienna perf. 19.viii.1858.
Rienzi: 1st Vienna perf. 30.v.1871.

[76] FW, p. 33, quotes an extract from Wolf's diary that not only introduces a Wagner item but also illuminates the musical activities of the Conservatoire's staff:

"Wednesday, 9th February 1876, concert by Marie Baumayer, with the assistance of Herren Hellmesberger and Wallnöfer. Hellmesberger and Baumayer played the A major Sonata of Bach. Wallnöfer sang Bach, Brahms, and finally a song from *Die Walküre,* which was magnificent. In conclusion Baumayer and Epstein played the *Hungarian Fantasy* with great success."

[Adolf Wallnöfer, born in 1854, was a Viennese singer. He had been a composition pupil of Franz Krenn.]

[77] In 1880, for example, at Maierling, Wolf, in bad weather, "used to play to his house companions for hours on end. We hear no more about Brahms, but a good deal about Wagner; the *Ring,* *Die Meistersinger,* and *Tristan,* of which the last had not yet been produced in Vienna, were performed by Wolf from the piano

scores" (FW, p. 103). NBL, p. 2, remembers a performance on the piano of the prelude to *Die Meistersinger* by the student Mahler. As Gerald Abraham pertinently observes, "... it is probably true to say that genuine understanding of Wagner was really only hammered out on the domestic pianos of Germany during the 'sixties and 'seventies" (*A Hundred Years of Music*, 2nd edtn., London, 1949, p. 131). But "genuine understanding" should not be taken to mean immediate stylistic assimilation by even the most enthusiastic of the young Wagnerian composers.

[78] See DN, pp. 1-13.

[79] In rather the same way, some of us have found our way back to Wagner through Mahler. Mahler's creative appreciation of Wagner, expressed in terms readily assimilable by contemporary and almost inevitably anti-Wagnerian ears, has helped us to recognize Wagner's specific genius. Mahler's far-sighted interpretation of his influential model has, as it were, prepared us for a better understanding of Wagner's achievement.

[80] FW, p. 33.

[81] FW, p. 31.

[82] FW, pp. 21-2, 30-2.

[83] FW, p. 20.

[84] A great deal of information about Vienna's concert life at this time may be found in R. von Perger, *Fünfzig Jahre Wiener Philharmoniker, 1860-1910*, Vienna and Leipzig, 1910. This work contains an invaluable statistical supplement.

[85] FW, p. 82.

[86] FW, p. 83.

[87] Mr. Walker points out that the address is now Weimarerstrasse, Vienna, XIX.

[88] HH², pp. 808-9.

[89] FW, p. 92.

[90] See n. 75, above.

[91] AM¹, p. 63; see also FW, p. 83, and n. 94 below.

[92] See HFR, p. 115; and my review of HFR in the *Musical Times*, June 1956, pp. 303-4.

[93] See FW, p. 83 and p. 106, n. 1.

[94] See, however, Chapter IV (*l*), pp. 139-40. Mr. Walker per-

tinently suggests in a private communication that "the best argument against the acceptance of Mrs. Mahler's story as something that occurred at this time would be that at that season of the year it would be too d——d cold for anyone to sleep on benches in the Ringstrasse"; but one cannot discount the possibility of a warm night in the early part of 1879 if Mahler and Wolf in fact lodged together for the "few months" mentioned by Mrs. Mahler.

[95] AM¹, p. 64.

[96] FW, pp. 130-1.

[97] AM¹, p. 63; Mahler was twenty when he accepted his first engagement, not eighteen as Mrs. Mahler states.

[98] To my knowledge, curious though it may appear as a biographical fact, Mahler only once visited Bayreuth and never conducted there, despite his eminence as a conductor of Wagner's operas. (Mrs Mahler (AM¹, p. 12) writes that "Cosima Wagner ... could not tolerate a Jew as director of the Opera in Vienna", wherein, I imagine, rests the explanation of Mahler's non-invitation to conduct at Bayreuth.) His solitary visit there occurred in July 1883, when he heard *Parsifal* at the *Festspielhaus* (see PS, p. 22, and GMB, p. 22). We know that Wolf heard *Parsifal* at Bayreuth at the same time (see FW, p. 141), and it may have been then that the incident took place to which Mrs. Mahler refers. If so, Mrs. Mahler's "many years later" needs adjustment— possibly her memory or her husband's played her false—and the Wolf-Mahler friendship cooled off more rapidly than is supposed (they are presumed still to have been on speaking terms in 1882). If not, then Bayreuth was not the place where their estrangement was given overt expression.

[99] 'Gustav Mahler and Hugo Wolf', *Chord and Discord*, New York, 1948, pp. 40-6; the biographical part of this article is now not to be trusted.

[100] *Musikwissenschaftlicher Verlag*, Leipzig and Vienna, 1936.

[101] Schumann, clearly, was a particularly prominent model in the conception of Mahler's and Wolf's first songs.

[102] Mahler, of course, was one of its major exponents, and I have more to say on the subject when it crops up, as part of the

discussion of his music. Ironic (or "Mahlerian") songs of Wolf that I have in mind are, for example:

Mörike Lieder

Der Tambour	*Nimmersatte Liebe*
Bei einer Trauung	*Nixe Binsefuss*
Auftrag	*Abschied*

Italienisches Liederbuch

Selig ihr Blinden	*Mein Liebster ist so klein*
Wie lange schon	*Hoffärtig seid Ihr, schönes Kind*

Goethe Lieder

Ritter Kurts Brautfahrt	*Cophtisches Lied II*
Gutmann und Gutweib	*Der Rattenfänger*
Genialisch Treiben	

Spanisches Liederbuch

Sie blasen zum Abmarsch	*Auf einem grünen Balkon*
Wer tat deinem Füsslein weh?	*Wer sein holdes Lieb verloren*

Eichendorff Lieder

Der Schreckenberger	*Der Musikant*

[103] FW, p. 415; see also NBL, p. 85, who records Wolf's profound admiration of Mahler's *Ring* performances in Vienna.

[104] AM[1], p. 177.

[105] AM[1], p. 239.

[106] See FW, pp. 83-7. Altogether, Brahms seems to have played an influential rôle behind the scenes in Vienna's musical life and to have crossed the paths, sometimes rather irascibly so, of many of the younger generation's rising talents. A study that measured his contribution to Viennese musical politics of his day would not come amiss.

[107] GA, p. 17. The occasion was a performance in Budapest of Mozart's *Don Giovanni*; Brahms thought it the best yet he had heard.

[108] BW[1], p. 93; AM, p. 138.

[109] AM[1], p. 236.

[110] AM[1], p. 238.

[111] NBL, p. 121.

[112] NBL, p. 133.

[113] Peter Latham, *Brahms*, London, 1948, pp. 39-40.

[114] AM[1], p. 239.

[115] NBL, p. 16. Mahler prophesied in the same conversation that posterity would have little love or understanding of Bruckner; his fears have scarcely been realized, especially in Austria and Germany, though there some of the motives promoting Bruckner's posthumous triumph would have confounded a more positive prophet, even had he been gifted with foresight.

[116] HFR, p. 12.

[117] HFR, pp. 12-17.

[118] HFR, p. 19.

[119] Romain Rolland, for example, in *Musicians of To-day*, trans. Mary Blaiklock, London, n.d., p. 219, writes that Mahler was "a pupil of Anton Bruckner at Vienna". The rumour was widespread in Mahler's lifetime. RS[3], p. 14, published in 1905, makes a point of stressing its untruth.

[120] GE, p. 21. His source is Max Auer, 'Bruckner and Mahler', trans. G. Engel, in *Bruckner-Blätter*, a publication of the *Internationale Bruckner-Gesellschaft*, Vienna, 1931, nos. 2–3. Auer states that the letter is unpublished and dates from 1902.

[121] Flesch, *op. cit.*, p. 27 (see n. 35, above).

[122] PS[O], p. 28.

[123] GE, p. 20.

[124] AM[1], p. 107.

[125] GA, p. 97.

[126] PS, p. 15.

[127] Werner Wolf, *Anton Bruckner, Rustic Genius*, New York, 1942, p. 81.

[128] Max Auer, *Bruckner*, Zürich-Leipzig-Vienna, 1923, pp. 177-9.

[129] See Auer, *op. cit.*, pp. 178-9, who attributes the piano-duet version to both Mahler and Krzyzanowski (the latter was Bruckner's organ pupil at the Conservatoire in 1877-8). PS, however (p. 16), makes no mention of the latter's contribution,

nor does GA (p. 97). How the honours are distributed on the printed edition, I do not know; I have not succeeded in tracking one down. DN, p. 106, tells us that Mahler's reduction "represents a more genuine version of Bruckner's original thought than the later 'cut' version".

130 PS, p. 16.

131 AM¹, p. 107.

132 Such facts tend to weaken one's confidence in the authenticity of reported conversation.

133 AM¹, p. 107; AMᴼ, p. 136. See also n. 69ᴵ, p. 293.

134 PS, p. 16.

135 For the subsequent history of the score, a page from which is reproduced in AMᴼ, between pp. 320-1, see HFR, p. 118, n. 1.

136 AM¹, p. 107.

137 PS, p. 16.

138 AM¹, p. 107.

139 PS, p. 15.

140 EK, p. 165.

141 Quoted in GE, p. 51, without source, whose source is Bruckner, *Briefe* (see n. 143 below), p. 329.

142 Respectively, 15 April 1892 (and again in 1893); 31 March 1893; 18 February 1895. HFR, p. 118, writes that Symphony IV was the work performed in 1895, but Symphony III, as given by Auer, *op. cit.*, p. 327 (see n. 128 above), seems more probable; he also appears to have the wrong date for Mahler's performance of the Mass (cf. Auer, p. 300).

143 These documents are quoted in DN, pp. 106-7; their source is Anton Bruckner, *Gesammelte Briefe*, Regensburg, 1924, Vol. II, pp. 329-30, and 387-8. I doubt whether Herr Zinne understood Mahler's "nervous" approach to Mozart.

144 AM¹, pp. 135-6.

145 Respectively on 28 January 1900; 24 February 1901.

146 HFR, p. 118.

147 AM¹, p. 108.

148 AM¹, p. 176. It is a matter of unfortunate fact that, in Austria and Germany between the wars, racial politics were as much bound up with Bruckner's canonization as with Mahler's

suppression—hence Mahler's relation to Bruckner has never received a fair measure of appreciation. Traces of the old feud smoulder on: in as recent a work as Alfred Orel's *Bruckner Brevier*, Vienna, 1953, Mahler's name is scarcely mentioned, and mentioned not at all in the comprehensive list of major and minor personalities who played a rôle in Bruckner's life.

[149] See AM[1], pp. 339-42.

[150] AM[1], p. 108.

[151] EK, pp. 162-3.

[152] A substantial body of serious opinion considers that the Austrian composer Franz Schmidt (1874-1939) was the last, but by no means the least, of musicians writing in the great Austro-German symphonic tradition. He has four symphonies to his credit.

[153] PS, p. 16.

III (1878-1880)

[1] PS, p. 19; HH[1], p. 451; GMB, p. 475, n. 17; NBL, p. 147.

[2] GMB, p. 492; p. 14, n. *.

[3] See p. 8.

[4] FW, pp. 92-3.

[5] FW, p. 112.

[6] EJ, I, p. 277, p. 245.

[7] American Columbia ML. 4295. It is impossible to give a meaningful impression of Mahler's playing on this disc. Perhaps two comments on his tempi—really the most interesting aspect of the performance—will convey something of the significance of this fascinating document. First, his tempi, while uniquely— incredibly—flexible (from the first bar onwards), are, none the less, strict where almost all other conductors of this movement, within my experience, are free (to the music's detriment, I have realized, since hearing Mahler's conception). Secondly, and arising out of the foregoing observation, his tempi, to a quite unprecedented degree, are an expression of the movement's structure. If Mahler conducted Beethoven, Wagner, or Mozart from as far inside the music as he conducted his own—hence the

startling clarity of this finale's outward shape—small wonder at his fame as an interpretative genius. Finally, let me testify to the character and immense verve of his piano playing, which reveals a rusty but commanding technique still capable of flashes of real pianistic brilliance. It may seem superfluous to write of the feeling that charges Mahler's performance, but I must point to the almost painful tenderness which steals into his playing with the onset of the E major concluding section, *Kein Musik ist ja nicht auf Erden*. It creates a luminous texture which shines through even the crippling technical defects of this antique method of recording.

[8] PS, pp. 18-19. There are no grounds, to my knowledge, for Engel's suggestion (GE, p. 17) that Epstein—Mahler's piano teacher at the Conservatoire—"purposely overlooked in this youth the possibilities of a world-stirring pianist, lest the exacting drudgery of scales and etudes take too great a toll of precious time that should be devoted to higher artistic purposes". Assuming these circumstances, surely his prize-winning career at the Conservatoire under Epstein's tuition was a peculiar form of purposeful neglect?

[9] GMB, pp. 473-4, n. 13.

[10] See IV/n. 10: the date of the orchestral version may be much later than the date of the cycle itself; and some sort of case could be made out for the instrumental mastery of *Das klagende Lied*, which preceded the cycle by almost four years.

[11] NBL, p. 2.

[12] Alfred Rosé, 'From Gustav Mahler's Storm and Stress Period', *Canadian Music Journal*, Winter, 1957, p. 21.

[13] NBL, p. 39: the entry is dated 21 June 1896.

[14] BW², p. 28; BW¹, p. 36.

[15] BW¹, p. 28.

[16] PS, p. 39.

[17] GMB, pp. 5-10.

[18] I have in my possession a postcard of Mahler's, addressed to Steiner in Vienna, dated 29 September 1876.

[19] GMB, p. 8, n. *. Grove V (p. 516) is mistaken in attributing the text to Mahler himself, following, perhaps, Pamer (Vol. XVI, p. 119, see IV/n. 146 below).

[20] See BW¹, pp. 61-2; BGM, pp. 26-7.

[21] GMB, p. 9; trans. DN, p. 111. "O meine vielgeliebte Erde" ('Oh my beloved earth') pre-echoes the climatic "Die liebe Erde" of *Das Lied*'s *Abschied*.

[22] DN, p. 112.

[23] HH², p. 810.

[24] Letter to Steiner; GMB, pp. 5-6; trans. DN, p. 111.

[25] Letter to Steiner; GMB, p. 5; trans. DN, p. 111.

[26] Trans. GE, p. 26.

[27] Presumably a leading motive associated with the opera's title figure. A few lines earlier Mahler writes of a "Song of Yearning" (*Das Lied der Sehnsucht*) ringing in his ears, which might be a reference to another part of the opera's music.

[28] GMB, pp. 7-8.

[29] PS, p. 19.

[30] GMB, pp. 9-10; trans. GE, p. 26.

[31] GMB, p. 6; trans. DN, p. 111. GMB, p. 10; trans. GE, p. 26.

[32] PS, p. 17.

[33] GMB, pp. 461-3.

[34] AM¹, p. 112.

[35] AM¹, p. 243. Adler co-founded the Wagner Society with Mottl and Karl Wolf. Mr. Erwin Stein, an unrivalled authority on the *minutiae* of the Mahler era, has confirmed that Mahler's attitude to Adler as a musicologist was scarcely an exalted one. Mr. Stein also contributes a further item of Adleriana apropos Schoenberg's first Chamber Symphony (1906): Adler was indignant at the introduction of the piccolo into 'chamber music'.

[36] LS, p. 14, n. *; PS⁰, p. 70.

[37] GE, p. 90, p. 114.

[38] PS, p. 15; GA, pp. 38-40; GAWW, pp. 95-100.

[39] See GMB, p. 472, n. 2.

[40] GdM¹. In AM only one brother is mentioned, and he is wrongly identified in the index as Heinrich. He is, without doubt, Rudolf (AM¹). Mrs. Mahler herself refers to the Kryzzanowski concerned as one of three "musicians" (AM¹, p. 63).

[41] HFR, p. 281, offers a queried 1859; RML, p. 687, 1862.

Whichever date is correct, Rudolf was almost an exact contemporary of Mahler's. See also GMB, p. 473, n. 8; and n. 93 *31*, pp. 295-6.

[42] See pp. 104-5, below.

[43] See GMB, p. 96 and pp. 123-4.

[44] At one time it appears that Löhr was going to collaborate with Bruno Walter in a book about Mahler; see PS⁰, p. 166.

[45] HFR, p. 281.

[46] HH², p. 807; HH¹, p. 455.

[47] GMB, p. 14.

[48] HFR, p. 282.

[49] HFR, p. 115.

[50] NBL, p. 137.

[51] AM¹, p. 107.

[52] AM¹, p. 8.

[53] NBL, p. 104; see also p. 148.

[54] One would expect the mother's feelings towards her son to display some of that ambivalence we have noted in the son's feelings towards his mother. See p. 8 and n. 101 in I, above.

[55] AM¹, p. 9.

[56] HFR, pp. 115-16.

[57] HFR, p. 116, n. 1.

[58] DN, p. 211.

[59] See BW³, pp. 159-63.

[60] GMB, pp. 279-87.

[61] DN, p. 120; see also H. F. Redlich, *Gustav Mahler*, Nuremberg, 1919, pp. 12-14.

[62] GMB, pp. 214-15; trans. DN, p. 121; see also BW¹, pp. 36-7.

[63] Erich Heller, *The Disinherited Mind*, Cambridge, 1952, pp. 105-6.

[64] NBL, p. 20.

[65] BW³, p. 93; BW¹, p. 118.

[66] AM¹, pp. 18-19.

[67] AM¹, p. 225.

[68] BW¹, p. 118.

[69] BW³, p. 162.

[70] AM¹, pp. 25-6; for a friendlier view of him, see BW³, pp. 159-63.

[71] DN, p. 122.

[72] PS, pp. 49-51.

[73] Trans. in DN, p. 122; see also BW³, pp. 162-3. In a letter to his wife written from Toblach in June 1909 Mahler refers to his happiness at having cleared away whatever cloud it was marring his friendship with Lipiner (AM⁰, p. 435); thus the reconciliation was effected, or at least prepared, somewhat earlier than is suggested in BW³, pp. 162-3. There is no doubt that Mahler esteemed Lipiner highly and that their estrangement was a grief to him. PS, p. 18, recording Mahler's affection for Lipiner, writes that he "constantly returned to this youthful friendship": even to the extent of returning to it after he had left it.

[74] GMB, p. 13.

[75] See pp. 55-6.

[76] In HH², pp. 812-13, this letter has no year, but Wolf's letter of December 1879 (FW, p. 92) enables us to place it decisively in 1879.

[77] HH², p. 809.

[78] See p. 88.

[79] NBL, p. 104.

[80] HH¹, p. 454.

[81] PS, p. 20.

[82] GMB, p. 415, trans. BW¹, p. 131.

[83] GMB, p. 461; trans. GE, p. 115.

[84] Communication from H. F. Redlich.

[85] PS, p. 21.

[86] HH¹, p. 455. See Plate VI(b).

[87] These details of Mahler's appointment at Bad Hall are to be found in Baldrian, *op. cit.* (see n. 3 in II, above).

[88] Baldrian, *op. cit.* (see n. 3 in II, above). I query Mrs. Mahler's description of Zwerenz as director of the theatre since Baldrian states that Viktor Berthal was director when Mahler was conductor, and Baldrian has doubtless examined the theatre's archives. It seems clear that Zwerenz was not in charge of the *Kurtheater* but director of the company that played there. See also HG, p. 76.

[89] AM¹, pp. 108-9.

[90] In various letters, Lewy's name is variously spelt—e.g.,

Löwy, Levi, Löwi—but the same well-known theatrical and concert agent was the recipient, Gustav Lewy.

[91] See p. 23.

[92] PS, p. 21; while conducting at Bad Hall, Mahler lived in Pfarrkirchen, a village south-west of the Spa.

[93] GA, p. 12.

[94] AM[1], p. 109; AM[O], pp. 138–9.

[95] GMB, p. 15.

[96] GMB, p. 14; trans. GE, p. 30.

[97] GMB, pp. 14-15; see also pp. 48-9.

[98] PS, p. 17.

[99] PS, p. 201.

[100] DN, p. 162.

[101] AM[1], p. 43. There is, on the other hand, the testament of Bruno Walter, e.g., "He had a warm feeling for all living things and felt a loving concern for dogs, cats, birds, and all the creatures of the woods. He watched them with sympathy and understanding . . ." (BW[1], p. 35). I am sure Mahler's feeling for animals was profound—much more than theoretical; but when they disturbed his meditations or his composing, he was ruthless in exterminating the sources of disturbance. When Mahler required Nature creatively, the degree of sympathetic identification was undeniably intensive; when Nature—in possibly the very same manifestation—hindered his creativity, he stamped out the intrusion quite dispassionately. There is no paradox here: merely a logical subservience, in either case, to the needs of his creative ego. Mahler did not, it is true, shoot, or shoot at, noisy humans; but we know of the persistent war he waged against trespassers upon his creative peace from Bauer-Lechner (pp. 37-8); and clangorous children, despite Mahler's well-known devotion to children, were as unwelcome as vocal dogs, cats, hens, or geese. Mahler, of course, like most major artists, was an exacting egotist and totalitarian: it would be a gross error to consider him a combination of St. Francis and Dr. Barnardo.

[102] PS, p. 17.

[103] BW[3], p. 93.

[104] *Encyclopædia Britannica.*

[105] Karl Ekman, *Jean Sibelius, His Life and Personality*, trans. Edward Birse, London, 1926, p. 176.

[106] GA, p. 97.

IV *The Early Works*

[1] See also n. 21 in II, above.

[2] I am indebted to private communications from Mr. Alfred Rosé for many of the data contained within this table.

[3] GA, p. 97; RS[2], p. 48, offers 1900. The publishers, "from the printing", assume the year of publication to be 1900, though in the *Catalogue of the Paul Hirsch Music Library*, Cambridge, 1947, 2nd Series, Vol. IV, p. 305, the work is dated 1902. But there seems no doubt that the cantata was in print before its *première* in 1901. See n. 8 below.

[4] GA, pp. 75-6.

[5] NBL, pp. 106-7.

[6] NBL, pp. 106-7; AN, p. 67.

[7] GA, p. 97. See also p. 152.

[8] See N. Slonimsky, *Music Since 1900*, 3rd edtn., New York, 1949, pp. 14-15. The year is also confirmed in GMB, p. 273, letter to Bruno Walter, Vienna, February 1901. Mrs. Mahler, remembering a performance of *Das klagende Lied* in Vienna, propagates a misleading date, 12 January 1902, in AM[1], p. 30, the date upon which Symphony IV received its Vienna *première*; but *Das klagende Lied* was not part of the programme of that concert, as Mrs. Mahler states, but of an Extraordinary Concert of the *Wiener Singakademie* held a few days later, on 20 January, when Symphony IV was *repeated* and *Das klagende Lied* received its *second* performance in Vienna; both works were conducted by the composer. Richard v. Perger's *Fünfzig Jahre Wiener Philharmoniker, 1860-1910*, Vienna and Leipzig, 1910, pp. 86-7, a valuable source of data about performances in Vienna from this period, lists the details of the cantata's *première* (1901) and its second performance (1902). The soloists on the first occasion were: Elise Elizza, Anna v. Mildenburg, Edith Walker (it is

surprising to find a famous American singer participating in a Mahler *première* in Vienna, but she was, of course, a prominent soloist with a big European reputation) and Fritz Schrödter. The chorus was assembled from the *Singakademie* and *Schubert-bund*. At the second performance Schrödter was not one of the soloists; his place was taken by Erik Schmedes, while Hermine Kittel reinforced the ladies.

⇨ [9] NBL, p. 30; PS°, p. 56; the first performance of the cycle, according to E. O. Nodnagel, *Jenseits von Wagner und Liszt,* Königsberg, 1902, p. 6. It is probable that he meant the first performance of the orchestral version, thus indirectly supporting NBL (see n. 10, below). It is scarcely possible to believe that the songs were not performed with piano, somewhere or other, before the Berlin *première* in 1896. RS³, pp. 15-16, allots the cycle (with orchestra) to 1883, but this is a poorly documented date which does not fit any set of facts.

[10] It has been widely assumed that the *Lieder eines fahrenden Gesellen* were conceived as an orchestral song-cycle, not as a cycle with piano. Doubt is thrown on this assumption by NBL, p. 30, who writes quite unequivocally that Mahler instrumented the songs, and gave them their first performance in this guise, for the Berlin concert of his own music on 16 March 1896.

⇨ There is no autograph MS. available of the orchestral score, hence the point cannot be settled without further investigation. Mr. A. Rosé possesses a MS. of the songs in a piano version, which he describes as follows (I had passed on to him my query arising from the statement in NBL):

> "I do not know the date of the orchestral version of the *Lieder eines fahrenden Gesellen*, but I feel that it was originally conceived for orchestra since Mahler in my copy specifically notes *Clavierauszug zu 2 Händen.* On the front page we actually find the title:
>
> *Geschichte von einem fahrenden Gesellen in 4 Gesängen*
> *für eine tiefe Stimme mit Begleitung des Orchesters*
> *von Gustav Mahler.*
>
> Then follows: *Lieder des fahrenden Gesellen—ein Cyclus.* I think my autograph is the first clean original piano reduction of the

original orchestral score. I do not think that Mahler waited 12 years before orchestrating a work that he so obviously conceived instrumentally."

One must, of course, respect Mr. Rosé's opinion. Unfortunately, although his MS discloses some fascinating information (e.g., the evolution of the title as we know it today—note that the four *Gesänge* became *Lieder* in the final version), it does not help us out with dates. In the absence of precise documentation, it is my view that we cannot altogether exclude the possibility that Bauer-Lechner's facts are correct. It has often struck me as odd that Mahler, having presumably composed a cycle for voice and orchestra, returned to songs with piano accompaniment (in the two later books of the *Jugendzeit Lieder*, which were written *after* the *Gesellen* cycle). It would make more sense if the latter had been conceived with piano, with the perfection of its later instrumental guise emerging from Mahler's experience in Symphony I (with which instrumental style the cycle has much more to do than that of *Das klagende Lied*, the cycle's closest and most relevant predecessor). This chronology is absolutely straightforward, providing NBL's information is accurate. Another odd aspect of the matter is the cycle's long-postponed publication; nothing happened in this sphere between 1885 and 1897 (a copy of the copyright contract in my possession, signed by Mahler, is dated Vienna, 27 September 1897), during which period all three books of the *Jugendzeit Lieder* appeared in print, songs composed both before and after the *Gesellen* cycle. Yet within a few months of the Berlin concert—which admittedly drew attention to the cycle—a publisher was found. Could it be that it was the orchestral version which did the trick?

[11] GE, p. 13; PS⁰, p. 29: "But for the *Klagende Lied*, he destroyed everything."

[12] PS, p. 13.

[13] See p. 19.

[14] PS, p. 16.

[15] NBL, p. 39, p. 66.

[16] GA, pp. 96-7.

[17] See p. 157.

[18] PS°, pp. 29-30.

[19] H. T. O. Graedener (in some sources Grädener), 1844-1929, German violinist, composer, teacher and organist. He was Bruckner's successor at the University of Vienna and also taught harmony and counterpoint at the Conservatoire.

[20] Th. Billroth was a famous Viennese physician, a close friend of Brahms's, and a well-known amateur musician and chamber-music player.

[21] NBL, p. 39.

[22] See p. 39.

[23] PS°, p. 29.

[24] GA, pp. 96-7.

[25] HFR, p. 172.

[26] GA, pp. 96-7.

[27] TR, pp. 315-20.

[28] In a personal communication.

[29] Another version of the Conservatoire rehearsal was given by Heinrich Schlosser, Neue Zürcher Zeitung, 22 May 1911, quoted in Die Musik, Berlin, 1910-11, no. 18, p. 384; but there the prize-winning substitute was a string Quintet, not a Suite for piano. Could the Quintet have anything to do with (l) below? It seems highly improbable. This is the only mention known to me of a *string* Quintet by Mahler.

[30] NBL, p. 1.

[31] NBL, p. 39.

[32] See, however, n. 29, above.

[33] NBL, p. 1.

[34] GA, p. 98.

[35] RS³, p. 17.

[36] PS°, p. 104.

[37] PS, p. 21.

[38] Perhaps he may. Mahler seems to have read the book in advance of publication and would surely have objected to a statement of this kind had it been without foundation? See GMB, pp. 261-2.

[39] RS³, p. 17.

[40] HH², p. 813.

[41] See pp. 57–8. Redlich is mistaken in implying (HFR, p. 172) that Wolf thought specifically of *Rübezahl*. The choice was the result of mutual discussion of the fairy-opera idea, which *was* Wolf's own, if Mrs. Mahler's account (AM¹, p. 64) is correct.

[42] A remark of Mahler's to Bruno Walter about Humperdinck's *Hänsel und Gretel*—"masterly in execution, but not really a fairy tale" (BW¹, p. 19)—gives us a negative clue to *Rübezahl*'s character. Probably Mahler's fairy tale was more fantastic and less cosily sophisticated than Humperdinck's.

[43] HH¹, p. 456. See also HFR, *op. cit.* (n. 61 in III, above), pp. 8-12, who rightly testifies to Mahler's Weber heritage but heavily overestimates the actual influence of Weber upon the style of the early works, in particular upon *Das klagende Lied*.

[44] HFR, p. 172.

[45] A. Loewenberg, *op. cit.* (n. 75 in II, above), p. 231, p. 657.

[46] GMB, p. 473, n. 9.

[47] GMB, p. 25 and n. *.

[48] NBL, p. 104.

[49] FW, p. 130.

[50] GMB, pp. 196-7. See also a post-1900 mention of the work in BGM, p. 12.

[51] See AM¹, pp. 143-4, and AMᵒ, p. 417, n. *.

[52] AM¹, p. 63.

[53] See, however, n. 29, above.

[54] FW, p. 83.

[55] HFR is wide of the mark (p. 115) in relating this *Quartettsatz* to the piano Quartet movement of 1876.

[56] PS, p. 51.

[57] LK, p. 131.

[58] DN, p. 115.

[59] PS, p. 91.

[60] GA, p. 76.

[61] HFR, p. 174.

[62] GE, p. 23.

[63] E. O. Nodnagel, *op. cit.* (n. 9, above), p. 191.

[64] BW¹, p. 85.

[65] GdM¹. It is perhaps worth mentioning that Hans Holländer, who was involved in the Brno performance of the cantata's unpublished first part, has suggested that Mahler may have heard the fairy tale as a child—"he was deeply impressed, so it is said, by the fairy stories told him by a kitchen maid in a neighbour's house"—before "his later reading of Bechstein's collection . . . brought about the final establishment of the plot". (From a MS. article.) In HH¹, p. 453, we learn that Mahler would have had the fratricidal character of the tale stressed early on, since it appears that he heard it from the servant as a "Ballade vom Brudermord". (The Bechstein version offers a brother and sister.)

[66] L. Bechstein, *Neues deutsches Märchenbuch*, Leipzig and Pesth, 1856, no. 3, *Das klagende Lied*, pp. 16-23.

[67] *Der singende Knochen* and *Von dem Machandelboom* (nos. 28 and 47) in *Kinder- und Hausmärchen der Brüder Grimm*, Berlin, 1870, pp. 116-18 and pp. 180-8.

[68] See, however, n. 65 above.

[69] The hunting of a notorious wild boar. The flower motive does also occur in Grimm, however, in *Jorinda and Joringel*; perhaps that is why Nodnagel cited the story as a source.

[70] Oxford, 1923, pp. 436-8.

[71] The elucidation of this claim requires specialist knowledge and treatment. I much hope that a musician with the necessary psychological qualifications will take the point up. I have no doubt that he would find a comparative survey of the sources of the cantata's text and its final version most illuminating. Doubtless not only the motives behind the variants would be revealed, but also the reasons which determined Mahler's choice of fairy tale (see, too, pp. 129-30).

[72] GE, p. 23.

[73] PS, p. 90.

[74] HFR, pp. 173-4.

[75] HH², p. 808.

[76] GA, p. 76.

[77] NBL, p. 104.

78 GE, pp. 28-30.

79 LK, p. 90.

80 E. Hanslick, *Aus neuer und neuester Zeit*, Berlin, 1900, pp. 76-7. For further information of Mahler's relations with Hanslick, see LK, pp. 77-8.

81 LK, pp. 36-8, 43-6.

82 E. J. Dent, *Ferruccio Busoni, 1866-1924*, London, 1933, p. 123. There is something wrong with Dent's date. Busoni played first under Mahler in Vienna in 1899 not 1898 (Beethoven's 'Emperor' Concerto). He cannot have minded the "lesson", appearing again with Mahler in 1900, this time in Weber's *Konzertstück*. For further information of Mahler's relation with Richter, see LK, pp. 65-71, 158-66, 271-6, and BWW, pp. 186-7.

83 GMB, p. 15.

84 See GA, p. 97, PS, p. 21.

85 GMB, p. 14.

86 GdM² is the source of all my information about the sittings and constitution of the Beethoven Prize committees.

87 The other members were: Joseph Hellmesberger (the Conservatoire's director), Franz Krenn (Mahler's composition teacher!), Wilhelm Gericke, the conductor (1845-1925), Johann Nepomuk Fuchs (1842-99), teacher, conductor, and brother of the prize-winning candidate (!). My notes specify 'R.' Goldmark, but the initial must be either misprinted in the records or I misread R. for K. There can be no doubt that the Goldmark involved was Karl, the composer.

88 GA, p. 97.

89 PS, p. 21.

90 GMB, p. 201.

91 GA, p. 97.

92 NBL, pp. 106-7. It is not clear to me what Mahler meant in telling Bauer-Lechner that he had "lost" the original version of Part III (or that passage in which the two orchestras are employed). As we know, a complete autograph score of the cantata in its original form has survived, and Mahler must have been ◁ aware of its existence.

93 AN, p. 67.

[94] I am much indebted to Professor Erwin Ratz for sending me detailed information of this MS., a photostat of which is in the Vienna archives of the International Mahler Society.

[95] GA, pp. 75-6.

[96] See pp. 220-4 and n. 158 below.

[97] See. n. 158 below.

⇨   [98] Who was Kralik? He is quaintly inscribed on these pages of *Das klagende Lied* and makes a fleeting appearance in NBL, p. 2, from which it is clear that he was one of Mahler's early acquaintances. But these references apart, the record is a blank.

[99] As I have pointed out in (c) above, the autograph of the first movement of the piano Quartet (1876) is similarly disfigured, though not to the degree of *Das klagende Lied*'s FS. I am not sure that this proves Mahler's doodling to have been a long-standing habit. He may, at some later stage have used an old MS. to scribble on. The type of word inscribed on the cantata's FS reminds me very much of the improbable vocabulary of the copperplate writing books one used at school. Perhaps there is a clue here?

[100] All such references are to the published score of the revised version.

[101] NBL, p. 34; the account in GE, pp. 27-8, is a sensationalized paraphrase of Bauer-Lechner's information.

[102] Mahler is inconsistent and uses both Exx. 1 and 2 in FS; but only Ex. 2 appears in RV.

[103] See, however, p. 193, and n. 118 below.

[104] This revision, in essence, makes for instrumental consistency. The themes and motives concerned (Exx. 11 and 13 combined!) have been heard before in the winds and they are demonstrably of that instrumental character: they lie uneasily on the strings. Mahler obviously realized this himself, hence the transfer which, like so much of the revising of the cantata, simply brings a passage into line with a precedent that has its roots in SK or FS.

[105] Mahler's footnote reads: "In this passage the third trombone player must provide himself with a bass tuba to execute the bars from * to *."

[106] HFR, p. 175.

[107] EK, p. 187 and p. 189.

[108] See pp. 52-3.

[109] EK, p. 189.

[110] To be absolutely just, Křenek does appear to make some sort of distinction when, in the passage quoted on p. 169, he writes of "drawing . . . conclusions" from the early "reaction", conclusions which, one must assume, formed the basis of the (technical) "reaction" explicit in the late symphonies. None the less the history, character, and eventual metamorphosis of Křenek's reaction remain somewhat mysterious.

[111] PS, p. 90.

[112] See, for instance, Fig. 23 of the RV and also n. 104 above.

[113] DN, p. 116.

[114] Performing version of the draft by Deryck Cooke, AMP/ Faber, 1976.

[115] DN, p. 117.

[116] See n. 10 above, and the new note to nn. 9 and 10 on p. 320.

[117] This culminating unison from the soloists reminds me of some pertinent information from Mr. Erwin Stein: that Mahler in his performances, to achieve maximum power, would sometimes allot more than one soloist to a solo part (for example, in the finale of his Symphony II: it seems that four soloists (the score requires two) took part in a performance of the work in Vienna in February 1907). In the present instance, the doubling is written in; but what Mr. Stein says may very well apply to *Das klagende Lied*'s first performance in which, if the records are correct, more soloists participated than the published score demands: four to three for the *première*, five to three for the repeat performance in Vienna in January 1902. (See n. 8 above.)

[118] See p. 165. It would seem almost certain that the introduction of the soprano at this climactic point is related to the abandoned idea of having the flute sing with a boy's voice (*Knabenstimme*) at an earlier stage (in Part I); it must have eventually occurred to Mahler that this device should be reserved for the *dénouement*.

[119] DN, pp. 117-18.

[120] HFR, p. 175.

[121] EJ, II, p. 89.

[122] GMB, p. 15.

[123] GMB, p. 201.

[124] HFR, p. 172; GA, p. 97.

[125] GA, p. 97.

[126] NBL, p. 39.

[127] PS, p. 16.

[128] RML, p. 772.

[129] NBL, p. 39.

[130] Private communication.

[131] See pp. 180–1, above.

[132] PS°, p. 104. See also p. 135 above.

[133] Books II and III were composed later—probably after 1888—and published in 1892. (See GA, p. 98, p. 100.) The whereabouts of the MSS. of Books II and III are not known. The publishers thought they possessed them still, but upon inspection drew a blank. Mr. Rosé's MS. may be the original autograph of Book I. Where are the others?

[134] GdM³.

[135] GA, p. 76.

[136] See, however, n. 138 below.

[137] An entry in the Music Catalogue of the British Museum specifies "14 Lieder und Gesänge, Aus der Jugendzeit, U.E., Vienna, 1912". (G. 1033 (1.).)

[138] This title is found on the title page of the *Philharmonia* pocket score, Vienna, 1926, which acknowledges the copyright of 1905 (C. F. Kahnt's). The cover, on the other hand, possibly for the sake of brevity, offers *Sieben letzte Lieder*, which sometimes crops up as an alternative title. The voice and piano versions are simply entitled *Lieder*. Adler (p. 103) states that *Fünf Lieder nach Rückert* were published in 1905, and does not mention the two *Wunderhorn* songs, composed earlier, as part of the eventual set of seven. Once again *aus letzter Zeit* seems to be no more than a device for keeping the catalogue straight, with one collection of *Lieder* plainly marked off from another. In any event,

aus letzter Zeit obviously could not have been Mahler's conception. It was his untimely death that endowed these songs with
their classification. It seems most probable that the complementary
aus der Jugendzeit was equally a publisher's invention.

[139] NBL, p. 142.

[140] GA, p. 98.

[141] GA, pp. 75-6.

[142] In a conversation with Alfredo Casella. See Abraham,
op. cit. (I/n. 88 above), pp. 392-3.

[143] DN, p. 125.

[144] "Unpublished", according to Pamer (Vol. XVII, p. 121, see
n. 146 below), which suggests that a MS. may exist somewhere.
Dr. Newlin's mention (p. 125) of the "guitar-like" accompaniment to *Serenade* is mysterious. Can she have had *Phantasie* in
mind? See also HG, pp. 739-40.

[145] HFR, p. 176.

[146] F. E. Pamer, 'Gustav Mahlers Lieder', *Studien zur Musik-
wissenschaft*, Vienna, 1929 and 1930, Vol. XVI, pp. 116-38, Vol.
XVII, pp. 105-27; Alfred Rosé, private communication.

[147] NBL, p. 142.

[148] See pp. 68-9.

[149] HFR, p. 176, suggests that Bruckner's trio influenced
another *Jugendzeit* song, *Frühlingsmorgen*, but I have been unable
to trace the parallel.

[150] See H. C. Robbins Landon, *The Symphonies of Joseph Haydn*,
London, 1955, p. 569.

[151] Smetana, however, had his influence on Mahler.

[152] H. Keller, 'Holland: Music's New-Found Land', *Musical
Opinion*, London, October 1955, p. 17.

[153] E. Stein, 'Mahler's Ninth Symphony', *Orpheus in New
Guises*, London, 1953, p. 22.

[154] HFR, p. 176.

[155] NBL, p. 161; quoted in DN, p. 188.

[156] See pp. 192-4 above.

[157] It appears from a communication of Mr. Alfred Rosé that
two of the three unpublished songs, *Im Lenz* and *Winterlied*—
whose composition certainly preceded that of *Erinnerung*—

progress tonally, i.e., he informs me that the "key sequences" of the songs are:

Im Lenz—F major: F minor: C major.
Winterlied—A major: C minor: F major.

Hans und Grethe, which follows, is concentric, in F major. If Pamer is correct (*op. cit.*, Vol. XVI, pp. 120-1, see n. 146 above), the intended five songs were conceived as a set, of which *Im Lenz* was to be no. 4 and *Winterlied* no. 5. *Hans und Grethe* was not placed. The circling about F lends even the three extant songs a certain hanging-togetherness.

It is Pamer (*op. cit.*, Vol. XVII, p. 117) who notes—not more —*Erinnerung*'s unconventional tonal structure (as of other songs by Mahler). He seems to have accepted this 'indifference' to the concept of tonal order as a general tendency in Mahler's music, without recognition of any new principle involved.

Pamer further mentions (Vol. XVI, pp. 120-1) that *Hans und Grethe* was, at an early stage, written in D; that F represented a later development. The MS. Pamer appears to have seen (one in the possession of Mahler's sister, Justine) one would have thought to be the same autograph in the possession of Mr. Rosé—on family grounds alone, though it is true Mr. Rosé offers no information about the sequence of the songs in the projected cycle, which discrepancy may rest in the existence of MS. sources other than that listed in the chronological table. If such is, or was, the case, the difference in key could be easily explained.

[158] The term is Dika Newlin's. She divulged it in DN, p. 129 (and thenceforth used it throughout her book), along with the term's opposite—also her invention—'concentric tonality'. Her concept of progressive tonality was criticized by Hans Tischler in 'Mahler's Impact on the Crisis of Tonality', *Music Review*, XII/2, 1951, pp. 114-15, whose suggested alternative term, 'dramatic key symbolism', was criticized, in turn, by Hans Keller in *Music Survey*, IV/2, 1952, pp. 433-4, in a review of Tischler's article, which, at the same time, contains some valuable thoughts upon the history of progressive tonality. Mr. Keller comments further upon the term—and introduces a qualification of it: he

would split progressive tonalities into " 'progressive' and 're-gressive' tonalities according to whether the tonal structure in question goes up or down the circle of fifths": 'The *Entführung*'s "Vaudeville" ', *Music Review*, XVII/4, 1956, pp. 304-13. Another view of progressive tonality is expressed by Mr. Harold Truscott in 'Some Aspects of·Mahler's Tonality', *Monthly Musical Record*, Nov.-Dec., 1957, pp. 203-8.

[159] See n. 158 above.

[160] The Danish composer, Carl Nielsen (1865-1931), employed progressive tonality in his Symphony I (op. 7), composed in 1892 (and in subsequent symphonies). The finale of Mahler's Symphony I, a work composed between 1883 (at the earliest) and 1888, shows that the seeds of progressive tonality—which had already, as it were, flowered in the *Lieder eines fahrenden Gesellen* (1883-5)—were about to fertilize his symphonic music. Symphony II (C minor→E flat) was composed between 1887 and 1894. It is probable, then, that Dr. Robert Simpson is correct in stating that Nielsen's op. 7 was "the first symphony to end in a key other than that in which it started" (*Carl Nielsen*, London, 1952, p. 9). That both Nielsen and Mahler—contemporaries, but with nothing in common as musical personalities—should have alighted upon progressive tonality at about the same time without mutual stimulation (it is doubtful whether Mahler knew of Nielsen's existence, while Nielsen, though he probably became familiar with Mahler's music, reveals no Mahlerian traits)—the coincidence is proof that the historical stage was set for the emergence of the principle, that progressive tonality was, so to speak, in the air, and not the copyright of any one composer. See also n. 163 below.

[161] 'Schumann after Freud', *The Listener*, London, 26 July 1956. (The quotation has been slightly reformulated by the author.)

[162] I am not an expert on Schumann.   ◁

[163] This qualification is important. Mussorgsky (1839-81) wrote songs which progress tonally much before Mahler, for example in his song-cycle, *Sunless*, composed in 1874. In 1867 it seems that he was thinking of writing a tone-poem which "begins in F sharp minor but ends in D major". (The project

came to nothing.) All this is further evidence that progressive tonality was part of the musical atmosphere towards the end of the nineteenth century (see n. 160 above), even the atmosphere of Asia. But Mussorgsky can hardly be accounted an influence so far as the young Mahler was concerned. See M. D. Calvocoressi, *Modest Mussorgsky, His Life and Works*, London, p. 75 and pp. 293-4.

[164] DN, p. 129.

[165] Since the C#[7] close of *Im wunderschönen Monat Mai* is already implicit in the first bars of the song—the very first note heard is C sharp—one might say, enharmonically speaking, that the cycle is contained within a kind of concentric outer frame. One is reminded of the framing function of the A minor introduction to the F major first movement of Schumann's A minor string Quartet.

[166] RS², p. 46.

[167] GA, p. 98.

[168] PS, p. 16.

[169] HH², p. 812.

[170] 'A German Comic Opera', *The Listener*, 22 August 1957.

[171] *Encyclopædia Britannica.*

[172] *Der Trompeter von Säkkingen*, Stuttgart, 1888, p. 109.

[173] RS², p. 46.

[174] GMB, pp. 27-8.

[175] GMB, p. 34.

[176] PS⁰, p. 36.

[177] Loewenberg, *op. cit.* (see n. 75 in II, above).

[178] NBL, p. 173.

[179] FW, p. 102.

[180] Mosco Carner, *Of Men and Music*, London, n.d., p. 110 ('Mahler's Visit to London').

APPENDIX

by

Paul Banks and David Matthews*

* Notes attributed to D.M., however,
are by Donald Mitchell

Chapter 1

*page
and line*

1 *18*   A detailed description of the village and birthplace is given in HG, p. 8.

1 *22*   According to HG, p. 9, the family moved to Jihlava on 22 October 1860. A number of photographs of Jihlava are to be found in KB².

2 *26*   During his early years in Vienna, however, Mahler was closely associated with a circle of aspiring politicians centred around Victor Adler and Engelbert Pernerstorfer; they were drawn together by a common interest in Wagner and ideas for social regeneration. Years later Mahler again made his socialist sympathies clear by voting for Adler in the 1901 parliamentary elections (see KB², p. 225).

4 *17*   This reference by Alma Mahler to the removal of restrictions is problematic because of the difficulty of identifying the legislation to which she refers. HG, p. 9, refers to a *Heimatschein*:

> "In the autumn of 1860, he [Bernard Mahler] obtained a privilege for which he had certainly been maneuvering for some time, a *Heimatschein*, a sort of passport delivered in Humpolec which for four years allowed him to change his domicile as he wished. In order to renew it four years later, he had, on paper, to move from Iglau [Jihlava] while actually, thanks to this [i.e. the possession of the passport], he brought his family there on October 22, 1860."

KB², on the other hand, reproduces the *Kaiserliches Manifest* of 20 October 1860 and comments:

> "This proclamation ushered in the decline of absolute

power in the countries ruled by the Emperor Franz Joseph. As a result Jews were granted the right of domicile in places which previously had either been closed to them altogether or permitted only a limited number of Jewish settlers." (KB², pl. 5.)

It would seem, however, that Alma was probably correct, but that the changes occurred before 20 October 1860. The first (see *Verordnung des Ministeriums des Innern* of 13 January 1860, published on 17 January 1860) repealed laws restricting the trades open to Jews, in particular those excluding Jews from brewing and the sale of alcohol in certain Crown Lands. Although this occupation was encouraged among Jews in some areas (especially Galicia, see C. A. Macartney: *The Habsburg Empire 1790–1918*, London, 1969, p. 63, n. 3), the leasing of *Schank- und Wirthhäuser* to Jews had been prohibited in Moravia (see *Hofdekret*, 9 June 1791, published in Moravia on 21 June 1791). The new legislation was no doubt held to remove this restriction.

The significance of the second legislative change is less clear: the *Verordnung des Ministeriums des Innern* of 14 January 1860 repealed the laws prohibiting the residence of Jews in *Bergorten*. As a *Bergstadt*, Iglau (Jihlava) had for many years no official Jewish population, although a number of surrounding towns and villages did have such communities (see the figures for the early 1830s in Hieronymus von Scari: *Systematische Darstellung der im Betreff der Juden in Mähren und im K. K. Antheile Schlesiens erlassenen Gesetze und Verordnungen*, Brünn, 1835, pp. 5f.). By 1861, however, a Jewish community was established in Iglau and a Synagogue was consecrated in 1863 (see KB², pl. 13). The uncertainty is due to the fact that the *Verordnung* refers specifically to Bohemia, Hungary, Croatia, Slovenia, Banat and Voivodina, and the Siebenberg, but not to Moravia. The date of the establishment of the community in Iglau suggests, however, that the relaxation did apply to, or was soon extended to, the Margravate.

It is clear, therefore, that before 1860 it would have been impossible for Bernard Mahler to have moved to Iglau and continued his trade there, despite the fact that freedom of movement had been granted to Jews in 1849.

4 *22*   Mahler's awareness of anti-Semitic pressures is made clear in his letter of 21 December 1896 to Edmund von Mihalovics:

> "In Vienna the problem of a conductor-director is acute. At the moment I am high on the list of candidates, but two factors are against me, it seems: my 'madness', which my enemies mention whenever they want to put difficulties in my path, and the fact that I was born a Jew. . . ." (Quoted in HG, pp. 389–90.)

4 *35*   The place of Bernard's birth is open to doubt, Kaliště and Lipnice (Lipnitz) being the two possible locations (see HG, p. 7 and p. 839, n. 17). The uncertainty is apparently resolved by the fact that Bernard's father, Simon Mahler, was expelled from Lipnice in 1832 and did not settle in Kaliště until *c.* 1833.

5 *5*   However, HG, p. 412, states that Mahler was "brought up in an orthodox Jewish family". See n. 9 *17* below for a further discussion of Mahler's religious background.

5 *9*   For a detailed account of Mahler's family, see HG, chapter 1.

8 *11*   In recent years Mahler's supposed sexual abstinence before his marriage (see also p. 78) has been the subject of some speculation and debate. HG, pp. 339f. and MK, p. 45, take the view that the affair with Anna von Mildenburg was consummated. HG has much to say about Mahler's early love affairs, e.g. with Johanna Richter.

9 *17*   This account of Mahler's parents is inevitably one-sided, since Mahler, the only witness, was far more

attached to his mother than to his father. Bernard's side of the affair is put into historical and social perspective by a fascinating letter (7 December 1958) to Donald Mitchell from the late H. C. Stevens, at one time music critic of *The Jewish Chronicle*:

". . . We have to accept that the marriage was one of 'convenience'. But, in fact, almost all Jewish marriages of that time were such, especially where disposal of the daughter was concerned. Bernard was in his early thirties, his wife just past twenty. The reason why he married her is simple: he needed her dowry. A father was only too glad to get rid of a daughter who was likely to be left on his hands (Jewish daughters were considered to be undisposable if they were not married by the age of twenty), and in this case he would provide a reasonable dowry for Marie. The marriage would be arranged between Bernard and his future father-in-law without reference to Marie; she would be expected to do as her father told her.

"The dowry, as well as the family link-up, would be useful to Bernard, who was obviously out to get on. On the other hand, it is, I think, wrong to assume that there was a considerable social difference between Bernard and his father-in-law. This was no case of 'Schmul and Goldenberg': Bernard was a trader, his father-in-law a soap manufacturer. But a man who kept a tavern in a small provincial town like Kaliste [*sic*; *recte* Jihlava] was socially the equal of a soap manufacturer in the same town. Here again, we have to see 'soap manufacturer' in true prospective. 'Soap manufacturers' and 'candle-makers' existed in many such provincial towns; their means of production were primitive, and their productions too were primitive. A Jew would make tallow candles in his kitchen; soap would be made in an outhouse. The father-in-law might be a local lord within his community, but in that case he would not dream of marrying even an unwanted daughter to a man socially very much inferior. No, here we have a couple of fairly hard-headed local merchant-class Jews out to make a bargain.

"And Bernard Mahler had the worst of the bargain.

"The wife in the Jewish household of the time was the woman of all work, at least in such a milieu. That Marie was ailing, lame, almost an invalid possibly, would not be taken into account – except in one sense. Having taken her with a dowry, Bernard could not do anything about it. Except take it out of her. And that was his prerogative as husband: wife-beating was not particularly abnormal in those days and milieus. . . . Children, too, were beaten; flogging was the common treatment for them. . . .

"Can one say at all that it was Bernard's desire to join the ranks of the cultivated that made him marry Marie? I don't think so. The cultural differences between the two families were almost non-existent, so far as Bernard was concerned. From what little we know of Bernard it is probable that he was in fact more cultivated than his wife, in terms of outlook, reading, intellectual capacity, etc. The point to be remembered here is that the women of such a provincial Jewish community were extremely orthodox (for we have no reason to assume that Marie's family was at all free-thinking, and the entry in the Jewish register confirms to some extent that even Bernard had to conform outwardly to the main rites of his community). To speak of a provincial Jewish merchant's home as 'cultivated' in the sense in which you use the term is wrong: Marie might have exalted ideas, but Bernard would not regard her family as particularly far above himself in cultural respects, probably just the reverse. . . .

"Here we have the second cause of conflict between him and his wife: orthodoxy. She would bring her orthodoxy into the home, he would fight it. But the Jewish community of the day being what it was, he could only fight it openly to his own detriment, if he were prepared to be put 'outside the pale'. Because his business life involved relations with his fellow Jews, he could not face that. So, once more, he took it out on his wife.

"There is a reflection of this in the incident of 1880 [see p. 111], when Gustav could not accept the Kapellmeister post at [Jihlava], 'because of my family'. That could not be a reference to his father directly, who, as a free-thinker, would not be troubled by the fact that the post would involve working on the Sabbath eve and the Sabbath. 'Family' here can only refer to Marie and her side. He could not bring obloquy on his family, having them pointed at by the community as having a son who was an apostate. . . .

"It is worth noting that he was able to conduct one performance at Iglau in 1882 because the date, Sept. 12, 1882, fell on a Tuesday, probably just before the High Holidays."

In view of Stevens's references to the orthodoxy of Jewish wives, it is fascinating to find that Mahler's only recorded visit to the synagogue was made in the company of his mother:

"Among the anecdotes about Mahler's childhood, one of the most amusing without doubt is that in which he relates one of his first visits to the synagogue, where, hidden in his mother's skirts, he interrupted the community's hymn singing with howls, shouting 'Be quiet! Be quiet! It's horrible!' Then, when he had finally managed to quiet everyone, he started to sing at the top of his voice one of his favourite songs: 'Eits a binkel Kasi (Hrasi)'." (HG, p. 15.)

9 35   Recent research has revealed that Marie Mahler bore 14 children in all: Isidor (22. iii. 1858–1859); Gustav (7. vii. 1860–18. v. 1911); Ernst (1861–13. iv. 1874); Leopoldine (18. v. 1863–27. ix. 1889); Karl (?. viii. 1864–28. xii. 1865); Rudolf (17. viii. 1865–21. ii. 1866); Louis (Alois), later Hans Christian (6. x. 1867–192?); Justine (15. xii. 1868–1938); Arnold (19. xii. 1869–15. xii. 1871); Friedrich (23. iv. 1871–14. xii. 1871); Alfred (22. iv. 1872–6. v. 1873); Otto (18. vi. 1873–6. ii. 1895); Emma (19. x. 1875–15. v. 1933); and Konrad (17. iv. 1879–9. i. 1881). Of these, seven died in infancy, though only one—Konrad—of diphtheria. See HG, pp. 11–12.

12 15   Mr. Knud Martner (in a letter in *Music and Musicians*, No. 266, October 1974, p. 4) has drawn attention to the fact that, owing to faulty translation, the works

mentioned by Walter have been incorrectly attributed to Otto Mahler; they were in fact those works completed by Gustav up to 1895: the First Symphony, performed at Budapest, Hamburg and Weimar; the Second, the first three movements of which were heard in Berlin in March 1895; and the Third which was not completed until 1896. The orchestral songs were the first seven of the *Wunderhornlieder* and the three books of songs were the *Lieder und Gesänge* published in 1892.

13 *20*   See n. 22 *8* below.

16 *13*   In a private communication to Donald Mitchell dated 30 May 1959 Ernst Křenek wrote:

> ". . . my uncle who hailed from Iglau [Jihlava] and was approximately of Mahler's age remembered the family well. He pointed out with some glee that the father of the high and mighty Director of the Hofoper had run a *Schnapps-Butik*, which used to be a kind of low-class saloon frequented by coachmen."

This description of Bernard Mahler's retail outlet is in close agreement with that given in HG (Chapter 1).

18 *2*   On the other hand, Bernard's estate at his death in 1889 was valued at the considerable sum of 28,000 florins (about £2,000), which was probably a conservative estimate (see HG, p. 10).

22 *6*   According to Pavel Eckstein ("Gustav Mahler stammte aus. . .", in *Wir und Sie*, Czechoslovakische Monatschrifte, April 1963, p. 20), Mahler's first teacher was J. Žižka, a violinist and *Stadtkapellmeister*.

22 *8*   Franz Viktorin left Iglau in 1868 and, after conducting at Budweis, Kracow and Bielitz, worked as *Kapellmeister* at the Deutsches Theater in Pest from 1874 to 1878. He then left theatrical work until 1880, when he was appointed first *Kapellmeister* at the Carl Schultze Theater in Hamburg. After a further gap of two years Viktorin began work at the Neues Friedrich Wilhelmstädtisches Theater in Berlin in 1883 and remained there

until his death on 8 April 1888. It is quite possible that Mahler studied with Viktorin and Brosch at the same time, since they ran a Musik-Institut at Jihlava together (see HG, p. 840, n. 13). Johannes Brosch was a violinist in the *Stadtkapelle* (see C. d'Elvert: *Geschichte der Musik in Mähren und Oesterr.-Schlesien mit Rücksicht auf die allgemeine böhmische und österreichische Musik-Geschichte*, Brünn, 1873, vol. II, p. 93).

Wenzel Pressburg (1824–1906) also taught Mahler piano and music theory. Pressburg, a Viennese, was a pedagogue and prolific composer of waltzes; a man, it seems, of doubtful artistic integrity, though in 1883 he requested and received from Mahler a document testifying to his abilities as a teacher, conductor and pianist to be used, no doubt, to bolster an unspectacular career (HG, p. 840, n. 14).

23 7   This report, which appeared on 16 October 1870, was followed on the 20th of the same month by a public vote of thanks to, and recommendation of, Wenzel Pressburg, which was inserted into *Der Vermittler* by Bernard Mahler (HG, p. 840, n. 14). Clearly Pressburg was annoyed that only his pupil's former teacher had been mentioned in the report of the concert, and had asked Bernard Mahler to redress the balance.

23 13   The only instance of Mahler's accompanying Milla von Ott (Ottenfeld) that has been traced is the concert given in Iglau on 11 August 1883, at which she played Wieniawski's *Fantaisie sur Faust*, op. 20, and the "Kreutzer" Sonata (HG, p. 107).

24 22   According to HG, p. 23, Grünfeld *père* was a wealthy leather merchant.

26 5   Another outsider, a farm manager by the name of Gustav Schwarz, was involved in the decision to send Mahler to Vienna, and according to his account, it was he who took Mahler there (KB[1], pp. 25f., HG, pp. 27f., and KB[2], p. 151).

Chapter II

28 *34*   Nevertheless, some of the political, social and philosophical influences experienced by Mahler at this time have been discussed in detail by W. J. McGrath in his remarkable book, *Dionysian Art and Populist Politics in Austria*, New Haven, Conn., 1974, which brilliantly articulates and illumines the communal intellectual life of the period, in Vienna particularly.

29 *19*   The fees payable by students at the Conservatoire were by no means insignificant—that of the piano course, for example, being 120 fl. per annum—but there is some uncertainty about the amounts paid by Mahler. When he completed his application form on 10 September 1875, no mention was made of a request for exemption from payment, and the *Matrikel* for 1875/76 indicates that he paid 120 fl. for the whole year. However, the *Matrikel* covering the three years of his study at the Conservatoire (pl. A, p. 283) states quite clearly that he was *halb-befreit* in all three years. Thus in his last two years at the institution, Mahler's annual fees were 60 fl. The anomaly of Mahler's first-year fee may be explained by reference to the Conservatoire regulations (GdM[4]; though there is some confusion as to their precise nature in 1875; for an exhaustive discussion of this problem, see PWB, Chapter II). The 120 fl. fee for the piano course attended by Mahler in 1875/76 covered that course, and also all the subsidiary courses prescribed by the regulations, but *not* the composition course which in 1875/76 was in no way connected with the first year of the piano course. Moreover, the composition course could apparently only be taken as a principal subject, the fee for which was again 120 fl. Mahler therefore studied two principal subjects in 1875/76, costing 240 fl.; but, since he was exempt from paying half the fees, had only to find 120 fl. In 1876/77, composition *was* a prescribed subsidiary course for students attending the

second year of the piano course (GdM[5], 1876/77) and so, although Mahler again took both subjects, his total fee was only 120 fl.; in his final year his principal subject was composition, the fee for which was once again 120 fl. Thus in his last two years, Mahler paid, after exemption, only 60 fl. for his courses.

It should also be pointed out here that students who applied successfully for exemption from payment of fees were expected to repay the unpaid amount in annual instalments of 100 fl. as soon as their income reached 2000 fl. per annum. It is uncertain how much Mahler spent on food and rent etc. while a student, but in 1878 Hugo Wolf was paying 15 fl. per month (i.e. 180 fl. per annum) for accommodation; so the annual cost of keeping Mahler at the Conservatoire must have been well over 300 fl. Precisely how much of a strain such fees and expenses placed on Bernard Mahler's resources it is difficult to determine, but the family's poverty should not be over-emphasized (see also the note on Bernard's estate, n. 18 *2*, p. 274).

29 *26*   As explained above, the *Matrikel* for 1875–8 (pl. A) indicates that Mahler was on half-fees from the academic year 1875/76, his first year at the Conservatoire. See n. 29 *19* above.

31 *28*   Mahler himself told Bauer-Lechner that he had heard Marie Wilt (a famous soprano for whom Rudolf Krzyzanowski acted as accompanist in 1878) from the fourth gallery (NBL, p. 79). Wolf saw her perform at the *Hofoper* a number of times in October 1875 (FW, p. 21); she left that institution in March 1878.

32 *10*   For the report on Mahler's first and unsuccessful attempt at the examination, see KB[2], p. 154.

32 *16*   Actually, German literature and the history of art. See KB[2], pl. 38, which reproduces the form on which Mahler registered at the Faculty of Philosophy in 1877.

34 *26*   Not so: see n. 116 *4*, pp. 299–300.

34 *34*   But see n. 35 *32* below.

35 *18*   An explanation of the Conservatoire record's apparent inconsistency can be offered here. It would seem that works submitted for the composition competition were not automatically performed; or if they were, the performers' names were not given in GdM[1]: such details were only supplied for works heard at the *Schlussproduction* (an entirely separate event, a "leavers' concert") which only included prize-winning compositions by students in their final year. The paucity of information about the Quintet of 1876 is, therefore, a result of the editorial policy employed in compiling GdM[1], rather than an error.

35 *32*   While it is not yet possible to reach any definite conclusions, it now seems more likely that the existing Piano Quartet movement was neither the prizewinner nor the piece performed at Jihlava. Since 1958 the advertisement for the concert at Jihlava has come to light (reproduced in KB[2], pl. 30): it confuses the issue by stating that the ensemble works by Krzyzanowski and Mahler were both for piano, two violins and viola; and, indeed, no cellist is listed among the performers. The review which appeared in the *Mährischer Grenzbote* of 17 September 1876 (see KB[2], p. 153) speaks, however, of a Piano *Quintet* by Mahler and comments "that it was awarded the first prize at the Conservatoire in Vienna". As Professor Blaukopf points out, the work by Krzyzanowski, also described as a Piano Quintet by the reviewer, was almost certainly the same movement as that performed at a Conservatoire concert on 22 December 1875. So the suspicion arises that there were after all five performers at the concert (though even the reviewer only mentions four). It would seem, therefore, that the reviewer may well be correct in his description of the work as the prize-winning (Piano) Quintet of 1876 (the Conservatoire records (see GdM[1], p. 87) do not specify a *Piano* Quintet, but the review would seem to confirm that this is what it was).

(Another, more radical suggestion: perhaps both works performed at the concert were arrangements for piano, two violins and viola, of piano quintets, arrangements brought about by the difficulty of finding a cellist. If the cello parts were as closely linked to the piano l. h. as that of Mahler's Piano Quartet movement, the simple omission of the parts would not have involved too great a loss. On the other hand, it is difficult to believe that a town possessing a theatre orchestra could not have provided one reasonably proficient cellist.)

It should further be noted that the evidence for dating the Piano Quartet movement 1876—a date which has hitherto never been questioned—turns out, in fact, to be rather slight. The evidence is, of course, the date on the title page of the MS (see p. 123 above); but this was added some time after the autograph title and signature, almost certainly by Alma Mahler, who also wrote the inscription "frühe Compositionen" on the folder containing the MS. We do not know when she did this, nor where her information for dating the work came from. Presumably it came from Mahler himself; but, as we know, he can hardly be relied on for such detailed accuracy of information (nor, for that matter, can Alma).

If there is no absolute need to assign the Piano Quartet to 1876, it is tempting to speculate that this might have been the piece that Mahler told Bauer-Lechner he wrote at the close of his student period and submitted for a prize competition in Russia (see p. 128 above). Dr. Gerald Abraham informs us that the St. Petersburg Society for Chamber Music announced a competition for a chamber work open to composers of all nations in 1877 (it has so far proved impossible to discover the closing date for submission of entries). Ninety-five works were submitted; none got the first prize but the second went to Bernhard Scholz of

Breslau (1835–1916). It must surely have been this competition that Mahler entered, as the next one was not until 1890. Mahler said that the MS went astray; but he may only have meant the copy he submitted, which Dr. Abraham suggests would have been most unlikely to have been returned. If Mahler thought this piece one of the best of his youthful compositions it might explain why, if it was the existing Piano Quartet movement, this alone of his chamber works has survived.

(Another small piece of evidence may be cited here. A letter of Mahler's to Julius Epstein, undated, but assigned by Mr. Martner to July 1877, includes, in a sentence full of musical metaphors, the phrase 'ungemein rubato' (see GMB¹, p. 53). This unusual direction occurs towards the end of the Piano Quartet movement, so it might suggest that Mahler had recently composed this passage when he wrote the letter.)

36 1   HG, p. 50, incorrectly gives the date as 20 June.

36 6   Mahler's registration form for 1876/77 (see SW, p. 50) indicates that in his second year he also took a subsidiary course in German Literary History (*Deutsche Literaturgeschichte*).

36 15   In fact Mahler did express regrets: see DM¹, n. 30, pp. 374–5, and n. 37 *34* below.

37 33   But see n. 35 *32* above.

37 34   Hirschfeld had, in fact, undertaken extensive research for his contribution to the *Geschichte der K. K. Gesellschaft der Musikfreunde in Wien* which was published in 1912. In this work Hirschfeld traced the Conservatoire careers of the most famous ex-students, and, curiously, tells the whole story of Mahler's study of counterpoint (which was such "a great secret" according to his letter to Karpath!):

"The view that Gustav Mahler was excused the counterpoint classes is erroneous. It may appear striking that in the yearly report for 1876/77 Gustav Mahler certainly is included amongst the students in the first counterpoint class, but it is not shown in the final report. The puzzle is easily solved as Gustav Mahler was only given the third progress grade in counterpoint: this is clear from the records (No. 286 C 1877). Thus it is very probable that he was a pupil of Anton Bruckner (a fact at present being questioned), who at that time was the only other teacher of counterpoint besides Krenn; but that, apparently on account of his unsatisfactory progress, he did not complete the year's course and is therefore not named in the final report among those attending the first counterpoint class. This fact, in itself of no consequence, would not have been adduced here were it not for the reproaches of unreliability that have been directed at the yearly report, which was only being discreet." (*Op. cit.*, p. 156.)

To date, Stefan's account (see p. 36 above), has been accepted and Hirschfeld's dismissed as malicious; and not without justification, for this passage, from an apparently 'objective' history of a national institution, represents one of the most invidious and subtle examples of musical invective ever aimed at Mahler. The whole statement is riddled with hints, half-truths and untruths: why, for instance, does Hirschfeld assume that Mahler studied with Bruckner and not Krenn? The Conservatoire's records show quite clearly (see below) that Mahler studied counterpoint in 1876/77 with the latter, as Hirschfeld must have known. It is also clear from GdM[1] (1876/77, p. 57) that only those students who attained first grade were named in the examination results. Unless, therefore, Hirschfeld was simply jumping to the most malicious conclusion, he must have been familiar with the document quoted below which clearly names Krenn as Mahler's teacher. There is plenty of evidence (see also HG, p. 559) of Hirschfeld's anti-Mahler bias; but as the following extract from the *Matrikel* of the Conservatoire shows, his chief assertion, that Mahler did not complete the course, is near the truth:

Second year: Half fees   Academic year 1876–77

Piano (Epstein)	compulsory	1	First Prize in Competition
Choir training	compulsory		Did not attend
Chamber music	compuslory		
Orchestral training	compulsory		
Counterpoint (Krenn)	optional	3	Supplementary exam., 14 June. 1st exercise handed in late, 2nd exercise not ready, 3rd no year's assignment produced and a 1st part of a fictitious [sic] work handed in: therefore not permitted to compete for the Prize for Composition.
Composition (Krenn)	optional	1	

(Based on KB², p. 154 and an examination of a photocopy of the original (reproduced as pl. A opposite). The published version is inaccurate, and has been corrected here.) Unfortunately this information, important though it is, does not unravel the Gordian knot of confusion which surrounds Mahler's study of counterpoint. The first point to be noted is that in order to study composition with Krenn in 1875/76, Mahler had already to be familiar with the contents of the first year of the counterpoint course (see GdM⁵ for 1875/76), and his ability in that subject was no doubt tested in the entrance examinations held towards the end of September (see GdM⁴, 1876). In any case, the demands of the counterpoint course were minimal: students were only expected to study simple and double counterpoint at the octave, imitation, and simple fugue, in the first year. The second year of the course—which involved the study of three- and four-part counterpoint, fugue with more

Ausbildungsschule.

Dem Schüler waren nachbenannte Lehrgegenstände vorgeschrieben: (Der erste Gegenstand ist das **Hauptfach**, die folgenden sind die Nebenfächer)	Das Nebenfach war obligat, facultativ, frei oder ausserordentlich	Classificationsnote	Prüfungsbefund		Note	Anmerkungen über nicht abgelegte Prüfungen, über Nichtzulassung zum Concurs mit Angabe der Gründe. — Sonstige.
			Eignung			
			zum Fortgang	zur Wiederholung	über den Besuch der Uebungen	über die Conduite	

1. Jahrgang. *Halb befreit* Schuljahr 1875 1876

Clavier (Epstein)		1				Concurs I Preis einstimmig
Harmonielehre (Fuchs)	oblg					nicht besucht
Chorübung	"					
Kammermusik	"					nicht besucht
Gesch. d. Musik	"					nicht besucht
Literatur	fac					
Composition (Krenn)	fr. a. o.	1				Concurs I einstimmig

Hat beim Concurs einen **1** Preis erlangt. *einstimmig Clavier, für Composition I Preis a. fg.*

Erhielt ____ Verweise; ____ Rügen; wesshalb?

II. Jahrgang. *Halb befreit* Schuljahr 1876 1877

Clavier (Epstein)		1				Concurs I Preis
Chorübung	oblg					nicht besucht
Kammermusik	"					
Orchesterübung						
Contrapunkt (Krenn)	fr. a. o.	3				
Composition (Krenn)	fr. a. o.	1				

Hat beim Concurs einen ____ Preis erlangt.

Erhielt ____ Verweise; ____ Rügen; wesshalb?

III. Jahrgang. Schuljahr 1877 1878

Clavier (Epstein)						
Chorübung	oblg					
Kammermusik	"					
Orchesterübung	"					
Composition (Krenn)	fr. a. o.					
Gesch. d. Musik	fac					

Hat beim Concurs einen **I** Preis erlangt.

Erhielt ____ Verweise; ____ Rügen; wesshalb?

A The *Matrikel* covering Mahler's three years of study (1875–8) at the
Vienna Conservatoire.

than one subject, and canon—was, in 1875/76, a *facultiv* subsidiary course for students taking the first year of the composition course as their main subject (i.e. they were examined in the subject, but did not have to attend the classes); but it appears that the administration was alert to the fact that Mahler was in the exceptional position of studying two main subjects (see n. 29 *19* above) and could hardly be expected to attend subsidiary courses for both.

By 1876/77, Counterpoint II was merely a *frei* subsidiary course for first-year composition students (i.e. it required neither attendance, nor examination); while for those, like Mahler, who were in their second year of the composition course, there was no obligation to attend any counterpoint classes (see GdM[5], 1876/77; in any case, Mahler was studying composition as a subsidiary subject), and in Mahler's registration form for 1876/77 (see SW, p. 50) Counterpoint I is listed as a *frei* subsidiary course, which it was for students in the second and third years of the piano course. Thus Mahler's unhappy participation in the first year of the counterpoint examination was the result of his following the piano course, and had nothing to do with his study of composition. It is therefore difficult to see why his evident misbehaviour in the counterpoint class should have led to his exclusion from the composition competition. Moreover, GdM[4] makes it clear that although a grade 3 was considered a "fail" in principal subjects, it was a "pass" mark in subsidiaries and sufficient to allow the student to enter the annual competitions: students who were excluded from competitions because of non-attendance of, or failure in, subsidiary courses were distinguished as such in GdM[1]; but the note explaining Mahler's non-participation in the 1877 composition competition is unique in reading:

"Those designated thus ★ ★ [Mahler was the *only* student

thus designated] have withdrawn from participation in the competition." (GdM[1], 1876/77, p. 64.)

It would appear, therefore, that the official responsible for the completion of the *Matrikel* quoted above may himself have been confused by the complexities of the administrative system.

A careful reading of the *Matrikel* report on Mahler's counterpoint studies, with particular reference to the dates, suggests that the first sentence refers to the last event: that the three exercises comprised the main annual counterpoint examination which Mahler failed and that as a result he was required to sit a subsidiary examination. The truth would seem to be that Mahler did little or no work in Krenn's counterpoint class, and that in the early summer of 1877 his problems were multiplied by the fact that he had to return to Jihlava in May in order to sit his *Matura* (see p. 32 above). The results in the latter were, almost without exception, unsatisfactory; and the luckless student had to resit the examination the following September. By 14 June he had returned to Vienna to sit the supplementary counterpoint examination, and a week later, on 21 June, participated in the annual piano competition where he achieved his only success of the year.

One of the curious features of Mahler's reminiscences about his time as a student at the Conservatoire is his reference to numerous "prize-winning" works which almost certainly did not win prizes at that institution. The suspicion arises that memories of this period carried an affective charge which led to these exaggerations; and this is perhaps confirmed by the revealing comments Mahler made to Ferdinand Pfohl while at Hamburg (FP, p. 39; see also DM[1], p. 375):

"Before the impending performance of the C minor Symphony, the Second, in Berlin, Mahler came to me and played the Symphony, which made a strong impression on me, though without being able to convince me completely, as Mahler's eclecticism emerged unmistakably throughout the first movement. He seems to have been reminded by a counterpoint of the violins in the first movement of the fact that during his time as a student at the Vienna Conservatoire he had failed his examination because of a contrapuntal exercise. He triumphantly pointed out this line in his orchestral score and called out: 'What do you say to that counterpoint!? That really is counterpoint!' "

To this may be added his later conversation with Natalie Bauer-Lechner:

"Now I understand why Schubert, so it is said, shortly before his death, had a wish to study counterpoint. He felt how much it was lacking. And I know how he felt, since I myself feel this same lack of ability and of the proper application to hundreds of contrapuntal exercises from my student years." (NBL, p. 138.)

Now that the truth about Mahler's counterpoint studies is known, these comments, far from being awkward inconsistencies as they previously appeared to be, provide crucial evidence that his lack of success in this subject lies at the root of Mahler's psychological complex—this is not too strong a word to use—and in this sense allow us a clearer understanding of his statements about his early attempts at composition. That this apparently trivial event should have had such a profound, indeed traumatic, effect is quite understandable when Mahler's position is recalled: a young immature, provincial boy, probably (if we accept David Holbrook's view, in *Gustav Mahler and the Courage To Be*, London, 1975) suffering from identity problems, who at seventeen had pretensions of becoming a composer. There could be little more damaging for his ego than a failure such as this. To have been so unsuccessful in an undemanding counterpoint course is hardly significant in view of his subsequent mastery, however idiosyncratic, of the art; but the young composer must have viewed the event from a very different perspective.

38 *9*   In a letter to Gustav Schwarz (Jihlava, 6 September 1877) Mahler writes that the examination will take place on 12 September (KB², p. 155).

Some idea of Mahler's academic work at this time may be formed from two essays written by him in 1877. These were first published by Hans Holländer—whose early Mahler source studies brought much of significance to light and should be gratefully remembered—in an article for the *Neues Wiener Journal* entitled "Gustav Mahler in der Schule" which appeared on 10 June 1929; only part of the second essay has previously appeared in an English translation (KB², p. 154).

In his introduction to the essays Holländer wrote:

"For the final examination of the eighth form's winter term (10 February 1877), Mahler was set, as a German essay, the subject of 'The Influence of the Orient on German Literature'. He took as his subject certain remarks by appropriate authors, such as Friedrich Schlegel, on the language and wisdom of the Indians, Sakuntala, Rustum and Sohrab, Savitri and others, yet did not succeed in working up his information. First and foremost the subject stimulated him in its general aspects – he gives a philosophical and aesthetical survey of the genesis of the various kinds of poetry, in which the boldness of many of his thoughts and their perspective of greatness already reveal the creator of the Third and Eighth Symphonies. The set time apparently available for this essay was responsible for its incompleteness and probably also explains the disjointedness of many of his trains of thought.

"His knowledge about the Wallenstein question which formed the subject of his summer term essay (14 July 1877) was based on less pertinent foundations. The uncongenial subject is arbitrarily given a different slant. In place of 'What motives caused the various followers of Wallenstein to defect from him?' Mahler, with abrupt resolution, substitutes 'On the motives that brought about Wallenstein's Decline'. Instead of the Schillerian answer to the question, he offers a Mahlerian fantasy expressing much that is true, indeed even original, but certainly in part making use of that examination trick which consists of glossing over the unknown facts with verbosity and sententiousness.

"Mahler took his school-leaving examination on 12 September 1877, after withdrawing from a first attempt on 6 July of the same year. The result was an overall 'fair'; only in scripture and preliminary studies in philosophy was his work judged 'satisfactory'.

'*German Essay*
'*The Influence of the Orient on German Literature*

'Perhaps the most productive influence on a people that has already developed a distinctive national identity and consequently an individual character, is that exercised by a knowledge of the intellectual products of other peoples. For in this way a nation's horizons are extended and will develop a comprehensive outlook which is the source of humanity and of the conditions for the creation of art, and in particular of poetry. A cautionary example is that of the Chinese who, though once a very important race from the original point of view, have barred the way for culture and enlightenment in their realm by rejecting everything that is foreign.

'If I may be permitted a brief digression on the origins of poetry, I would call this precisely the inevitable result of the human spirit. Man indeed feels impelled to give expression to whatever mood he happens to find himself in, and this in as beautiful a way as he possibly can: thus does lyric poetry come into being. In like manner, he wants to tell of what has happened to him, what he has done or what his fellow men have experienced; here we find the origins of epic poetry. Dramatic poetry, the acme of the art, probably developed last. But we must also take into account the individuality of each artist. For everything that man thinks and does is always founded in his personal character, and so it is with his poetry. Thus it is quite natural that every race imprints its literature with its own, its national character, and then what we have is world literature. And almost invariably we find that the further races are distinct from each other in the geographical respect, hence the more different are their climates and locations, the more different will be the nature of their literature, and the more strange will be the impression it makes of the peoples themselves. And yet we find an attraction in what is strange. Let us now recall our opening words: "What is most productive for a people is the knowledge of the literature of other peoples . . ."

'It is above all the German mind which aspires to a comprehensive outlook; through the assimilation of the product of different nations there emerges, with regard to ideas of form. . . . [The essay breaks off here.]

'Summer Term Essay, July 1877
'On the motives that brought about Wallenstein's Decline

'Often, when a man is alone with only his imagination for company, he makes plans without at all dreaming of putting them into practice; they are as though a mere offspring of his poetic fantasy: he may dream of future greatness, of luxury and splendour, and will gradually come to imagine that his lofty ideas and his daring plans are real, even though when he considers them in a sober frame of mind they seem to him merely ridiculous. In this way he creates a pattern of ideas which make him utterly oblivious of the outside world. If he is now, by some chance event, snatched out of this mood, then he will calmly go about his business and perhaps in the next hour will no longer know what he had so recently felt and thought in the intoxication of his brain. But woe to the man who is so pleased with these ideas of his that, by frequently coming back to them, he forgets all the absurdities and incoherences they contain! For by virtue of the fact that a certain mental image emerges from this chaos, he becomes a slave to his imagination, and despite never at all dreaming of putting

289

his plans into practice, he has gradually imagined them real to the extent that a certain dark hope enters the heart. Either people become really irresponsible in such circumstances, that is, their mental images are irreconcilable with common practice, or else hope becomes more definite and ideas loom larger and soon he believes he can already realize them. Thus too with Wallenstein. His imagination showed him pictures of royal diadems and the crowns of princes; in the power of his imagination he already saw himself as a ruler as he distributed fiefs and favours. Certainly he well knew that this was something completely impossible, but he could not bring himself to forgo the pleasure of toying a little with his plans. Indeed he even did everything that could contribute to their realization. Gradually he appeared to be genuinely getting closer to the goal and the rest followed from this. Now he approached in reality what he previously had scarcely dared think of, and his hope held him in sway. However, hope is a treacherous ship sailing boldly and easily on the sea of humanity. Its progress ploughs deep and leaves long furrows in which whirlpools play their tricks. It is the lot of only a few mortals to be sucked up out of these and thrown on to a safe footing. Most are pulled down to the depths by them and thus meet their destruction. Wallenstein too, for whom at the beginning free choice still remained – "he could still do as he wished" – had later to succumb to the bitter compulsion. For him there was no turning back, since others had already been dragged along with him; for this reason he finally yielded to his destiny. His passage to Sweden was the crossing of the Rubicon: "Alea jacta est".'

"The first essay was marked 'barely adequate', and the teacher added the comment: 'The problem not solved – the introduction too far fetched – in the accompanying draft there are perhaps indications of a knowledge of the facts which ought to have come into the question. Handed in after one and a half hours.'

"The second essay was marked by the teacher as 'Subject altered quite arbitrarily. Not satisfactory.' "

[*Translated by Bill Hopkins.*]

39 *18* Ed. Rosenblum was Eduard Rosé, the brother of Arnold Rosé. See n. 39, p. 232.

42 *14* The answer that may now be supplied is a tentative "No". The orchestral and choral rehearsals, which all students were expected to attend, performed the dual function of providing an opportunity for the students to perform together while learning the repertory and offering composition students the chance to conduct. It seems probable that, as Mahler took composition as his single main subject in 1877–8, it was only in that year that he conducted the student orchestra. He can hardly have been an outstanding success, however, for he was not one of the students allowed on to the podium at a public concert (see GdM⁵ and GdM¹).

43 *3* It has now been published in KB², p. 154.

46 *11* The teachers of composition at the Conservatoire were at that time Krenn, Fuchs and Hermann Grädener (1844–1929). It seems inexplicable that Brahms could have regarded their music as too modern. Indeed an examination of Krenn's music suggests that Brahms's opinion was probably similar to that of Mahler and Wolf, for, as a composer, Krenn was remarkable only for a superficiality, lack of imagination, an incomplete mastery of the craft of composition and a marked conservatism, even from a Brahmsian standpoint. It is possible that Brahms did have Bruckner in mind and the reference to the "teaching of composition" was a slip of the pen.

47 *15* Some information is now to be found in HG, Chapter 4.

49 *13* We should note, however, that in this same essay Wagner had also enthusiastically expounded the philosophic ideas of Schopenhauer, with whose thinking Mahler was certainly very well acquainted in later years.

50 *6* Wagner was in Vienna in March, but of course it was not until September that Wolf and Mahler entered the Conservatoire.

50 *16* These performances, attended by the student Mahler,

were conducted by Hans Richter, who was serving at the Vienna Opera when Mahler was eventually appointed Director there—and soon departed. By a further ironic chance, it was *Lohengrin* that Mahler performed at the Vienna Opera in 1897, his first appearance at the Opera and one in which he scored an immediate success. Mr. Philip Winters (New York) points out that the performance of *Tannhäuser* on 22 November 1875 was the first occasion that the opera was given with the Overture leading directly into the Venusberg Music (though the revised Overture and Venusberg Music had been heard before at a concert that Wagner directed in Vienna on 12 May 1872). In the Paris version of 1861 the revised Venusberg scene began after the original Overture had finished.

51 *18* On 2 March 1876 Wagner himself conducted *Lohengrin*. It is hard to imagine that Mahler would not have been present on this occasion, which was perhaps the only opportunity he would have had to experience Wagner as a conductor.

53 *33* Perhaps it should be noted here that Mahler had taught the piano as a child (from the age of eight) and as a youth (see HG, pp. 19–20 and p. 33).

57 *5* But see n. 35 *32* on pp. 278-80.

62 *25* For a discussion of possible Brahmsian influences in Mahler's symphonies, see Rosamond McGuinness: 'Mahler und Brahms: Gedanken zu "Reminiszenzen" in Mahlers Sinfonien' in *Melos/NZfM.*, 3 Jahrg., Heft 3, May/June 1977, pp. 215f.

63 *20* HG deals extensively with Mahler's attitude to, and relations with, Brahms. See particularly the accounts of Mahler's meeting with Brahms (which were more frequent than was ever supposed) on pp. 220–1, 304–5, 331 and 373–4.

66 *9* Rott studied with Bruckner from 1874 until 1877, as did Rudolf Krzyzanowski from 1876 to 1878.

68 4   Actually, at the beginning of 1880. See DM¹, p. 69, and KB², p. 155.

68 19   It seems that this remark was made not to Mahler but to Hermann Behn, who had come to Vienna to study composition with Bruckner and offered to transcribe manuscripts for him. See HG, p. 47.

68 23   A confusion that has been finally (and brilliantly) elucidated by the late Deryck Cooke (*Musical Times*, January, February, April, May 1969).

69 1   There is some evidence that this title has been misinterpreted (see AG, IV/1, p. 532) and that Mahler's being a Jew may have caused Bruckner some concern. For many Catholics, Jews were the originators and prime representatives of the "modern spirit, the spirit of rationalism and materialism, of the science which denies the existence of God and creation" (D. van Arkel: *Antisemitism in Austria*, Leiden, 1966, pp. 5–6).

70 10   The precise date was 20 April. Bruckner's Scherzo was one of no less than twenty-eight pieces Mahler conducted at this concert. For more details see HG, p. 143.

70 31   The *Te Deum* was in fact performed three times, and the symphony was no. IV.

73 3   Alma was mistaken: Mahler conducted only the Fourth Symphony of Bruckner in America.

Chapter III

75 8   According to HG, p. 54, Mahler left the University in the autumn of 1878 and did not return until the spring of 1880. See also n. 106 *13*, pp. 297-8.

75 13   No longer, fortunately, with the publication of the first volume of M. de La Grange's biography.

77 28   See, however, DM¹, pp. 169f. and n. 25, p. 373, where Mahler's relation to Ives is discussed, in more detail— and with appropriate seriousness!—and Robert P. Morgan, 'Ives and Mahler: Mutual Responses at the

End of an Era', *19th Century Music*, Berkeley, Calif., Vol. II, No. 1, July 1978, pp. 72–81.

78 *11*   But see n. 8 *11*, p. 270.

79 *17*   But see n. 75 *8* above.

80 *6*   Mr. Walker was misinformed. Bauer-Lechner played viola and not second violin (information from Mr. Knud Martner).

81 *15*   Mahler in fact made four pianola rolls, using the Welte-Mignon system. Three of them were made on 9 November 1905: recordings of *Ich ging mit Lust*; *Ging heut' morgens übers Feld*; and *Das himmlische Leben*. It has not proved possible to discover when the fourth roll was made: this was a recording of the first movement of the Fifth Symphony (an extraordinarily vivid performance), which is available on a record published in the U.S.A. called "Great Composers Play Their Own Works" (The Keyboard Immortal Series, KBI 9: Stereo 4-AO72-5). (See also n. 7, pp. 247–248; and the list of Mahler's metronome marks for *Das himmlische Leben* given in DM¹, pp. 424–5.)

82 *1*   A number of these important performing scores may be seen in the Anna Mahler collection in the Library of the University of Southampton.

82 *5*   To the list of conductors, Willem Mengelberg and Oskar Fried should be added.

83 *5*   One should not, however, neglect to mention the Bach Suite of 1909 (see DM¹, pp. 350–60) which has an important keyboard part; or the Rückert song *Um Mitternacht*.

84 *13*   The complex chronology of the *Gesellen* songs is dealt with at some length in DM¹ (see especially pp. 119–23). See also the preface, by Donald Mitchell, to the latest edition of the vocal score, ed. Colin Matthews (Weinberger, London, 1977).

86 *26*   For further information about this early associate, see DM¹, pp. 54–6 and p. 118.

89 *4*   A few years later, in December 1884, Mahler wrote

two poems which foreshadow the text of the last song of *Das Lied von der Erde*. The last stanza of "Die Sonne spinnt ihr farbig Netz" anticipates, in general mood and imagery, the end of the cycle:

"Was ruhest Du mein müder Fuss?
Fahr' weiter stillen Leids Gefährte!
Über alle Schönheit ich wandern muss,
Ach, über die grüne, grüne Erde."

while the third and fourth lines of the other poem, "Die Nacht blickt mild aus stummen":

"Und müde Menschen schliessen ihre Lider,
Im Schlaf, auf's Neu vergessnes Glück zu lernen."

reappear in *Der Abschied* as follows:

". . . die müden Menschen geh'n heimwärts,
Um im Schlaf vergess'nes Glück
und Jugend neu zu lernen!"

Both these passages from *Der Abschied* were additions by Mahler to the original text. The two 1884 poems are given in full in HG, pp. 831–2; see also DM[1], p. 124 and p. 249, n. 16. See Arthur Wenk, 'The Composer as Poet in *Das Lied von der Erde*', *19th Century Music*, Berkeley, California, Vol. I, No. 1, July 1977, pp. 33–47.

89 27 A rhetoric that was certainly influenced by Mahler's favourite writer at this period of his life, the novelist Jean Paul. See DM[1], pp. 225–35.

90 3 Also (and perhaps most strikingly) Symphony III/1.

92 5 Much more information about these people has now come to light. For a detailed account of Mahler's relationship with Adler, see ER[1+2]. J. B. Foerster's autobiography, *Der Pilger: Erinnerungen eines Musikers*, Prague, 1955 (an abridged German translation of the two-volume Czech edition), contains some important reminiscences of Mahler. For Schmidt, see Carl Nemeth: *Franz Schmidt*, Zürich-Leipzig-Vienna, 1957.

93 31 For a short biography of Rudolf Krzyzanowski, see

PWB. The following information and correction may be added here: Krzyzanowski was born at Cheb (Eger) on 5 April 1862 and studied at the Vienna Conservatoire from 1872 until 1878. His first theatrical post was apparently at Laibach (Ljubljana) in 1883 and was followed by similar appointments at Wurzbach (1884–1885), Halle (1887–9), Elberfeld-Barmen (1889–91), Prague (1892–5) and Weimar (1895–6). In 1896 Krzyzanowski was engaged as *Kapellmeister* at Hamburg where he worked with Mahler and where his wife, Ida Doxat, a mediocre dramatic soprano, was a member of the company. Two years later he was offered, and accepted, the post of *Hofkapellmeister* at Weimar, which he held until his death at Graz on 20 June 1911, although his duties were carried out by Peter Raabe for the last two years, probably because of Krzyzanowski's ill health. Only two works by Krzyzanowski, a set of five songs (see n. 197 *32* below) and a fugue for piano, have been traced (the MSS are in the *Österreichische National-bibliothek* and the *Stadtbibliothek* in Vienna) and it is unlikely that he devoted much energy to composition during his later years. According to the unanimous opinion of contemporary critics, his conducting was able, but uninspired.

94 *22*   For further details, see PWB. Anton Valentin Ferdinand Krisper was born at Laibach (Ljubljana) on 28 December 1859 and studied at the Vienna Conservatoire for two years, 1876–8, without completing either year's study. Despite exhaustive researches no information about the opera supposedly performed at Prague has been uncovered and its existence now seems very doubtful. One work by Krisper survives, a Piano Sonata, which is to be found in the National Library and University, Ljubljana. This would appear to be an uninspired product of Krisper's youth.

95 *9*   Rott studied composition with Krenn in 1876/77 and 1877/8 (GdM[1]).

95 *10*   Rott studied organ with Bruckner from 1874 to 1877 and took his *Abitur* in that subject (GdM[1]).

96 *23*   The latter hypothesis now seems unlikely: the competition referred to was almost certainly one of the annual composition competitions at the Conservatoire. For an account of both composers' involvement in the Beethoven prize, see pp. 145f.

97 *2*   According to HG (p. 847, n. 14 and pl. 12), Krisper died insane and Heinrich Krzyzanowski spent some time in an asylum. Another of Mahler's acquaintances, Alfred Stross (born *c.* 1860) also died insane in Vienna (after 1885?). (See PWB, Chapter 4.)

97 *36*   The visit took place on 17 September 1880, after Wolf's interview with Brahms. Rott's sanity collapsed on 21 or 22 October 1880, and he was confined until his death on 25 June 1884.

98 *23*   Further information about Rott's tragically short life is supplied by HG and PWB. Next to Mahler and Wolf, Rott was certainly the most talented composer in this small group: his Symphony in E major (1878–80) was known to Mahler and the remarkable similarities between some of its ideas and passages in Mahler's Second, Third and Fifth Symphonies show the extent of its influence on him. All of Rott's surviving MSS may be seen in the *Österreichische Nationalbibliothek* (see Leopold Nowak, 'Die Kompositionen und Skizzen von Hans Rott in der Musiksammlung der Österreichische Nationalbibliothek', *Beiträge zur Musik dokumentation, Franz Grasberger zum 60 Geburtstag,* ed. Günther Brosche, Tutzing, 1975, pp. 273f).

99 *11*   For a further discussion of Mahler's conception of Nature as revealed in the programme of Symphony III, see DM[1], pp. 286–7.

103 *22*   The most extensive new account of Mahler's interest in Lipiner and Nietzsche appears in McGrath, *op. cit.*

105 *17*   But see n. 42 *14*, p. 291.

106 *13*   On 1 April 1880, soon after the completion of "Der

Spielmann", the second part of the original *Klagende Lied*, Mahler re-entered the University and at about the same time made his first attempt to find some sort of musical post. Little is known of the appointment he sought or the negotiations he undertook, but it is clear from the following letter from F. Schaumann (in later years Chairman of the *Wiener akademischen Wagner-Verein* and *Obmann* of the *Akademischer Gesang-verein*) to Guido Adler, that the latter was already, in 1880, offering practical help to the young composer:

"No 81 [Schaumann's identifying number]   Vienna
                                                        10 April 1880
Dear Adler:

In reply to your letter of the 8th of the month, permit me to inform you that, although the choirmaster post is not yet definitely filled, an individual is already under consideration for it; Mahler, whose artistic aspiration is well-known to me, would, with the exception of the direction of the concerts, hardly find a [suitable] sphere of activity; for in such positions it is less a matter of artistic ability than of a rather mechanical musician's experience.

Just because of the friendly opinion that I cherish of Mahler's talent, I would advise against such a post, simply because of his competence; for he would certainly be dis-illusioned in the first weeks.

With cordial greetings,
Yours,
F. Schaumann"

A month later, on 12 May 1880, Mahler signed a five-year contract with the agent Gustav Lewy, under which the latter was to receive 5% of Mahler's fees from theatrical work. Lewy remained Mahler's agent until 1890. (HG, pp. 74–5; ER[1], p. 441 (from which source the translation of Schaumann's letter is taken); KB[2], p. 160.)

108 *31* This advice was given during Mahler's only meeting with Berg, at a Grinzing Gasthaus (Schoenberg,

Zemlinsky, Webern and Jalowetz were also present). The conversation, as communicated by H. F. Redlich to Donald Mitchell, ran thus:

"Mahler: 'Und Sie wollen auch Kapellmeister werden?'
Berg: 'Nein.'
Mahler: 'Da haben Sie recht. Wenn Sie komponieren wollen, durfen Sie nicht zum Theater gehen.' "

"Mahler: 'And do you want to become a Kapellmeister too?'
Berg: 'No.'
Mahler: 'You are right. If you want to compose, you should not go into the theatre.' "

110 7   Mr. Martner informs us that Mizzi Zwerenz was four years old in 1880, so it is rather unlikely that Mahler would have wheeled her in a pram. (Or was it a push-chair?)

111 9   Zwerenz became Director of the *Stadttheater* in Jihlava in the winter of 1881 (HG, p. 76). For a further possible explanation of Mahler's refusal of this post, see n. 9 *17* on pp. 270–3.

111 24   The precise duration of Mahler's engagement at Bad Hall is uncertain, but according to Zoltan Roman's review of HG (*Musical Quarterly*, July 1974), "there are extant in Bad Hall semi-monthly paysheets for the entire period from June 1 to September 1 1880, showing in each instance Mahler's signature in receipt of the corresponding portion of his salary."

Chapter IV

116   See pp. 322–4 for complete revised list of the Early Works.

116 *4*   An earlier performance of the Violin Sonata was given by Mahler and Richard Schramml at a concert of the *Städtische Musikkapelle* at Jihlava on 31 July 1876, when

Mahler also performed Schubert's "Wanderer" Fantasy (see HG, pp. 36 and 719).

Another lost chamber work may be mentioned here: a *Nocturne* for cello (and presumably piano), mentioned by Bauer-Lechner (see HG, p. 706) without comment.

116 *10* First modern performance, in an edition by Dika Newlin: New York, 12 February 1964. The movement, together with the G minor Scherzo fragment, has also been edited by Peter Ruzicka and published by Hans Sikorski, Hamburg, 1973 (see DM¹, p. 54).

117 *22* For a description of this MS (not an autograph but a copyist's MS), which is now at Yale, see DM¹, pp. 79–81, n. 2.

118 *12* Mr. Martner's researches have revealed that it was the complete *Das klagende Lied* that was performed, in Czech, on 28 November 1934. The details given for the 2 December broadcast are, however, correct: only *Waldmärchen* was performed.

For details of the first performances of *Waldmärchen* in England and the U.S.A., see DM¹, p. 81, n. 3. A vocal score of *Waldmärchen*, with a foreword by Jack Diether, has been published by Belwin-Mills, New York, 1973. An orchestral score is available from the same source.

118 *16* In fact the score seems not to have been published until 1902. See DM¹, p. 120.

118 *27* This autograph of the Revised Version is now in the Pierpont Morgan Library in New York.

120 *6* While at Cassel, Mahler wrote at least two other occasional works: a *Vorspiel mit Chor*; and *Das Volkslied*, choral arrangements of folksongs (see HG, pp. 716–17). There is also a reference in Josef Stransky's reminiscences of Mahler, published in 1911, to a *Trauerhymne für die Kaiserin Maria Anna* that Mahler may have composed in 1884 (the Empress died on 4 May 1884). See KB², p. 171 and KB³, pp. 356–7.

122 *17* Bauer-Lechner mentions a *Polka with Introductory*

Funeral March, composed by Mahler as a child (see HG, pp. 25 and 719).

122 *19* See n. 116 4, p. 299 above.

122 *34* Bauer-Lechner's anecdote (NBL, pp. 65–6) must refer to the winter of 1875–6, as Winkler, the friend of Mahler mentioned in the anecdote, left the Conservatoire in the summer of 1876. So it would appear that the Violin Sonata was composed during Mahler's first winter as a student (see n. 132 *2* below).

123 *13* For the reasons why this statement is now open to doubt, see n. 35 *32* on pp. 278–80.

123 *21* It may mean, as HG suggests (p. 721), that Mahler submitted the score to the firm of Rättig at about the same time as they published his arrangement of Bruckner's Symphony III; though this would have been more likely had the Bruckner arrangement been published in 1878, as M. de La Grange states, instead of 1880, as we now know to have been the case (see n. 68 *4*, p. 293).

124 *32* The three main themes of the movement (*A, B, C*) are shown overleaf. The similarity of theme *C* to the main theme of the A minor first movement of Symphony VI (see Ex. 2), as well as the presence in the latter of motive *x* from *A*, have been remarked on by Dika Newlin, and help to justify Stefan's suggestion quoted above.

125 *2* Tedious, perhaps, in this particular instance: but the *method* is wholly characteristic—prophetic, indeed, of what was to be one of Mahler's principal compositional techniques. (D.M.)

127 *13* No longer unidentified: see n. 128 *10* below.

128 *2* See also II, pp. 52–3 and IV, pp. 169–70, for further comments on Wagner's influence on Mahler. The ill-digested *Tristan*-isms of the Heine fragment scarcely affect these arguments.

128 *10* For further information see JD, pp. 65–76 and DM[1], p. 54. The text of the D minor fragment is not a folk-song, as Mr. Diether states, but a poem, based on a folk

Ex.1

Ex.2

source, by F. von Zuccalmaglio (see also DM², pp. 29–30). The clumsiness of these settings, as well as the immaturity of the calligraphy (as compared, for example, with the Piano Quartet) both point to an early date of composition, 1875 or earlier, i.e. before Mahler had had much formal training. These songs would certainly appear to be his earliest surviving music.

128 *19* See n. 35 *32* on pp. 278–80.

129 *4*   As this Scherzo was written as a composition exercise it is not improbable that it was an isolated piece rather than one movement of a larger work.

129 *17* See III, p. 90.

129 *20* Mr. Martner writes in a private communication to Donald Mitchell:

> "The story of Herzog Ernst exists in many different versions. The first complete edition of the many versions was published in Vienna in 1869, in an edition by K. Bartsch (Das Volksbuch vom Herzog Ernst). I am inclined to believe that Mahler and Steiner used this book as the basis for their libretto, but they probably also knew Uhland's drama."

129 *24* According to Miss Annie Steiner (see DM[1], pp. 54–6), the libretto and some of the music were written in the summer of 1875 while Mahler and Josef Steiner were on holiday at Ronow; they apparently left the manuscript there and on returning next year found that it had been accidentally destroyed. This would perhaps seem rather unlikely: unless Mahler had already lost interest in the project, he would surely have taken the sketches away with him. HG, p. 27, states that Mahler played some of the opera to Gustav Schwarz.

130 *27* See also n. 132 *2* below.

132 *2*   A different version of what is clearly the same event is reported by Richard Specht (in *Die Musik*, VII, Jahrg. 1907/8, Heft 15, pp. 152–3). According to Specht, the rehearsal was sabotaged by Mahler's fellow pupils, who had inserted mistakes into the score and parts; and the new piece that Mahler hurriedly composed after this fiasco—in a single night in Specht's account—was a String Quintet movement rather than a Piano Suite. Specht states that this piece also (of course!) won a prize. A similar story is found in an anecdote of Bruckner's, as reported by Carl Hruby (CH, p. 13). Bruckner used to tell how Mahler once wrote a movement of a symphony for the *Jahresprüfung* of Krenn's

composition class; but it turned out that what was wanted was an instrumental sonata movement rather than an orchestral piece, so Mahler composed overnight a Sonata Andante, which Krenn said was "worthy to bear the name of the greatest master". This story may conceivably refer to another occasion; but from these various accounts it does seem reasonably certain that Mahler once produced a new and successful piece very rapidly from an unsuccessful orchestral movement. What new piece? Maybe Specht's String Quintet is the most likely; this would be the easiest to believe, as a String Quintet arrangement of an orchestral movement might well be produced very quickly, perhaps even overnight, by a young composer anxious to overcome an orchestral failure. What exactly went wrong at the rehearsal we can only guess; but we can hardly believe Specht's story that Mahler's fellow students were to blame. Perhaps the most reasonable explanation is that the original piece was incompetently written for the orchestra, which would not be surprising if it was Mahler's first attempt at orchestral composition. We may easily imagine the young Mahler anxious as soon as he got to Vienna (there is some evidence from Specht's account that the event took place as early as 1876) to compose something ambitious: a symphony, or at least part of one, would be the obvious choice; and we can imagine his humiliation when at the first hearing it turned out to be faulty work. What more natural than that he should work all night to salvage what he could in the shape of a new piece—String Quintet, Piano Suite or whatever? (In fact, since we know Mahler won a prize in the 1876 composition competition with a Piano Quintet (see n. 35 32 above), it may well be that Specht's String Quintet and Bauer-Lechner's Piano Suite both represent confused memories of this piece.) This is all, of course, mere speculation; but it is likely that some experience of this kind was responsible for Mahler's subsequent perfectionist approach to orchestration. Just as with his setback in the counterpoint examination (see n. 37 34 above), one small failure would have been enough to instil a fanatical determination to excel.

As this book was about to go to press we received from the *Österreichische Nationalbibliothek* a photocopy of a manuscript of extraordinary interest. It is a piano reduction (with some instrumental indications) of a Symphonic Prelude for orchestra in C minor, which, according to the title page, was made by one Heinrich Tschuppik from a fair copy (*Niederschrift*) by his distant relative Rudolf Krzyzanowski of a work "ostensibly by Bruckner" dating from 1876. The first thing to be said is that the piece is certainly not by Bruckner, though it begins in Bruckner-like fashion (except that Bruckner would never have introduced his main theme immediately) with a repeated quaver string pattern on C and the long build-up of its (Wagnerian) main theme towards an impressive C minor climax. After this opening, however, there is hardly any more Bruckner, but a great deal of undigested Wagner. The piece is roughly in sonata form; though there is no clearly defined second group and the recapitulation begins not with the main theme, but with a fugato on a subsidiary idea: the coda has an enormously protracted dominant pedal (Bruckner again here). Altogether the piece, apart from its stylistic inappropriateness, is far too crudely constructed for the mature composer who had just completed his Fifth Symphony, and the possibility that it is an earlier work of Bruckner's can also be ruled out on stylistic grounds. The piece— which, despite its faults, is far from worthless—is clearly the work of an inexperienced composer who had come under Bruckner's influence, and who was also a thoroughgoing Wagnerian. Presumably Tschuppik took it for Bruckner because of the opening, and because he knew Krzyzanowski had been a pupil of Bruckner. The full score Tschuppik was working from must have lost its title page and the music must simply have been headed "Sinfonisches Praeludium, 1876".

Recently (since the writing is in ball-point pen) someone has added at the foot of the title page "Could this be an examination work of Gustav Mahler's?" Could it indeed?! It would seem that its composer was one of the Bruckner circle in 1876. This effectively restricts the choice to Krzyzanowski himself, Rott, or Mahler. It is just possible that it might be by Hugo Wolf, though he was never a pupil of Bruckner and the music he was writing in 1876 shows no trace of Bruckner's influence. Krzyzanowski might seem at first to be the most likely candidate, but Tschuppik clearly was certain that the piece was not by him; and in any case the little that survives of Krzyzanowski's music hardly suggests that at this time he would have been able to compose with any success on a symphonic scale. Rott certainly would have been competent enough; but he was not influenced by Bruckner until later, and the orchestral pieces of his that we possess from this period are quite different in style. On stylistic grounds, and from the occasional moments of real creative power in the piece, Mahler seems the most probable of all. There is a considerable similarity between the relentless restatements of the Symphonic Prelude's main theme and an obstinate emphasis on C minor, and the similarly emphatic emphasis in the Piano Quartet on the main theme and its tonality of A minor. At other times there is a certain general similarity of composing technique and style—though the Prelude is far more Wagnerian than the Quartet. One wonders whether the passage opposite (from the Prelude's pseudo second-subject group) could not be said to prefigure, in the lush harmonies at the beginning, similar moments in *Das klagende Lied*; while at the same time is not the

Ex. 3

exposed writing for trumpet and horn under tremolo strings at the end a characteristic texture in the early symphonies?

If the Symphonic Prelude is by Mahler, and if we assume that it belongs to 1876 as Tschuppik's manuscript states (there is always the possibility that it is a slightly later piece; that it is perhaps the lost prelude to *Die Argonauten*: see n. 197 *15*), where does it fit into the chronology of Mahler's composing activities during his first year at the Conservatoire? Internal evidence suggests that, like the rehearsal reported by Bauer-Lechner and Specht, the events recorded by Hruby date from 1876 (see PWB, p. 334). It is, therefore, tempting to identify the Symphonic Prelude as the symphonic movement mentioned by Bruckner to Hruby. Even so, the number of works apparently composed by Mahler during the first eight months of 1876 could still be as many as seven, an improbably large number, viz:

(a) Symphonic Prelude
(b) Sonata Andante (the substitute for (a) in the examination)
(c) Violin Sonata
(d) Symphony
(e) Piano Suite or String Quintet
(f) Piano Quintet movement (the prize-winning work)
(g) Piano Quintet (performed at Jihlava)

However, as has been suggested above, the works listed at (e) are almost certainly garbled references to (f), while the latter was in all probability the piece performed at Jihlava (see n. 35 *32*). Also worth noting is the fact that the Violin Sonata is the *only* sonata by Mahler for which documentary evidence exists: given their close chronological proximity the Sonata Andante and the Violin Sonata must surely be related. If so, then in the light of

308

Winkler's testimony (see n. 122 *34*) the Sonata Andante, rather than being composed 'overnight', was probably written earlier in the winter of 1875/6. It would also mean that Mahler was partly right when he told Bauer-Lechner that the Violin Sonata won a prize (see p. 122), if it did at least gain for him first grade in the composition class. A final speculation: Mahler would surely not have abandoned a movement as impressive as the Symphonic Prelude. It is far more likely that he subsequently entered it for the annual competition.

Perhaps further evidence to confirm or refute these suggestions might yet be hidden somewhere in Viennese archives. Until such evidence is uncovered, the deductions offered here (and, in more detail, in PWB, Chapter VI) suggest that the references to a multitude of compositions dating from the first half of 1876 may well stem from only three works, the Symphonic Prelude, the Violin Sonata and the Piano Quintet.

133 *4* It should be noted here that Paul Stefan's account of four early Mahler symphonies that Willem Mengelberg was supposed to have discovered in Dresden (see DM¹, pp. 51-4) has now been shown to be open to question by Mr. Robert Becqué in a paper for the Dutch Section of the International Gustav Mahler Society, July 1976 (reproduced in DM², appendix A; see also *ibid.* pp. 1-3). In addition see *News About Mahler Research*, No. 3, July 1978, International GM Society, Vienna, pp. 7-8.

135 *4* See n. 139 *28* below.

135 *15* Callot was an etcher, not a painter, nor was he the author of "The Huntsman's Funeral". The woodcut of that title, which was quite possibly an inspiration for Mahler's movement, is by Moritz von Schwind. For a discussion of Schwind and Mahler's reference to Callot (and a reproduction of Schwind's woodcut) see DM¹, pp. 235-7.

137 *16* A letter of June 1880 to Albert Spiegler—a doctor

and close friend of Mahler from about 1878 onwards —proves that Mahler was working on *Rübezahl* in the winter of 1879–80 (see HG, p. 712 and GMB¹, Letter 10, p. 63).

139 *28* The libretto of *Rübezahl* turned up among Alma Mahler's papers after her death (see pl. B and C; also AM¹, pp. xxv–xxvi, and DM¹, p. 56). One of the choruses uses words from *Hans und Grethe* (see pl. B) and this was undoubtedly where Mahler incorporated the music of the song.

140 *10* This is indeed the tidiest solution. If it is true, and if the speculation in n. 35 *32* above is correct, then it is possible that Mahler only wrote one quartet—the A minor Piano Quartet, of which the surviving movement may well have been the only one completed.

142 *1* A pseudonym of the Bavarian poet Friedrich Hermann Frey. HG, p. 731, provides more information about him, and states that the work in question was a dramatic poem, which was performed by drama pupils at the Conservatoire.

144 *16* And has not died yet: see HG, pp. 732–3, and DM¹, p. 56.

144 *28* This MS is now at Yale University. See n. 117 *22*, p. 300.

145 *6* Ernst Decsey must also be held responsible for the dissemination of this tiresomely long-lived myth, though it is perhaps unjust to blame him for the weight that successive commentators have placed upon the brief mention he makes of this matter in an article, 'Stunden mit Mahler', in *Die Musik*, Vol. X, No. 18, June 1911, p. 355. (D.M.)

148 *7* Yugoslavia is, of course, a twentieth-century invention and in 1881 Laibach (now Ljubljana) was the capital of the Austrian Crown Land of Krain.

148 *12* Rott was, in fact, committed to an asylum on 23 October 1880. He died in 1884 (see n. 97 *36*, p. 297, and PWB, Chapter 4).

150 *1*   Mahler, according to HG, p. 150, started work at Olmütz in January 1883.

152 *25*   Mahler was working on the revision of the cantata in Hamburg at the end of 1892 (see HG, p. 731).

152 *34*   It is: see DM^1, pp. 79–81, n. 2, for a full account of the original manuscript.

153 *20*   See again DM^1, pp. 79–81, n. 2.

153 *24*   For much more information about *Waldmärchen*—which, with the publication of a vocal score (see n. 118 *12* above) is now no longer a matter for speculation—see DM^1, pp. 56–68, and also JD, pp. 3–65.

154 *14*   I should like to pay tribute to the excellence of Dr. Holländer's commentary, particularly in the light of my own scrutiny of *Waldmärchen*. His text is full of insight and I especially commend his paragraph on p. 155, lines 22–6. It seems to me now that he said almost everything that needed to be said—in the early 1930s. A complete translation of Dr. Holländer's text is given in JD, pp. 19–40. (D.M.)

155 *30*   On this particular point see AM^1, p. xxxiii.

155 *34*   Recte: *Langsam und traümerisch*.

156 *28*   See, however, nn. 153 *24* and 155 *30* above.

157 *34*   This is the score now at Yale (see n. 117 *22* on p. 300). It is possible that this copyist's MS was made from what is described as the first full score in line 12 above.

158 *8*   It included, for example, no less than six harps (see DM^1, pp. 79–80).

160 *12*   See again the account of the MS in DM^1, pp. 79–81.

167 *12*   We know now that this was not the case, that major restructuring was often part of the compositional process until a very late stage (see DM^1, p. 201).

167 *23*   Cf. however, just such a transfer in the *Gesellen* songs, in DM^1, pp. 98–9.

176 *10*   i.e. the thunderous unison spread out through the orchestra, and dotted rhythm.

177 *11*   They are!

180 *9*   In a private communication to Donald Mitchell,

Weiber (Kreisend)

Mit uns spiel und kos'!
Wir lassen dich nicht los!
Hast uns geschaffen – musst uns leiten –
Kannst dich nicht mehr von uns scheiden
– statt der Jungen – nur die Alten!

Emma Weicht von mir, ihr Spuk gestalten!

Weiber (Schwärmen...)

Seht doch, wie sie sich ziert – Feinliebchen!
Wir sind ihr zu schlecht, dem Zuckerpüppchen
(...)
Komm nur! Kannst noch so schrei'n!
Wir spielen Ringel reih'n!
(...)
Ringel ringel reih'n!
Wer fröhlich ist, der schlinge sich ein!
(...)

Rübezahl (kommt...)

Werdet zu Staub, aus dem ihr geschaffen!
In die Erde! Weiter zu schlafen!
(...)

B & C Two pages from the libretto of *Rübezahl*.   Plate B shows one
of the choruses which uses words from *Hans und Grethe*.

Deryck Cooke pointed out that the beginning of the
narration (Fig. 21) and the song itself (Fig. 26) are
given in embryo in bars 13–16 of the orchestral introduction.

180 *21* It seems likely that the song quotes from the cantata,
rather than the other way round, as the tempo direction
Noch einmal so langsam found in both is more appropriate

to the cantata than to the song; in the latter, it cannot really be understood without reference to the equivalent passage in the cantata.

182 *12* Cf. also the finale of Symphony VII, bars 51–2: not a minor triad this time but a similarly abrupt dislocation achieved in principle by the same means.

182 *19* But see also n. 180 *9* above.

183 *13* No longer the case: see DM¹, pp. 92f.

183 *18* See the preface to the new edition referred to in n. 84 *13*, p. 294.

184 *13* Deryck Cooke noted that the phrase has in fact already appeared *in toto* in bars 3–8 after Fig 19. See also *s* in Ex. 10, p. 173: an even earlier adumbration.

188 *19* See also DM¹, p. 80, for a detailed comment on the original constitution of the wind band in the cantata, and Mahler's predilection for the E flat clarinet. (See also GMB¹, Letter 189, p. 201).

196 *36* In a letter (1979) to Donald Mitchell, Dr. Felix Steiner refers to a MS libretto, apparently in his father Josef Steiner's hand with marginal comments in another handwriting, which he last saw in Vienna in 1938, shortly before he was forced to leave that city. This MS is now presumed lost: it was in *Stabreim* and dealt with the subject of Jason and Medea; thus it may well have been the libretto of *Die Argonauten*, which perhaps was another joint project by Mahler and Steiner, like *Herzog Ernst von Schwaben*.

197 *13* A letter of Mahler's to his sister Justine in November (?) 1908 seems to imply that whatever he had completed of *Die Argonauten* was still in existence then, as Knud Martner suggests.

197 *15* M. de La Grange strangely misinterprets this passage (see HG, p. 72). Hirschfeld, in the *Geschichte der K. K. Gesellschaft der Musikfreunde im Wien* (1912: quoted in KB², p. 158) states that Mahler submitted the prelude to *Die Argonauten* (unsuccessfully) for the Beethoven Prize in 1878, and that a copy of the opening theme is preserved in the files; Professor Blaukopf comments that the file for 1878 can no longer be found in the archives. (M. de La Grange's suggestion (HG, p. 80) that the rules of the Beethoven Prize debarred Mahler from entering for it until 1881 is incorrect.)

197 *32* Among them, HG (p. 720) records a song (*Die Türken*) based on a poem by Lessing, mentioned by Mahler to Bauer-Lechner; also a song composed for a

Ex.4

competition (yet another) at the Conservatoire. This
was a prize founded by the Austrian poet Vinzenz
Zusner for settings of his work (see also LK, p. 62
and PWB, Chapter 4). Göllerich (AG, IV/1, p.
450) mentions some songs by Mahler dedicated to
Marie Lorenz, and records that, according to Frau
Lorenz, Wolf once rated them above his own; but
since Göllerich refers to Frau Lorenz as Rudolf
Krzyzanowski's sister-in-law when she was in fact his
one-time fiancée, and since we do possess some songs

by Krzyzanowski dedicated to Marie Lorenz, we cannot be certain that those were not the songs in question—though it is of course perfectly conceivable that both Krzyzanowski and Mahler could have dedicated songs to the same young woman.

198 *11* The Josephine of the dedication was Josephine Poisl, the daughter of the Iglau postmaster, with whom Mahler was in love in 1879–80 (see HG, pp. 61–7). The fact that their relationship ended shortly after *Maitanz im Grünen* was composed was doubtless the reason why only three of the projected five songs were completed (see HG, pp. 724f: M. de La Grange prints texts and translations of the first two songs; he also describes them in full). Two poems by Mahler written in 1880 (published in HG, pp. 824–6) were almost certainly intended as texts for the remaining, never composed songs. Through the kindness of Professor Zoltan Roman it has been possible to examine the manuscript of the three extant songs. *Im Lenz*, which is very much in the style of *Das klagende Lied* and (as has been noted: see p. 180 above) quotes extensively from it, progresses by a rather bizarre series of key-changes from F major to A flat, not C as stated in n. 157, pp. 263–4. (HG, p. 725, describes the ending as in D flat, with the final A flat major chord a dominant of this key; but the tonality is not clearly enough established to draw this definite conclusion.) *Winterlied* is a more skilfully composed song, in alternating 6/8 and 9/8 with 'spinning-wheel' figuration. At bar 15f. there is a reminiscence of *Waldmärchen*. Ex. 4 shows the opening of its C minor middle section. Both songs certainly deserve occasional performance. *Maitanz im Grünen* is, as suspected, in D major, rather than the F of its otherwise near-identical successor, *Hans und Grethe* (see p. 264, line 16 *et seq.*).

198 *32* All three volumes were in fact published in 1892. See DM[1], p. 89 and p. 243 (where the advertisement for their publication is illustrated); also p. 114 for a

reproduction of the title-page of the first volume (the title pages of all three volumes are, in fact, identical).

199 *17* This score was published in April 1913 (information from Mr. Martner).

199 *25* This whole paragraph must be adjusted by the reader to conform with the chronological information given in n. 198 *32* above.

199 *29* The date should be 1892 (see n. 198 *32* above): the statement was already slightly misleading in the light of the already published piano-duet version of Bruckner's Symphony III (1880); and it should also be noted that Mahler's completion of *Die drei Pintos* was published in 1888.

200 *18* Mr. Martner informs us that in October 1887 there was a revival of Tirso de Molina's *Don Juan* at the Leipzig *Stadttheater*; it is highly probable that Mahler saw this performance and even possible that he wrote *Phantasie* and *Serenade* for inclusion in it (which would explain the instrumental indications). At any rate it would seem likely that the two Tirso de Molina settings date from this period, despite M. de La Grange's assertion to the contrary (HG. p. 740). See Knud Martner and Robert Becqué, 'Zwölf unbekannte Briefe Gustav Mahlers am Ludwig Strecker', *Archiv für Musik-Wissenschaft*, XXXIV/4, (1977), pp. 287f.

201 *25* In fact for these two Tirso de Molina songs Mahler used a German translation by Ludwig Braunfels *verbatim* (see HG, p. 740).

201 *36* An incomplete orchestration by Mahler of this song has recently come to light (see DM¹, pp. 144–5, and HG, p. 764).

204 *18* See HG, pp. 724–7 for the texts of *Im Lenz* and *Winterlied*; also pp. 824–37 where a number of other poems by Mahler are given.

205 *8* But see n. 139 *28* above.

205 *17* See DM¹, pp. 290–1, n. 84, who no longer inclines to this view.

208 *2* See DM¹, p. 292–3, for a discussion of the influence of Czech music on Mahler.

214 *23* The appearance of this motive in *Waldmärchen* is commented on and illustrated in DM¹, p. 64.

220 *11* See DM¹, p. 62, second paragraph.

222 *36* "Starting in A major" now strikes me as a very quaint way in which to describe a song, the opening bars of which are so emphatically ambiguous in tonality and suggest, if anything, F sharp minor. Admittedly, A major *is* the song's tonic, and is established as such. But if I were writing afresh now, I hope I should show a little more sophistication in this passage, and again in line 2, p. 224. (D.M.)

223 *1* In the original version of *Winterreise* the last song was in B minor.

223 *29* Originally, in fact, Schumann wrote his epilogue in C sharp minor, but rewrote it in D flat in order to simplify the notation.

226 *19* HG, p. 705, gives a list of the seven movements that comprised Mahler's incidental music (see also DM¹, n. 100, p. 300).

227 *16* No parts or score have yet turned up; it seems most likely that the originals were destroyed during the Second World War (see DM¹, p. 68). But one movement (probably that listed by M. de La Grange as the first number in the suite: "Ein Ständchen am Rhein") would seem to have survived as "Blumine"—the original second movement of Symphony I. (See DM¹, pp. 217–24, and p. 300, n. 101, where apologies are made for describing the continuation of the melody shown in Ex. 1 on p. 227 as "feeble".)

229 *15* Mr. Martner informs us that during Mahler's Hamburg years *Der Trompeter* was given 24 times, including the two London performances; but it was never conducted by Mahler, and it was Leo Feld who conducted it in London.

Notes

I (1860–1875)

230 n.9 *6*   Alma's mistake is understandable: there is an even smaller village (*c*. 200 inhabitants in 1855; see RL, p. 670) of the same name near Jihlava, on the Moravian side of the border.

233 n.82   The noun *Ziehharmonika* used by both Specht and Stefan can in fact mean either concertina or accordion.

II (1875–1878)

240 n.65 *11*   For "that the possession of a blanket authorizes a black to consider himself a white" read "that blacks were authorized through a *carte blanche* to consider themselves whites". This mis-translation by Ernest Newman has been corrected by Mr. Philip Winters.

243 n.98 *2*   Mahler visited Bayreuth on at least three other occasions: in July 1891, from 28 July to 4 August 1895, and in August 1896 (HG, pp. 236, 305 and 378). According to HFR, p. 253, Mahler also visited the town in August 1888 (see also ER[1], p. 443). During the last of these visits Mahler heard Siegfried Wagner conduct a *Ring* cycle and wrote of his impressions to Cosima (see Z. von Kraft: *Der Sohn Siegfried Wagners Leben und Umwelt*, Graz and Stuttgart, n.d., p. 80).

243 n.98 *5*   Mr. Winters points out that while Cosima's anti-Semitism cannot be brushed aside, the conductors she employed at Bayreuth had all been associated with Wagner himself or appeared as music assistants at festivals after Wagner's death and were, as Mr. Winters puts it, "part of the Bayreuth 'family'"—which Mahler, of course, never had been; nor was to be.

246 n.129	The published edition has since been tracked down, and its title page is reproduced in DM¹, p. 65. (See also *ibid.*, pp. 68–9.)
246 n.142 *2*	See n.70 *31* above. HFR in fact was right about Symphony IV.

III (1878–1880)

248 n.7	The original Columbia recording of 1957 is now a rare and expensive collector's item; but, fortunately, new and improved recordings of the rolls were made by Telefunken in 1969/70 (SLA 25057 – T/1–5).
248 n.10	See also n.84 *13*, p. 294. The "instrumental mastery" of *Das klagende Lied* as we now have it was of course only achieved after much revision over a lengthy period. See the discussion of the original version in DM¹, pp. 79–81.

IV The Early Works

253 n.3	See n.118 *16* on p. 300.
254 nn. 9 & 10	As has been mentioned above (see n. 84 *13*), the complex problems of the chronology of the *Gesellen* songs —with the conclusion that the orchestration was indeed long delayed—are dealt with comprehensively in DM¹, pp. 92–112 and 119–23.
254 n.10 *7*	No longer true: an early version of the full score is in the Willem Mengelberg-Stichting, Amsterdam (see DM¹, p. 97).
255 n.10 *16*	Also Symphonies II and III, both of which had been completed by 1897.
255 n.10 *23*	The contract is reproduced in DM¹, p. 91.
257 n.43	I think now that Redlich was more correct in his assessment of Weber's influence than I was in 1958. (D.M.)
257 n.55	But was he? See n.35 *32* on pp. 278–80.
258 n.71	For an approach along the lines suggested, see Robert Still, *Gustav Mahler and Psychoanalysis*, the *American*

Imago, Vol. 17, Fall, No. 3, 1960, pp. 223–5.

259 n.92 5	This is the Yale MS referred to in n.117 *22* on p. 300.
260 n.98	This question is answered in DM¹, p. 118.
261 n.117 7	Actually 24 November 1907. The soloists were Elizza, Mildenburg, Kittel and Bella Paalen (information from Mr. Martner).
262 n.133 2	See n.198 *32* on p. 316.
262 n.133 5	In fact, among MSS owned by the late Alfred Rosé were Mahler's nine early settings of *Wunderhorn* texts which comprised Books II and III of the *Lieder und Gesänge* (see DM¹, pp. 92–3).
263–4 n.157	See n.198 *11* above. As is pointed out there, *Maitanz im Grünen*, the early version of *Hans und Grethe*, is in D major not F, so the three songs cannot be said to show a "circling about F".
265 n.162	Clearly not. See n.222 *36* above. (D.M.)
266 n.163	For a suggestion of the influence of Mussorgsky on late Mahler, see DM¹, p. 383, n.48.

Revised List of Early Works

Surviving works are marked with an asterisk. Works whose existence at any time now seems doubtful are marked (?).

Works from original list on pp. 116–20 / Additional Works	Dates of Composition	References to new notes
(a) Other compositions for piano		
Polka mit einen Trauermarsch als Einleitung for piano	c. 1867? —1875	122 17
Song: *Die Türken* (Lessing) for voice and piano	c. 1870?	197 32
Song for the Zusner prize for voice and piano	1875?–1878?	197 32
Songs dedicated to Marie Lorenz (?)	1875?–1880?	197 32
Nocturne for cello (and piano?)	1875?–1878?	116 4
(b) Sonata for violin and piano	1875?–1876	116 4
(c) ★First movement of Quartet for piano and strings in A minor ★Fragment of Scherzo for piano quartet in G minor	1876?–1878?	35 32 · 116 10 · 124 32
★Two songs (fragments): (i) *Weder Glück noch Stern* (F. von Zuccalmaglio) (ii) *Im wunderschönen Monat Mai* (Heine)	1875?	128 10
(d) Quartet for piano and strings (?)	??	35 32
(e) Quintet for piano and strings	1875?–1876	35 32
Scherzo for piano quintet	1878	120 4

(f) *Herzog Ernst von Schwaben*, opera (Libretto: Josef Steiner)	1875	129 20, 129 24
(g) ★*Das klagende Lied*, text (Mahler)	1878	
(h) Suite for piano (?)		
(i) 'Conservatoire' Symphony	1876?	132 2
String Quintet } Sonata Andante (?) }		
(j) Symphony in A minor	1882?–1883?	
(k) *Rübezahl*, fairy-tale opera (★Libretto: Mahler)	1879?–1883?	137 16, 139 28
(l) Quartettsatz (?)	??	140 10
(m) ★*Das klagende Lied*, music	1878?–1880	117 22, 118 12, 118 16, 118 27, 152 25 to 188 19
(n) *Die Argonauten*, opera (Libretto: Mahler and Josef Steiner)	1878?–1880?	196 36, 197 13, 197 15
(o) ★3 Songs for tenor and piano (words by Mahler):		198 11
(i) *Im Lenz*	19 Feb. 1880	
(ii) *Winterlied*	27 Feb. 1880	
(iii) *Maitanz im Grünen*	5 March 1880	

Works from original list on pp. 116–20

Works from original list on pp. 116–20	Additional Works	Dates of Composition	References to new notes
*Fragment of Scherzo of Symphony I for piano duet		1880?–1883?	205 *17*
*Lieder und Gesänge (aus der Jugendzeit)—I:		1880–1887?	198 *32* to 201 *36*
(i) Frühlingsmorgen (R. Leander)			
(ii) Erinnerung (R. Leander)			
(iii) Hans und Grethe (Mahler)			
(iv) Serenade (Tirso de Molina's Don Juan)			
(v) Phantasie (Tirso de Molina's Don Juan)			
(p) Nordische Symphonie (or Suite?), for orchestra		1879?–1882	
(q) Incidental music to "living pictures" from Der Trompeter von Säkkingen, for orchestra			
	Vorspiel mit Chor, for chorus and orchestra	1884	{ 226 *19*, 227 *16*, 229 *15*
	Das Volkslied, for voices, chorus and orchestra (arrangements by Mahler)	1883	120 *6*
	Trauerhymne für die Kaiserin Maria Anna	1885	120 *6*
	Maria Anna	1884	120 *6*
(r) *Lieder eines fahrenden Gesellen		Dec. 1883–Jan. 1885	84 *13*

INDEXES

INDEX TO TEXT

Authors of works listed in the BIBLIOGRAPHY AND KEY (p. xvii) are indexed only where there is a biographical mention of them in the text or where their books are discussed.

Figures in Roman capitals refer to plates.

INDEX TO APPENDIX